10630625

# Paris-Roubaix

**1970.** That year was a true Paris-Roubaix, a muddy one. Eddy Merckx, despite flatting, was magnificent. He attacked solo with 31km to go, to finish more than five minutes ahead of his fellow Belgians Roger De Vlaeminck, Éric Leman (No. 37), and André Dierickx.

**1934.** The Sunday of Paris-Roubaix. It's the big family outing by car, even by baby carriage, for a picnic with friends. French rider Gaston Rebry and Roger Lapébie lead this group along the edge of the road. (pages 2–3)

**1988.** In the dust, you can't see anything and you fall. In the Wallers-Arenberg "trench," Swiss rider Alfred Achermann takes a hard tumble on the cobblestones. (pages 4–5)

# Paris-Roubaix
## A Journey Through Hell

Text:
**Philippe Bouvet**
**Pierre Callewaert**
**Jean-Luc Gatellier**
**Serge Laget**

Created by
Jacques Hennaux
(art direction)
and Serge Laget
under the direction of
Gérard Ejnès
with Pierre-Marie Descamps
and Yann Hildwein

Layout:
Philippe Le Men

Translation:
David Herlihy

## "L'Enfer du Américain"

BY BOB ROLL

Paris-Roubaix has captured the world's imagination more completely than any other single-day race. Both fascinating and fearsome, the Hell of the North (*L'Enfer du Nord*) is the one day outside the Tour de France when the whole world watches cycling. I myself first saw the great race on a network TV Sunday sports show and I was instantly hooked. I proclaimed to the East Bay club riders the next day that I would be in Paris-Roubaix soon! Never mind that I had been resoundingly pummeled on each and every piddly club ride up to that point. The guffaws and ridicule that ushered forth from the club riders' incredulity fell on my deafened-by-epic-images-of-bloodied-warriors-pounding-across-the-ancient-stones-like-centurion-ghosts ears. Imagine the club riders' surprise a couple years later when I emerged from the mud and dust of Paris-Roubaix as the only American finisher!

The photographic image captured by the legendary Graham Watson you see here of me off to the side of the cobbles was taken in 1988. I'm surrounded by some great racers in the thick of the madness. That year Paris-Roubaix was bone dry and it was only Graham who could find a patch of mud and only I who inadvertently went flying through it. The reason why Graham had found it is easy: He's a genius! My trajectory was a bit less glorious. I found the only patch of mud because our team never re-conned Paris-Roubaix one time! Nowadays all the teams look at the course for days and weeks beforehand, surveying every meter. When I came upon that spot I had no idea what danger lurked there, but I did see an opening in the wall of bodies and shot through. I made a great forward movement only to be delayed by Sean Kelly himself as even the great Irish champion came to grief on the pavé, crashing to the stones and having his left ear sliced in half by another falling rider's chainrings. That was also the year of the great escape by Dirk Demol and Thomas Wegmüller, who were never caught by the chasing peloton led in by Laurent Fignon.

American riders have had a great string of success at the Tour de France, but apart from George Hincapie's great successes, our palmarès are pretty thin at Paris-Roubaix. This photo of me by Graham brings back some of my best memories of my career to me and remains a potent testament to why I loved Paris-Roubaix so desperately. The race is so powerfully eternal that we are carried back in time to the very first edition in 1896 each year we see it. No matter what modern progress brings to the rest of life, Paris-Roubaix extracts the same measure of punishment to the riders and awe and delight to the fans as the very first editions of the race. We are immediately reconnected with our distant past and our ancestral struggles when we see the hardships the racers face with such resounding ferocity. There most certainly is no other bike race like Paris-Roubaix. There probably isn't any other contest on earth like it either. These images are so evocative and compelling, I'm sure you will enjoy them for years to come.

*This book is dedicated
to the people of the North,
who after having made
Paris-Roubaix their race
now preserve it with enthusiasm.*

**1954.** It's a beautiful Sunday for the well-dressed citizens of Saint-Just-en-Chaussée who cheer on the breakaways. After 69km, Frenchman Bernard Gauthier, Spaniard Miguel Poblet, Dutchman Gerrit Voorting, and six others have a two-minute lead. It's high noon. The race has gotten off to a great start....

# The prevailing winds

Coincidence or not, the Paris-Roubaix road race was born at the same time as the modern Olympic Games, in April 1896. That was also the golden age of velodromes. Today, those tracks have all but disappeared. Yet Paris-Roubaix, like the Olympic Games, endures as a classic.

The year 1896 was indeed a turning point in the history of sport. The idea of reviving the Olympic Games, first proposed four years earlier by the Baron Pierre de Coubertin under the auspices of the USFSA (l'Union des Sociétés Françaises des Sports Athlétiques), reached fruition on the grounds of Athens. At the same time, the cycling movement unleashed in 1891 by the journalists Maurice Martin and Pierre Giffard, who had created the classics Bordeaux-Paris and Paris-Brest-Paris, also saw its seeds bear fruit.

As French machines rapidly improved, cycling became more popular. And as the number of cyclists rose, so, too, did the number of French champions. With its inflatable tires and equal-sized wheels, the safety bicycle sparked a true revolution. More than just a sport, cycling became a social blessing and the bicycle a providential instrument of freedom. Racers could be counted in the hundreds, while, according to the Touring Club de France, Sunday cyclists numbered 150,000, including 8,000 women.

Spurred by fashion and social progress, France quickly embraced sports of all kinds in the wake of the safety bicycle, including gymnastics, archery, rowing, fencing, rugby, and soccer. Emulation, invention, and progress were all at play in a world in full effervescence. Cinema pulsated as if it were radioactive, and automobiles were slowly making their mark. All the while, the bicycle was rapidly infiltrating everyday life.

Such an animated environment gave rise to bicycle ambulances, fire-fighting bicycles, and military bicycles. Stronger forks and more efficient—at times almost invisible—brakes as well as lighter materials drove the evolution of the machine. Standardized fittings were introduced for improved tire inflation, along with better lights and toe-clips to prevent feet from slipping off the pedals.

Pierre Giffard's daily journal, *Le Vélo*, earned its edgy green color every day, for by now the new sport raised considerable expectations. Of course, "The Green" gave news about all sports, but cycling took precedence, and velodromes were its favorite haunts. Up to then, in fact, cycling competition was largely confined to the tracks, which, given the mediocre state of the roads, was no surprise. In a way, the racing bicycle was going around in circles, unsure of its destiny.

## An explosion of velodromes

Still, the spectacle was immensely popular—so popular that it was able to support two categories of racers: sprinters (the champions of short bursts) and stayers (the kings of endurance and specialists at breaking speed records while trailing bicycles powered by two, three, and four pacers). The velodromes were filled with spectators, and they multiplied rapidly across the country. In 1896, France welcomed new facilities with equally crowded stands in the southwest (Nantes, Saintes, Bordeaux, Toulouse), the southeast (Marseille, Nice, Béziers, Nîmes), and the northeast (Quimper and Caen).

In Paris, fans no longer knew which way to look. They could choose among the circuits at Vincennes, Neuilly (Buffalo), Levallois (the Seine), Clignancourt, and the Champ-de-Mars (The Vel' d'Hiv' in the Palace of Liberal Arts). Naturally, the rinks where one could learn to ride a bicycle, just as one learned to mount a horse, were also multiplying. The journals *Véloce-Sport* (which had just merged with *Bicyclette*) and *Paris-Vélo* feathered their nests by touting training tips, miracle products (Quinquina, Énergine, Bovril), puncture-proof tires, underwater cycles, and Six-Day individual races in New York, not to mention matches that pitted sprinters against stayers, and amateurs against professionals. To further enrich the spectacle, Tristan Bernard introduced the "revenue-generating" armband for sprinters, which stayers also quickly adopted.[1] The first holders were Edmond Jacquelin for sprints and Emile Bouhours for longer distances. The holders earned 20 francs a day (the cost of an annual subscription to *Vélo*), but they had to defend their superior status against all challengers. This gave rise to dramatic serialized write-ups in the press and to abundant gates.

---

(1) A symbolic armband that its owner, the best sprinter, had to defend. The bearer earned a daily income for as long as he held on to it.

## The very first start
## 1896

April 19. Easter Sunday. It's 5:30 A.M. at the Porte Maillot in Paris, where photographer Jules Beau immortalizes the start of the inaugural Paris-Roubaix. With armbands and cloth caps, the race favorites line up in the front row. The handlebars vary widely in size and shape, just like the riders gripping them. The future winner, Germany's Josef Fischer (in the center), is flanked by Welshman Arthur Linton and Frenchman Paul Guignard. On the extreme right, the prudent Lucien Stein has a bag of supplies strapped to his bars. Maurice Garin, who'll win the first Tour de France in 1903, is wearing a white jersey in the second row.

**Turmoil
1898**

That year motorcyclists and tricyclists had their own race, and at the same time could pace the cyclists. That caused a real mess at the start control. Here, they carry bicycles, gossip, and give engines a final tune-up. Paris-Roubaix is still searching for its true rhythm.

## Two hundred spectators at the finish of Bordeaux-Paris

As a result, only rebels, eccentrics, and inferior track racers could remain oblivious to the colossal prizes offered by the velodrome owners. Road events, on the other hand, were difficult to organize and had a meager pool of racers to draw from. Road racing was indeed a rich family's poor relative. At the Olympic Games in Athens, five out of the six races were held at the city's only velodrome. Only the track world had organized world championships. The games turned out so well, in fact, that the visionary organizers even put together continental championships. Capitals and other large cities had their own velodromes, too, with grand prizes for sprints or longer distances. There reigned the sprinters Morin, Bourrillon, Jacquelin, Jaap-Eden, and Huet, along with the stayers Huret, Riviere, Lesna, Michaël, and Linton. They were the masters of the Bol d'Or (Golden Cup), Chaînes (Chains), and Cuca Cocoa Challenge Cup. The best track racers were French, and all the authoritative journalists like Minart and Desgrange never ceased to celebrate track races, far less hazardous and complicated than the road variety. The latter were, after all, hampered by inequities and abuses due to the inevitable presence of the trainers, who at that time did whatever they could get away with to ease their racer's burden.

Ludovic Morin, a Breton, who won the grand prize of Paris and 6,000 francs, earned an average of 50,000 francs a year. In contrast, Charles Terront, the hero of Paris-Brest of 1891, had yet to reach the 10,000-franc mark after twenty years of road racing. The winner of Bordeaux-Paris 1896 claimed a purse amounting to only half that awarded to the winner of the Grand Prix of Paris (although, admittedly, the latter did more than a few laps, covering 591 kilometers). Indeed, road racing was not in style and when Arthur Linton and Gaston Rivière finished the 1896 Bordeaux-Paris in a tie, they were greeted by at most two hundred spectators! Nevertheless, the need for racing adventures grew, and the repetitive aspects of certain track races at the velodromes worked in favor of road racing, which was slowly developing.

To enliven their programs, some new owners of velodromes proposed to have road races finish at their tracks. In 1896, this was the case in Roubaix (on April 19) and in Tours (on May 17), giving birth to two road races almost simultaneously, Paris-Roubaix and Paris-Tours. The first was essentially reserved for professionals, the second for amateurs. In the northern city, the purse was but 1,000 francs. Forty-five starters (one hundred had registered) who were not afraid of the unknown vied for the prize. Not until early April had the journalist Victor Breyer even approved the route, which seemed rather ominous given the abundance of cobblestones, especially along the final section after Arras.

## A race sheltered from trickery

*Le Vélo* nonetheless prepared meticulously for the race, soliciting local cycling clubs, lining up six supportive bars and hotels in the area, and assigning all its correspondents to cover the event. But would its high hopes be realized? Would the Easter date, the opening of the season, attract racers eager to improve their form for Bordeaux-Paris one month later? There seemed some cause for optimism.

In the meantime, a special train that was supposed to leave Paris and follow from point to point was canceled due to a lack of inscriptions. Ironically, this setback turned out to be the key to the race's future, for it ensured right from the start that this would be primarily a northern rather than a Parisian affair. And its success that day was indisputably threefold. First, it was indeed popular—the velodrome in Roubaix, in fact, was so filled with workers, weavers, peasants, and other fans from the region that one section of grandstands collapsed under their weight. Second, it was athletically impressive; the average speed of the winner surpassed 30 kilometers an hour. Finally, the competition was international in character. A German (Josef Fischer) beat out a Dane (Charles Meyer) and an Italian (Maurice Garin, who had yet to become a French citizen).

Contested during daylight hours, and thus spared the nighttime trickery that had consistently marred Bordeaux-Paris, Paris-Roubaix quickly grew in stature. This event, conceived by Théodore Vienne and Victor Pérez, two spinning-mill owners from the region, became the race of the northern people. They appreciated good work, especially when the conditions were difficult. For them the race became more than a simple spectacle or a routine Sunday outing. It was a matter of respect, a communion with these pedaling workers, who were so well drubbed by their cobblestones and their earth that they wore a mask of mud, like grimy child miners.

This bond between the spectators and the racers has never changed. Whether the course passes through urban, industrial, or rural settings, the fans will always be there, weathering rain or wind. Even those northerners who have relocated to Paris for work make a point of presenting themselves at the start of "their" race, be it at Chatou or at Saint-Denis.

Paris-Roubaix quickly became a challenge all its own—a race so unique, so fitting, that it now belongs to the heritage of all of northern France. It no longer requires friends to watch over and sustain it. The

majority of the classics that were likewise born in 1896, like Paris-Mons or Paris-Royan, have long since disappeared. So, too, have the velodromes. But Paris-Roubaix is still here, with its notorious cobblestones and its champions. It gives witness to the fact that it is still *the* race—indeed, the great classic that can make one's eyes sparkle at the mere thought of it.

SERGE LAGET

**Apotheosis at Roubaix**
**1901**

After pacing the racers for a couple of years, automobiles became follow vehicles. But in 1901 they remain one of the attractions on the velodrome infield. After all, cars are still rare and mysterious. Behind the track, a bullring presents an intriguing sight.

# CHAPTER I

# A DAY UNLIKE ANY OTHER

This is the race that drives you crazy. Whether it evokes love, passion, and loyalty, or anger, fatigue, and resentment, it crushes both body and soul. Here begins the image of a legend, the timeless racer who has lived for over a century. He is everywhere and spans all eras. On those wretched cobblestones he has won, lost, struggled, and prevailed. He dutifully suffocates in the dust and ploughs his way through the mud. Let us now examine him, listen to him, and admire him. For he is the one who breathes life into the timeless spirit of Paris-Roubaix.

**In a tangle**
**1985**

The road is slick and the riders are still grouped. It doesn't take much for a rider to fall, taking others with him, to cause a chaotic melee in which it's difficult, if not impossible, to find your bike. Fons Van Katwijk (No. 194) has found his machine, but not Stefano Giuliani (No. 154), who's wondering which saint will help him out.

# The Queen of the Classics

The last thing he wants to do is to get out of the shower. He just wants to melt here, under the last drop of tepid water that slowly exposes wrinkles of flesh under his crust of earth. He wants to drown his last tears in the soapsuds that seal his eyelids. Like quick-drying cement, his lactic acid has fossilized in the thinnest recesses of his muscle fibers. But there's no point in cursing this pain, this mud, this dust. A short while ago at Warlaing or Cysoing, he no longer remembers exactly where, he acquired this coat. Now, lulled by the sound of streaming water and the muffled cries of his companions, he knows he's wearing a trophy, a prize for all his efforts.

He wants to lift his head. And if he could, he would see at every opening of the door another reptile covered in earth slither over the tiled floor and enter the steaming mist. All around him, heads without bodies peer over the walls of the heavy granite stalls, their round eyes full of ghosts from the race. Gradually, some of the racers manage to forget their ordeal as they let their road-warrior suits fall to the ground.

A few are already shaven, combed, and dressed. Purified. But others have fallen mummified, prostrated on wooden benches. Over there, another one, forgetting his bruises, has already jumped on his bike to ride home to Belgium. Our racer tells himself that these showers are good. He is comfortable in this familiar environment, as happy as a wet dog. It's as refreshing as sitting in a barber's chair. Every gesture is cushioned by the soft puree of steam. He is like a small boy who has tired of playing and is ready to go to bed, so that he can wake up the next morning transformed into a man.

Of course, he didn't win. That is, he didn't arrive first. So what? As usual, he had a number on his back and he managed to finish the race. A small inner voice almost dares to admit that it isn't such a bad thing to have had a number on his back and to have finished this race—it was an accomplishment just to get here. But he won't allow that, of course. A racer never admits as much, not even to himself, not even at the end of the race. But he knows deep down that it often requires greater mental strength to finish 138th than first. At least that's what he heard from a Flemish rider, who should know. That was this morning at the starting line. Was that at the Gillet café by the Porte Maillot in Paris, or Chatou, Saint-Denis, Chantilly, or maybe Compiègne? He simply doesn't remember. Everything is fluid in his head, so shaken was he by that race.

He swears, on the million cobblestones he had tried to crush that day, he will never do this again. Today was the last time, he vows, as he spits into the black water that swirls about his feet. Or maybe this was just his first time—he really doesn't know. It's always the same: he forgets all the wrongs the race did to him, because of all the good. Because of the intense excitement he felt when he bounded into the light of the velodrome, by that fluorescent carpet of grass that pierced his eyes. It all made a lasting impression: the blast of glacial air that penetrated his jersey, the hairs on his neck that stood up, the faded pink track, and the horizon of black lions speckled on the yellow banners hoisted by the Flemish fans. As always, he had just enough sugar left in the blood to make one and a half laps. The overflowing stands, his heart beating in unison with the regional bands on hand, the stiff hairs on his back . . . things that Flemish racer had also told him about.

Despite all these persistent sensations, he has trouble committing these images to memory. What shade are these memories—black and white or in color? He can't recall; all that is left is a vague taste of dust in his saliva. How did he get to Roubaix? Had he arrived alone, without even stirring the ducks at Barbieux park? Or had he sprinted from the top of avenue Villas, tearing away with three or four accomplices to steal ninth place like a thief in the night? Or had he made his triumphant arrival huddled in the vanquished peloton? And what place did he get— how far was he behind the hero? The man who would soon, in a long waltz, embrace his cobblestone-shaped trophy, his women, his blood brothers, and his directeur sportif. Was the gap 5 minutes and 21 seconds or 20 minutes? Or was it perhaps his next seven lives combined, or simply an eternity?

## Protruding cobblestones, protruding memories

The images of the start that morning slowly filter back into his head. The long wait, and the pervasive fear that radiated right through the derailleur cables. The silence. He smiled, but it was a sad smile, as the thought of those cleanly clad riders whose behinds had felt no more than minor vibrations emanating from the small, neatly aligned cobblestones in the square facing the palace of Compiègne. Before the morning had passed, they had quit without ever leaving the asphalt, without ever seeing Troisvilles. A royal procession of buses took them the rest of the way to the sign-in podium.

**The start**
**1975**

When the race starts at
Chantilly, a center for horse
racing in France, it seems to
take on the look of a fox hunt.
As soon as the bugle has
sounded and the tape is
dropped, the pack will
charge and Eddy Merckx
says he's determined to
shake everyone off his tail.

**The start
1925**

Luxembourg champion Nicolas Frantz (far left)
looks best prepared to tackle the Hell of the North.
Like the others he has a food bag, bottles, a spare
tire, long sleeves, and goggles; but he also has leg
warmers.

**Good-bye Paris
1936**

When the peloton leaves the capital and heads
north, it traverses the industrial suburbs where
smokestacks abound. But it's Sunday and no
one's working today: "Pass in peace, gentlemen,
you have enough to deal with in Hell. . . ."

He was beaten while turning into the wind at the crossroads of l'Arbre, where numerous wars have been waged, spilling streams of horse blood. For centuries now, a fourth of humanity in the region have been cut down in trenches, even on the Lord's Day. So pervasive is the aura of war at Bouvines,[1] it was said that if racing cyclists ever dared pass through, German horsemen would arise from out of nowhere to laugh in their faces, and refuse these pathetic foot soldiers the honor of slitting their throats.

He had spun out of control in a final spasm at Gruson, amidst a flurry of yellow flags raised by dead-drunk Flemish fans. Their stench, however, motivated him to push on, up the false flat past the tavern. Here he had to negotiate a laborious path lined by nutcases, with no possibility to ride along the shoulder. But he had no more than a shovelful of milestones left before the finish line. He remembered what Madiot[2] had told him: "I ached everywhere but I pulled myself together. My throat hurt and my muscles were contracting, but I could still keep going as long as I made the effort. I felt I had to, it was in my head." And he remembered what Duclos[3] had said at the crossroads of l'Arbre: "The best thing that can happen to you here is you take over the lead." Sure, they had experienced that ecstasy, those two. The best thing that had happened to him, he chuckled to himself, was that he got to sniff the aroma of fried sausages, knowing in the bottom of his belly that his nightmare would soon be over. It was as if, beyond the tavern, the sun would be dawning on a new day.

Earlier that morning, he had traversed the rugged hill at Mons-en-Pévèle over the wrinkles of stone. That was before the roads were tarred over. He had also skirted around it from below, over a detour of cobblestones stretching 3 kilometers and rising imperceptibly, with a crosswind so strong it had scared away the wild boars.

He was beaten near Wallers, in the woods of Raismes. The torsos of miners reemerged from the center of the earth just to watch him pass by. One year, in these showers where memories rebound, he had overheard his peers cursing one of their own, Stablinski. It was he who had proposed crossing the forest through that trench 3 meters wide and 2,400 meters long and straight, a third of that in descent. Here are the worst cobblestones in the world. Stablinski himself had descended into the bowels of the local coal mine, so he could ride reasonably well above it— but what about everyone else? All the old-timers advised him to enter that trench in the lead and position himself well, taking care to avoid the

stacks of tibias and broken forks. Then, they added, do your best there. You won't win anything here but you could lose everything.

Even before that, a little earlier on when he was a bit fresher, he was beaten at Troisvilles while trying his best to cross those wretched cobblestones awash with adrenaline. This was a wakeup call, the day's first stretch of cobblestone—or maybe the last, he doesn't know. At any rate, it scattered the peloton between two fields of endive.[4] He left the woods shaken up, but happy to be still in one piece, and feeling as though he had just won a stage. It occurred to him that the organizers should number the cobblestone sections in reverse order, just as some count down rosary beads to please the devil.

He had even launched a flurry of kicks for nothing, starting in the forest of Saint-Germain-en-Laye, then in Pontoise, Beauvais, Amiens, Arras, and Carvin. He pressed on until the last towns in the bicycle's northern hemisphere. The cement on the roads there has sealed off a kingdom of brick, the red blood of races past that has now been drained. Villages with smoking chimneys where the giants of carnivals, looming larger than the slag heaps, lean their big heads of papier-mâché over the cyclists' small silhouettes. Cities that mix their sweat and coal dust with the mud in ruts of the road. Cities that were once prosperous, well before the cobblestones exacted their revenge by becoming cherished souvenirs, much like the picturesque bows of gondolas. He had deftly evaded the shell-shaped craters that punctuate the road. He had done his duty as a messenger, formation after formation, just after the hill of Doullens, between Amiens and Arras, hauling himself up without a derailleur to the elevated plains of Artois. For this is also a race on roads subject to swift and strong winds. It is also a long and draining pursuit over an asphalt coat.

---

**(1)** On this plain on July 27, 1214, the troops of Philippe Auguste, the king of France, defeated a coalition comprising the German emperor Otto IV, the count of Flanders, and John of England, the king of England. They thus avoided the dismemberment of the French kingdom.

**(2)** Marc Madiot was the winner in 1985 and 1991 and later a directeur sportif.

**(3)** Gilbert Duclos-Lassalle was winner in 1992 and 1993.

**(4)** Known as *chicons* in northern France and Belgium.

**The start**
**1936**

They're on their way to the flying start. The
starter's flag is ready. One capped fan has spotted
a star. Everyone is ready to go, but make sure
there are no spectators in the way.

**Across the fields**
**1939**

The peloton passes by and the farmworkers lift
their heads for a moment. It's a brief rest that the
horses appreciate too. It's Sunday; but on the
road, as in the fields, they're hard at work.

## I was small, and you made me a giant

At last he had arrived at the velodrome. With lightning speed, the track
sewed up his wounds and soothed his pain. The velodrome—the place
where one no longer feels bad. And it wasn't a bad idea either, he tells
himself, to have practiced track riding beforehand. That helped. He
knew how to take advantage of the banking at the precise moment, how
to lunge toward the line, from near or far, and how to dispense with a
nearby foe.

Thus, all day long, until the last meter of the track, over the local
roads, in line formation, through Prières and Abattoirs,[5] he had dili-
gently persevered, gradually consuming his bitter medicine. Finally, he
took off his number. He told himself that everything was now okay.

He thinks back: not that long ago he was toiling in the plains of
Picardy, as slimy as the runny omelet of Maroille. Or perhaps rolling bar-
rels for his father, two at a time, at the ports of the Seine. Or slaving away
at the feet of tall furnaces hotter than hell. Or vaccinating cows' behinds
in the sticky furrows of his native Trentin. Or sweeping chimneys in the
Aosta valley like a monkey. Or hallowing out the stomach of the earth
even deeper to extract either coal or gold in Poland or Hainaut.
Whatever he had done previously, he had been insignificant. Then the
race made a majestic eagle out of him. He had been a peasant, and now
he was a lord. He had been small, and now he was a giant. He had been a
bike racer, and now he was a man.

It matters little where he was born. In Brakel, in Marseille, in Gistel,
in Milan, in New York, in Herentals[6]—he can't remember. In Mexico,

Poland, or Melbourne? And it matters even less where he will die, once
he is frozen on the cover of a beautiful book, where our dead breathe as if
still alive. Perhaps he will go down in glory, like the French airman
Lapize,[7] who was firing a hail of bullets from the sky one July 14, 1917.
But while he awaits his own fate, he can take all the time he wants to tell
his nightmares to those he plies with Lambic.[8] He can tell alarming tales
about cold mud, razor-sharp stones, and flat tires. He can take all the
time he needs to explain how he became a hero. Or he can just keep
quiet; that won't change anything.

Under the water that makes him sleepy, he recites only one haunting
refrain: I loved you, Paris-Roubaix. More than anything. Of course, I loved
Milan-San Remo to death, and a hundred times I had my way with it. I
loved Liège, and I loved the Tour of Flanders and its demons. I even loved
the interminable Bordeaux-Paris, and Paris-Brest and back; that goes without saying. Then, from its first day, I loved the Tour de France, which
replaced long distances with mountain climbs. But you, Paris-Roubaix, I
loved you like no other, if you allow me to speak of you as a woman.

Then he waits. He can wait a long time, even a lifetime. Be patient,
the old-timers tell him. He wants it that much. And to want it is the only
way to have it. He loves it like the Frenchman Madiot, who gave himself
no choice but to win it, and who won it twice. One can prepare to have
what it takes in the legs, he said, this Frenchman who speaks so well of it,
but above all you need to love it, to have it in your head.

He loves it like De Vlaeminck,[9] Mr. Paris-Roubaix himself, the only
nickname he ever liked. He was the perfect lover: faithful, savvy, robust,
and fluid. A true specialist who had an acute understanding of the race.
Four times he was the winner. Four masterpieces that no one will ever
approach. There's nothing more to say about him.

He loves it the way the Belgians have always loved it, ever since Van
Hauwaert.[10] He loves it like Raymond Poulidor who threw himself into
it eighteen times. Eighteen races! He allowed himself a fleeting thought
of wonder: what sort of classy athlete would compete eighteen times in
the toughest challenge of his discipline?

Naturally, he would prefer to love it while pretending that nothing
was going on, a bit like that Georges Claes. This good-looking kid, a big
Belgian, prepared himself down to his toes for several months a year, and
he won it twice[11] because, apart from a few exhibitions at fairs, he only
raced after her and no one else. The job of a full-time racer was for the
nutcases, he would say, laughing.

---

**(5)** The names of two sections through which the course passes.

**(6)** Brakel, Gistel, and Herentals are Flemish towns.

**(7)** Octave Lapize won Paris-Roubaix 1909–1911, as well as the 1910 Tour de France.

**(8)** A distinctive Belgian beer.

**(9)** Roger De Vlaeminck won in 1972, 1974, 1975, and 1977.

**(10)** Cyrille Van Hauwaert became the first Belgian to win the race in 1908.

**(11)** In 1946 and 1947.

**Onto the sidewalk
1937**

To avoid the worst of a pavé section, the riders voluntarily take to the sides, which are more inviting. Doing it this way, they are doing it just like the locals, who have even made a small access ramp from the street.

He loves it like the immense Merckx, who tamed it three times, while taking care to create three masterpieces.[12]

He would like to love her with all his devotion, like Duclos-Lassalle. A faithful lover, he came here seventeen times—from the age of 23 to almost 39—to gnash his teeth and bend his wheel rims on its muddy flanks. "I am made for this race," he would say, "but does she want me?" In fact, she gave in to him twice, two times in a row. Then, at last, he noted, "She gives you back everything you had to do to seduce her." He went so far out of his way for her that one morning before the race he started his march from the hotel without recognizing the face of his own son! He was ready to pay the ultimate sacrifice. But she knows how to give back, he would say. "You have to be strong with her. I was facing a monument of the bicycle. She wasn't going to give me any gifts, and I wasn't going to give her any either."

## When you love it, one day or another you will win it

Through the water that still streams from the showerhead, he recalls the infernal uproar of the peloton, a ruckus that sometimes wakes him at night. It's a cacophony comprising metallic clicks, the muffled sounds of pneumatic tires jumping over the crests of cobblestones, and the cries of racers in all the languages of the bicycle. His most somber nightmares find new life in the whirlpools of dust. This race scares him. She reminds him of his worst childhood stories about monsters hiding under his bed. Maybe the race has the same effect on those greats who no longer bother to come here. He must talk to them about that someday. He fears her like a mortal infection, this cursed thing. He hates her too, with a passion. For years, he had even spat upon her, before he finally dared to come here to measure himself out of respect for her. And to win.

Just like Hinault, the tough Breton with his rainbow jersey. A fool's paradise he said, pigs' play. In winning it, he necessarily made it bigger.[13] Or like Anquetil, who wanted to steal one at all costs. When he lost by a few pedal strokes at the velodrome, he could not admit defeat and he sang out his verdict: "It's a lottery!"

Or the wounded Italian, Ballerini. "I will never come back!" he swore when paralyzed by rage, after finishing behind Duclos by barely a

tire's width. Yet he would come back—and win twice![14] All he would say was, "You take your blows, but you must not repeat the same errors. And when you love it like I do, one day or another you will win it."

But for all these champions, wonders our racer in the shower, how many more have been unranked and anonymous nobodies, from obscure platoons, who simply did their job for very little pay? We, the small racers, we sometimes work harder than they, and with as much passion. They just happen to be gifted enough to win. But the press never speaks about us. And what does this profession do for us? The privilege of washing our wounds here in these ancient showers? The satisfaction of having finished Paris-Roubaix? If we're ever to become big, it's right here, in this foundry of heroes.

Besides, no directeur sportif is crazy enough to force us into this. We are volunteers here. We were the ones who, last winter, ticked off the Roubaix checkbox on our calendar. A big step forward. For whoever crosses the finish line first becomes a legend for all time. Even the smallest of the smalls, like Lucien Storme with his meager harvest of 14 professional victories.[15] Or small like Roger Rosiers,[16] who did not hesitate to throw himself into the wind of the north, joining a formation of greats that included Merckx. Or small like all those who win without ever becoming leaders the rest of the season. It's the rendezvous of workers, miners, weavers, metalworkers, and farmhands. That day, there's no more boss. Here, nothing is easy, not even for the greats. After all, what kind of idea is it to go and fracture a tibia in the icy mud, three months before the start of the Tour? Is that why the greats won't race here anymore? And is that why they are perhaps no longer so great?

He would just like to know a few secrets from the giants who founder here. "The route is not responsible for your problems," Madiot whispered in his ear. "It's you, and you alone. If you did not properly prepare for your campaign, you cannot win. You must think, live, eat, and sleep Paris-Roubaix. It must become obsessive. In a normal race, you can be agonizing and, in the final sprint, seize an opportunity. In Paris-

---

**(12)** In 1968, 1970, and 1973.

**(13)** In 1981.

**(14)** Franco Ballerini lost at the finish line in 1993 but prevailed in 1995 and 1998.

**(15)** First in 1938.

**(16)** The 1971 winner.

Here, you *have* to ride the cobblestones. We're in the heart of the Hell of the North. The focused riders have their hands on the drops, ready to brake. They don't want to fall here because still on the menu are the nasty cobblestones at Warlaing and Marchiennes.

Roubaix, it's not possible. You are either ready or not." Even De Vlaeminck had a dream one night: the secret, it's confidence. He left with the idea that he would win. He knew how to prepare for Paris-Roubaix. In the preceding week he made three outings on the order of 300 kilometers apiece. It's so simple, when you look at it that way.

All these fuzzy voices and faces come together to form the portrait of an ideal winner. What he has to become in order to shine. He would need a little experience. It's not easy to win for someone who has yet to cut his teeth. There's not much room here for those who want to go too fast. The race most often goes to a seasoned roadster, to a crafty old devil who knows the best angle of attack on each cobblestone. With age, the solid mixture of power and efficiency crystallizes.

He needs a bit of panache to become an outstanding warrior. To acquire a taste for excessive work. To desire to do his work under the rain or sleet. To want to eat wind and dust. To orient all this training toward the classics, without waiting for the sunny month of July. He might also need more culture, a greater knowledge of the history of this race, something that forges dreams and inspires imagination. But also maps out an itinerary culminating in success.

## A reconnaissance mission to exorcize the fear

In any case, he doesn't have to become an eater of cobblestones to win Paris-Roubaix. He just needs to be a very good racer. Hinault and Raas[17] won because they were great racers, but they were not especially talented when it came to cobblestones. Just ask De Vlaeminck. Even Merckx wasn't made for the cobblestones. Yet he won three times because he was Merckx.

He would also like to acquire a killer instinct. Madiot was said to have that, a knack for killing others. Win Paris-Roubaix and you will gain the peloton's absolute respect. And in order to win, you have to kill them. To survive, you have to hurt your peers. But to do that, you have to transform yourself. Grow to survive. It's the eternal lesson that little boys learn when their training wheels are removed and they scrape their knees.

He knows he needs to develop his talent for this race by accepting an idea of racing like one almost never races anywhere else. He must stay in front over the several dozen kilometers of cobblestone, and design his race like no other. It's impossible to find shelter. Do what it takes no mat-

ter the price, work with others more than against them. Get in front to get the best perception of the bending trajectory, the ruts, the rails. If possible, try to stay on the elevated part of the road. Once back into the full wind, he must know how to hide himself, to employ wise calculations of economy to space out his tired spells while enjoying occasional reprieves.

In the week preceding the race, he should conduct a reconnaissance mission. Perhaps on Thursday, for two or three hours. Go over just a few cobblestone sections—more to exorcize the fear than to study up on all the nasty turns. After all, what's the point of trying to remove the slightest enigma? You can't break through the mystery of women just by looking up their dresses.

If he had the time, he would come here one day in the summer, leave his bicycle in the tall grass, and continue along the cobblestone road on foot. He would then discover the charming mineral of blue shale or the ginger plants impossible to cut, having been planted there four centuries ago. He would study the delicate blue of the Côtes-d'Armor granite, which has shown through the clay since the eighteenth century. Or the very pretty rose of Perros-Guirrec, which landed in Dunkerque and was brought here by cart. The bluish black of Tarn, the blue of Tournaisis.... But who bothers to stop here? At first, all this went unnoticed. The roads of France were once full of such things. The journalists who followed the first editions barely even noticed these things. They were much more inclined to point out the sporadic, and very modern, paved sections. One attentive eccentric simply cited in his report a few bad cobblestone stretches between Seclin and Lesquin, not far from the finish line.

What stood out most at that time about this race was its comparatively short length—less than 300 kilometers. That was rather an original idea on the part of the organizers, the directors of the newspaper *L'Auto*.[18] Little by little, with the passing of time, the cobblestones disappeared under a coat of tar without much fanfare. The riverside residents found that the cobblestones caused too much noise and were too dangerous to drive over. And once city folk began to move here into newly constructed country homes, they showed nothing but disdain for the cobblestones.

---

**(17)** In 1982, Jan Raas succeeded Bernard Hinault as reigning champion.

**(18)** The ancestor of *L'Équipe*.

**Hide-and-seek**
**1988**

When there's no mud, there has to be dust to preserve the event's legendary status. It's certainly the case here, where the riders search for the road and the fans for the riders.

**Ancient and modern**
**1992**

Perhaps the duel isn't classic, but it is unique. You stick to the ridge of the pavé on a conventional bike, while you test the grass verge if you have shock absorbers.

Finally, by the 1965 edition, only 22 kilometers of cobblestone remained in the course. The average winning speed rose to over 45 kilometers an hour. Pavement threatened to turn this classic into a moribund banality. The realization of the need to restore its unique character bore fruit in 1968—the year of cobblestones. At a time when Paris would shortly pave over the whims of revolt, Paris-Roubaix invented (the way paleontologists "invent" brontosaurs) its legend of granite. The profile of the course was reconfigured to wind its way toward Valenciennes, to uncover with an excavator all the lost cobblestone sections. By then the restoration of the cobblestones was working to everyone's advantage. In the traversed regions, the image of the Hell of the North, which previously had not excited the locals in the least, suddenly became endearing to them. How could they attract visitors with these frightful images? Precisely, they told themselves: for us, the answer is Paris-Roubaix. If we lose our cobblestones, we lose Paris-Roubaix.

## It's not pure luck if you don't flat

So, the locals resolved, let us restore the cobblestones as much as we can. Let us preserve our heritage. Let us remove the tar, then send out agricultural high school students to scrape off the moss that gnaws at the mortar between the cobblestones. Let's sprinkle a few pebbles here and there where the racers' wheels will pass. Today, at Roubaix, the path along the avenue Alfred-Motte, the last section of the race, has been paved with good souvenirs and rebaptized Charles Crupelandt, after the local hero who won at Barbieux park in 1912 and 1914. Will some crazy inventor one day lay the foundation for a velodrome track covered with cobblestones?

Our racer in the shower continues to reflect. To prepare for war, his mechanic had mounted a choice artillery: two chainrings, with forty-six and fifty-three teeth. After all, you don't go out hunting for boar armed with carnival darts. No need for the little ring of thirty-nine, kid, his mechanic had said. Roubaix is flat, so leave the alpine sprockets for those who want to climb Mont Ventoux. Besides, you'll see in the morning, at the start, they'll all switch to this to avoid rubbing. With these two big chainrings, your chain won't hop off as soon as you attack the cobblestones. And if it starts to jump as you leave the stones, just get on the flat

and the chain will click into place. You won't have to fret anymore about it. In the rear, I put on a straight block with an eleven-tooth sprocket so you can devour the cement at the velodrome. I've also put on 25-centimeter tubular tires, inflated to eight bars. If it's wet, we'll deflate them a bit.

At least, he tells himself, we did as much as we could to transform this adventure into an exact science.

The equipment has become his obsession. He has seen and tried everything over the years. When the race was born, the bicycle was barely ten years old. The pneumatic tire was even younger. He had seen characters who, in order to change sprockets, had to jump off their machines and rotate the rear wheel. He had seen Van Looy[19] put his shifters at the ends of his handlebars. He had seen an enraged Bauer[20] throw his bicycle into a ditch in the middle of the race after his chain acted up. He had seen racers use telescopic forks pinched from mountain bikes, shocks in front and rear, and cyclocross cantilever brakes. Today, it's the frame of his machine that is studied to absorb the millions of electrical charges that all these blocks of granite send to his nerves.

Designers adapt bicycles specifically for Roubaix the way they streamline surface-to-air missiles. They devise details such as wider dropouts to evacuate the mud, frames extended to absorb shock, greater fork rakes to stabilize the machine over the swell of cobblestones, possibly even a double layer of handlebar tape—the only possible airbag for the hands. The problem of not flatting, or flatting as seldom as possible, remains. Madiot preferred to see his bicycle as a friend; when you don't flat it's not luck, you paid attention to it.

Then you have to try to pilot your bicycle. Attack the cobblestones with the teeth in front. Don't let it dictate its law. Constantly maintain a firm grip. Be your bicycle. If you let the cobblestones have their way, you will bounce around. It's a question of gears, Madiot says. You mustn't go with one too small or you will get jostled, nor one too big or you will stumble. There is no ideal position, but you mustn't be too stiff in order to cushion a maximum of vibrations. Your body must become one with your bicycle. Think of it before you think of yourself.

**(19)** Rik Van Looy, the winner in 1961, 1962, and 1965.

**(20)** Steve Bauer came in second in 1990 and he conceived, with the help of Eddy Merckx Cycles, a particularly innovative bicycle that allowed him to sit farther back.

**Mud train
2001**

How is the pilot fish able to find the way? Apparently, his eyes are so blocked by the mud that he's riding by radar. But, between his eyelashes, can he even see his front wheel?

He wanted to glide, to be supple, to be in top form for this race. To pilot, after all, is to cushion the shocks. Avoid the puddles that hide potholes and dangerous ruts, and know how, when necessary, to ignore the temptations of comfortable shoulders where the flint shows through. Keep only your reptilian brain awake. Let yourself go completely. He must no longer calculate the trajectories, or ponder the tactics to employ. There is nothing left but vibrations. He senses in a thousandth of a second everything that will happen, where he needs to pass, to rest his legs. He has the impression that he and his bicycle will jump in all directions. He becomes so into the race after ten or fifteen seconds that the cobblestones are no longer a deciding factor. If he takes a good look around, he comes to the conclusion that it's always the same racers who survive on these cobblestones, and often the same ones who languish here. "Every time I won Paris-Roubaix, I never flatted," says De Vlaeminck. There's a simple explanation: one rarely punctures when one is in great shape, because one becomes more lucid and more selective about one's trajectories.

## The elusive supersonic parade of racers

Our racer in the showers has a recurring vision: he sees all the people who were amassed on the sidewalks, in the ditches, and in the trees. While the racer has to earn his victory, those on the side of the road who watch them pass by must also pay a high price for this entertainment. The fans have to bide their time under hail, cold rain, or dust, their boots sinking into the puree of old beets that rot at the bottom of the ditches. They amuse themselves by pouring the dregs of their tankards on the trailing cars, as they slalom between ruts and crevasses. The helicopter approaches; its rotor announces the pack of muddied faces is about to make its charge. Before the racers' arrival, the fans perch along the cobblestones on their toes, as if on the edge of a diving board. They bend their backbones to get closer to the faces of the racers. Flashes of color pass in one breath. Orders are cried from top to bottom of the peloton, in Flemish, Italian, and French. The fans hear the chinks of metal, chains, cables, derailleurs, and sprockets. Once the racket vanishes, they sit down again. They pretend to have had perfectly dissected, in slow motion, the elusive supersonic parade of racers. Moncassin,[21]

he's doing well, isn't he? Boonen! Did you see how he's still fresh? And Van Petegem?[22] I didn't see him. Where is he, did he flat? They had come to await the racers, not necessarily to get a good look at them but to talk about them.

If he racks his memory, this character whose mud splotches are slowly dissipating under the shower, he realizes that he has become this evening the spitting image of those who represent effort, adventure, and durability. He was 10 years old in 1896 or in 2006, he doesn't remember well. He had read about this race in gazettes; this incredible adventure in which consenting victims naively subject themselves to the fatigue of galley slaves. A battle of free men. Words translate into images. He had watched the race on television, which did not hide the truth. The images they gathered in the North proved that those who had commented on the harshness of the race had not exaggerated a whit. As in all legends, the magic of the race is this: the contemporary images of Paris-Roubaix have been preceded and amplified by all the ghosts of its storied past.

That evening our racer never wanted to leave his shower. He wanted to continue talking to himself. Until the race started to listen to him. Until the race had something to say. If you knew how much I really love you, he says to himself in a final murmur, you would be afraid. And me, if I really knew how to love you, I think I would no longer fear anything. Because you never give anything away for nothing. I know you will never sell yourself, because you are far too classy. Yes, you give away nothing. Look, it's only me, a small gutsy racer in the shower, but I only want you. Stop breaking my heart. I am no longer so young and you, you are not very beautiful either, but I'm okay with that. Look here around me, look deep into the eyes of all those you sent on their way: haunted by ghosts. Listen to their silence. Give me a chance and I will vanquish my fears. Help me just a bit, take my hand. I am freezing and it is late.

PIERRE CALLEWAERT

---

**(21)** Frédéric Moncassin finished fifth in 1998.

**(22)** Peter Van Petegem and Tom Boonen, the winners in 2003 and 2005 respectively, are the two great Flemish rivals in the early 2000s.

**On the cobblestones**
**1922**

Roadworks after World War I.
The cobbles are still there at
Pontoise, and the riders are
still jolted around.

**On the tarmac
1938**

The cobbles have been tarred over and the ride through Pontoise is much faster now. You can't halt progress. Also, modern sedans have replaced the old bangers of the 1920s.

**Abandon
1938**

Belgian Romain Maës, winner of the 1935 Tour de France, abandons the race while his bike is unceremoniously dumped in a follow car. Since he was "tricked" out of the Roubaix victory by Georges Speicher in 1936, Maës has been disillusioned.

**In the ditch**
**1961**

These five fans can easily rescue the still-shocked Belgian Frans Demulder from the ditch. Is his bike broken? And he's probably thinking, what's ahead to master on the pavé?

## Dancing in the rain
## 1966

The riders seem to search out the puddle jumper on the sidewalk. Panicked, he avoids the first cyclist, but his side step takes him into the wheel of another who has already fallen. It's an acrobatic feat worthy of a Jacques Tati movie.

## On the canvas
## 1973

A rider has fallen heavily on the ground, forcing Belgium's Marc Demeyer to put a foot down, while his teammate Freddy Maertens is waiting to help.

### Railroad crossing
### 1961

A barrier is raised and the spectacle begins as everyone sets off again. One tries to take an advantage on foot as another finds his balance. And a photographer goes to capture the image, first looking to see if another train is arriving.

### Traffic cop
### 1958

You hesitate a moment. But it's the same whether you go to the left or right. It's only a traffic island. You'll find the others at the exit, which marks the entry to the pavé. Thank you, officer!

**A broken wheel
1953**

The defending champion
Rik Van Steenbergen has
broken his wheel. There's
panic: a gendarme whistles,
a motorcyclist swerves,
and someone helps the
rider run to his bike.
Perched on a bridge,
spectators lap it up. No, the
great Rik isn't going to win
his third Paris-Roubaix today.

**Slag heap**
**1961**

From the factories of the Paris suburbs to the mining villages of the North, the warm-up doesn't last long. And it's only here, at the end of the straightaway, that the race really begins. We've arrived at the mine pit.

**Pileup**
**1966**

A racer skids sideways into
the spectators. In the breach
where he went flying, he gets
up more easily than the
granny he bowled over. More
fear than injury, though, as is
usually the case.

## Drama
### 1975

Paris-Roubaix is one long drama, in which the racers, particularly the stars, are the major players; but also playing an occasional and helpful role are the motor cop, the Good Samaritan, the photographer, and the spectator giving first aid.

## Barry Hoban and the umbrella
### 1966

Englishman Barry Hoban, who has just given his wheel to help his team leader Raymond Poulidor, waits for help under the scrutiny of an elegant spectator wearing a beret and tie, with an umbrella in hand. He seems to be asking himself: Should I do something? Shelter the rider? Help with his repair? But with what?

### Running with the bulls
### 1966

No, it's not the festival in Pamplona, but now and then a wayward racer veers onto the sidewalk and collides with a spectator; this time it's a young girl. Thanks for the muddy leg, mister! There's a moment of fright, but nothing serious.

### A helping hand
### 1966

Hand lift, slip, zigzag, and also drop, encourage, share, and take Communion. So much so that, sometimes, a hand helps a racer onto his bike to get back in the action. Hands that applaud, hands that push…Paris-Roubaix has a thousand and one hands.

**The party**
**2005**
Walls of joyous fans at fever pitch and racers filing fearlessly between them. Flags slapping in the wind. Spectators standing atop balanced haystacks. This is also Paris-Roubaix: a party, a Flemish kermesse.

**In the trenches**
**1992**
They've entered the Arenberg trench like big cats in a cage, but they will get out again at the end of this endless straightaway. Until then, these big cats roar and have a hard time with those who cry and whimper.

# CHAPTER II

# BENEATH THE COBBLESTONES, THE NORTH...

Long threatened, the route of Paris-Roubaix has become a legacy to which the people of the region are now very attached. The legend stems from a small stone block some 20 centimeters deep with a surface about 14 centimeters square: the pavé of the North.

**The backbone**
**2001**

The cobblestones—the pavés—make up the backbone of this event from another age. It's an almost prehistoric race that can make the spectators look like paleontologists. And whether ancient or new cobblestones, the helmeted racers almost swallow them up like pythons.

# The stones are eternal

It is gray or blue, depending on whether it comes from the granite basin of Brittany or the quarries of Hainaut province in Belgium, or whether it's sandstone from Artois. It's often referred to with over-the-top expressions like "sugar lump" or "bowler hat" when nicely rounded, "baby's head" or even "barnum," an evident allusion to the circus it generates as soon as the race takes off on this monumental rattletrap. It has given rise to a quite a few expressions. To stay on "top of the pavé," for example, refers to taking the privileged path in the center of the road, not on the sides where mud and water gather. Alternatively, one might be "thrown in the pond," an allusion to those side channels. Either way, this cycling hell is known for being "paved with bad intentions." Finally, when a tiring racer can no longer cross the pavé at a good clip, he is condemned to "counting the cobblestones."

These back roads of the North, which sink to the level of the fields and are sometimes buried by thick earth, are the vestiges of another time. Their cobblestones resound to the deep memories of a region. In the gray dawn, it's the clatter of miners' clogs that suddenly rises to the surface. Under a low sky, the pavé returns the echo of cartwheels, belonging to peasants or weavers, who once went as far as the spinning-mills of Roubaix. Beneath the cobblestones, the North....

The pavé is not tender; it does not wilt like roses. "A cobblestone, that's eternal," says Alain Bernard, president of the Friends of Paris-Roubaix, an association that continues to play an important role in safeguarding this legacy. "The only enemy of the pavé is water," Bernard continues. "The blue sandstone cobbles are more fragile; they sometimes split when water infiltrates, and in winter, when it freezes, they crack. But the Brittany cobblestone is indestructible." If it has survived, that's witness to a frame of mind transmitted through the ages. "In the North, people have always worked hard, and the cobblestone represents that work ethic," affirms François Doulcier, vice president of the Friends of Paris-Roubaix, and one of the most ardent defenders of this course that recalls a hardworking past.

One must recognize, however, that the vocabulary of Paris-Roubaix has also borrowed heavily from that of World War I (1914–1918): words such as *trench*, *breach*, and *chaos*. Indeed, in the aftermath of that conflict, to prepare for the race's return in 1919, Victor Breyer, the special correspondent for the sponsoring newspaper, *L'Auto*, accompanied by the champion cyclist Eugène Christophe, toured the countryside devastated by myriad shells and bomb holes. Breyer coined a phrase that has passed into posterity: "the Hell of the North."

At that time cobblestones were by no means specific to the North. There are still some scattered all over France, especially in towns. But if, elsewhere, the major roads were made of dirt, the pavé recalled that the North, apart from its industrial past, has always been a land of transit, where invasions were commonplace. The cobblestones reflect an obvious military interest, because they render the roads passable in all weather conditions. Indeed, later on, when the first roads of the North region were paved over with tarmac, they were referred to as "strategic pavement."

## Only 22 kilometers of cobblestones in 1965!

When Paris-Roubaix was created in 1896, cobblestones were hardly quaint. Indeed, the press did not even mention their presence along the route until the following year, when it singled out the "poor" cobblestone stretch between Seclin and Lesquin. On the contrary, the chroniclers of that era took pleasure in citing the rare stretches of asphalt. What truly stood out about this race back then were not its cobblestones but its relatively short distance—about 280 kilometers. This length contrasted sharply with the typical long-distance classics of the day, such as the 600-kilometer Bordeaux-Paris, upon which racers built their reputations.

In the aftermath of World War I, authorities in the North went about repairing the roads damaged during that apocalyptic conflict. The main roads, as far as Amiens, were paved with bitumen. From 1922 to 1939, the great restructuring of the national French highway network took place. And was it a coincidence that as the roads between Paris and Roubaix gradually improved, so did the Belgians strengthen their domination over the event?

The countryside, for its part, was barely affected by this modernization project. The national and departmental roads were still composed of nice cobblestones. In general, they were in good shape, except for a few bad stretches, notably around Wattignies, Seclin, Hénin-Liétard, and Lesquin. To be sure, some secondary roads were in miserable shape, but they were still superior to roads made of pebbles,

**Urban cobblestones**
**1914**

It's often forgotten that in the Belle Époque all the streets in the towns along the race route are cobbled, like this one that passes the city walls of Paris and is laced with tram rails.

**The ruins of war 1919**

Paris-Roubaix has become the Hell of the North . . . of France because it traverses the terrain battered by the Great War of 1914–1918. Writer Victor Breyer penned the terrible "Hell of the North" phrase after seeing the ruined buildings and shelled streets during a reconnaissance of the 1919 racecourse.

resembling the gravel driveways one sometimes sees today leading up to a grand French château.

In the long history of resurfacing the roads between Paris and Roubaix, the year 1939 marks a turning point. That year, the race's first kilometer of cobblestones, between Forest-sur-Marque and Hem, disappeared under concrete. No one despaired; on the contrary, they rejoiced. Progress was on the march. A director of the Highways and Bridges department went so far as to predict, "In six years, all the roads of Paris-Roubaix will be modernized." It took the intervention of another war to retard this inevitable prospect.

When the race resumed in 1943, few paid attention to the 2 new kilometers eaten up by tar, between Lesquin and Ascq, in the suburbs of Lille. Still, the tendency was by now irreversible. Initially, the route had included some 60 kilometers of cobblestone roads, a third of which were through the cities of Saint-Germain-en-Laye, Pontoise, Breteuil, and Amiens. The balance was an uninterrupted stretch of 40 kilometers from Hénin-Liétard to Roubaix. By 1955, however, the length of the pavé sections was nearly halved, with only 31 kilometers remaining. Ten years later, at the lowest point, the total had fallen to just 22 kilometers. The year before, 1964, was marked by a disturbing development: the Dutchman Peter Post won the race averaging 45.120 kilometers per hour, collecting the "yellow ribbon of the road" for setting a speed record in a classic longer than 200 kilometers.

Hell was rapidly becoming softer than its reputation. "It had become much less difficult, less hostile than it is today," says Jean-Marie Leblanc, the race director of the Tour de France (and Paris-Roubaix) until 2006 and a staunch northerner. "From Doullens on, the national roads were paved. They were normal traffic routes, wider than those employed in the race today. They invariably had adjacent bicycle paths made of cinder, and the racers alternated freely between the road and the bike paths. That's how they crossed the region during those years."

In fact, the number of races that ended in sprints on the velodrome multiplied over the years. The race lost much of its allure. From 1955 on, one had to comb the countryside to find any remaining cobblestone roads. One explored, for example, Pévèle, a region whose name derives from *pève*, the old French word for *pavé*, the cobblestone. Finally, in 1968, came the cobblestone revolution. In May of that year, French authorities collected cobblestones to build barricades in Paris, to quell the student uprising. But more to the point, a month earlier, the race's

technical director, Albert Bouvet, had sent the Paris-Roubaix racers over the famous course we know today, mostly back roads and abandoned farm tracks. Bouvet had been commissioned to find the cobblestones at any cost by race director Jacques Goddet, who was keenly aware that this masterpiece of a race was on the endangered list. Bouvet found that, yes, cobblestones still existed, and not just any cobblestones! All he had to do was bend the route toward Valenciennes, where the principal sectors awaited.

## Under a shroud of tar

At the same time as it uncovered the forest of Wallers, in 1968, Paris-Roubaix acquired what was arguably an excess of cobblestones. Paradoxically, however, it was this anachronism that helped make the race very modern and highly newsworthy. "Before, you only got to see the last 30 kilometers on television," observes François Doulcier. "Then came coverage of the Wallers-Arenberg section during the midday news hour. Now they broadcast all the cobblestone sections without interruption."

Still, in the 1970s, the "race against time" that haunted Bouvet's sleep was far from won—not as long as the tar-spraying machines stayed active. "Every election, more cobblestones would disappear, as mayors kept their pledges to lay more pavement," recalls Jean-Marie Vallaeys, who initiated the creation of the Friends of Paris-Roubaix. This resident of Roubaix, devoted to all cycling causes, launched the formidable crusade that led to the present policy of preserving cobblestone sections rather than systematically destroying them.

Here's one example of the resistance to cobblestones. In 1972, the mayor of Nomain, Raymond Vandermesse, launched a poster campaign coinciding with the race—which was assumed to give the North a wretched image. "They don't deserve this," ran the message over a background of abominable cobblestones stagnating in a filthy pool.

The president of the Friends of Paris-Roubaix remembers this era when tar was synonymous with the comfort of the residents, and new housing developments were springing up in every village. "Cobblestones were not particularly bothersome for the locals," explains Alain Bernard. "But those who had arrived from cities to live in the countryside

**Crossing Montdidier
1920**

Not one house is standing in this sinister-looking town. Building stones have been lifted to the side to allow traffic to circulate, although the cobblestones themselves remain intact.

demanded that the cobblestone roads be tarred, triggering a gradual erosion. The newcomers wanted the comfort of their city streets."

Thus the "reserves" of cobblestones were disappearing before one's eyes. Bouvet warned his friend Vallaeys, "Soon we're going to have to call the race Paris-Valenciennes!" He really wasn't kidding. One day, in the course of a casual conversation, Leblanc, then a journalist with *L'Équipe*, politely suggested to the president of Lille's urban commission, Pierre Mauroy, that he consider saving the cobblestones. "Forget about it," snapped Mauroy, expressing the prevailing attitude of the time. "It's negative for the North department's image."

The situation was becoming desperate and the future of the race was directly threatened. The writer René Fallet, who chronicled Paris-Roubaix for *L'Équipe*, wrote, "You lucky climbers, no one will ever take your mountains away from you. Pity the poor cobblestone racers who are threatened with unemployment."

Then came the freeways and the TGV (bullet train), which cut through the suburbs around Lille. These massive engineering projects made entire sectors of cobblestone disappear, and broke up others with no possibility of reconnecting them. Little by little, the cobblestones of the North were disappearing under a shroud of tar.

## "No more cobblestones, no more Paris-Roubaix"

Happily, the winds would eventually shift. Encouraged by Vallaeys, Leblanc wrote a book titled *Les Pavés du Nord* (The Cobblestones of the North), published by La Table Ronde in 1982, which struck a loud chord in the region. More importantly, Vallaeys's lobbying was beginning to pay off. Starting in 1979, the mayors of the towns on the Paris-Roubaix route were polled. A large majority (80 percent) favored the race passing through their territory. Moreover, they declared themselves willing to slow down the tarring process in order to preserve the race, even if they were concerned about maintaining the cobblestone byways. All the same, there appeared to be a certain awakening of conscience. "People were beginning to realize that if there were no more cobblestones there would no Paris-Roubaix either, a disturbing proposition," recalls Leblanc. "And, moreover, it was the time when people were beginning to talk about the environment, ecology, and legacy. All of a sudden, politi-

cians began to listen to our proposals, to the point where the interests of the North region overlapped with those of the race."

The increasing press coverage devoted to an event that stirred the imagination as far away as America, where they relished the images of racers covered in mud, gave the race a decisive boost. "That played in our favor," acknowledges Leblanc, who became the director of the race in 1989. "The Northerners reclaimed Paris-Roubaix. They also became more attached to their roots and by now they recognized that, without Paris-Roubaix, the legacy of the cobblestones would disappear entirely. They became extremely proud of hosting it once a year—so much so that the indifference of the 1970s gave way to a passionate commitment."

Since then, the initiatives to protect the race have multiplied, most of them started by the Friends of Paris-Roubaix. Even if the proposal to classify the route as a national landmark, filed in 1993 with Ségolène Royal, then minister of the environment, has languished, the Northerners themselves have come to the race's defense. Over here a volunteer repairs a cobblestone, over there another one fills some potholes. The Friends of Paris-Roubaix do not hesitate to intervene like this and put their know-how to work on-site. "We reposition the stones and pack down the earth. We go away exhausted but happy that we have participated in the adventure of Paris-Roubaix, even if only for a few square meters," explains its president, Alain Bernard. "But this isn't just patching things up. We believe this restoration will lead to Paris-Roubaix 2050 and will allow us to recall what the North was like in the nineteenth century."

Some Belgian and British friends of the race also willingly participate in these repaving operations. The reclamation of the pavés is well under way, and everyone gives what he or she can. A high priority is to repair those sections where the cobblestones are in dangerous condition. The horticultural schools of the region, including those at Raismes and Lomme, allow their students to participate so that they can take their course work in the great outdoors, learning practical skills. An agreement was signed among the different communities, which supply the materials, and the Friends of Paris-Roubaix, who supervise the students. The General Council of the North, for its part, provides the primary material, the cobblestones, from its large stockpile accumulated from various work projects. "The existing stock can cover many kilometers of road," says a gleeful Doulcier.

**Roadwork 2000**
The grass is getting green so Paris-Roubaix can't be far off. And volunteers are hard at work to repair the damage caused by the winter weather and the influx of mud from the fields.

Thanks to the filled holes and rehabilitated shoulders, which provide proper drainage, the route of Paris-Roubaix is slowly coming back to life. It's not about making an entirely smooth surface, but rather eliminating the pitfalls that can make the race too dangerous. At the same time, this work permits local residents to use their cars on the cobblestone roads and thus helps to overcome any lingering opposition at the local level.

## One kilometer of pavé every 3 kilometers

Even better, some cobblestones lost over time have sprung back to life. The best example of this is at the Moulin de Vertain, a difficult 500-meter stretch in the town of Templeuve that was exhumed in 2002. "That was my greatest find," rejoices Jean-François Pescheux, who has succeeded Albert Bouvet as director of competitions for Amaury Sports Organisation (ASO), owner of the Paris-Roubaix race. He knows the route like the back of his hand, but to tell the truth, this happy discovery of the Vertain sector, named after a nearby windmill, is due to Madame Farine, the secretary to the mayor of Templeuve. She remembered that her own mother, years before, crossed the cobblestones when she cycled to that place. "She was convinced that the cobblestones were still there, so we got a mechanical digger to come and, as they were simply covered by earth, they came to light," relates Pescheux, who, over the years, has developed close ties with the local populace, who are increasingly interested in saving the route. In one sense, it's archaeology, digging up people's memories. "Today we are no longer losing cobblestones," says Pescheux with a sense of relief. "On the contrary, we have the possibility of rediscovering more."

Pescheux has become something of a celebrity in the North. One day while scouting out the route, a week before the race, he was unpleasantly surprised to find the course blocked by roadwork outside a housing development in Wallers. But the bulldozer operator recognized him right away and shouted, "Don't worry, Monsieur Pescheux! We'll have it all done by Sunday." It seems that everyone is doing his part to clear the way for Paris-Roubaix.

At this point, the main objective is to rehabilitate cobblestone sections found within a band about 20 kilometers wide, whether or not the roads are used in the race. To this end, with the continued support of the Friends of Paris-Roubaix, the General Council of the North has commissioned a detailed study to assess the amount of cobblestones available, and the technical requirements needed to restore them to good order. This document is especially useful for the sporting services of ASO. To be exact, there are 165.7 kilometers of pavés within the area concerned. But often, alas, perfect sections of cobblestones are isolated in fields, with no prospect of leading anywhere. Consequently, only about 75 kilometers of road are serviceable for the race. Fortunately, that's still more than enough to guarantee the future of the event. "We need about 50 kilometers of cobblestone in the last 150 kilometers of the race," Pescheux maintains. "Ideally, we should have 1 kilometer of pavé every 3 kilometers. It's this mix of sectors that gives Paris-Roubaix its character."

They are not far from this goal. The 2005 edition included 54.3 kilometers of pavé, spread out over twenty-six sections. "You might say we no longer have a problem," admits Pescheux. "The only concern is between Orchies and the finish line. There, we have no more choice. But we still have 18 kilometers in eleven sections, and that's okay."

For some time to come, Paris-Roubaix seems destined to flatter the Northern sense of pride, to such an extent that it ranks second on the list of annual events most cherished by the region's populace, right behind the Great Fair of Lille and ahead of the Carnival of Dunquerque. The phenomenon of rejection that once plagued the race has been completely reversed. "Once the people of the North were almost embarrassed by the race; now they proudly consider it part of their heritage," emphasizes Leblanc. "All that cannot be swept away by modernity. Nor can I see how anyone down the road can revisit these words: history, patrimony, environment...."

To sum up, let us defer to the president of the Friends of Paris-Roubaix, who happily speaks on behalf of all his dedicated members, particularly Vallaeys. In Bernard's succinct words describing a well-deserved outcome, "Paris-Roubaix has won the race!"

PHILIPPE BOUVET

**Reconnaissance
1955**

You can never know the
route of Paris-Roubaix too
well. Here, Jean Bobet leads
his champion brother
Louison on a scouting trip a
few days before the race.
Riding the gravel sides, their
hands on the tops, they
make a detailed inspection
of the mining zone, where
the race really begins.

**Crossing Clermont de l'Oise 1950**

Cobblestones still carpet the streets of many towns. It's the increase of vehicles, causing residents to complain about the noise of their tires on the bumpy surface, that triggers their disappearance.

**Crossing Clermont de l'Oise 1951**

A year later, the cobblestones have gone, except on the sidewalks. The gendarmerie is there to police two new traffic islands, and in the side street there are three vehicles, not two. That's quite a change in just twelve months.

## Albert Bouvet,
## the guarantor
## 1980

Champion cyclist turned organizing official, Albert Bouvet knows that the pavé is the soul of the race. Starting from 1965, when the race bottomed out with just 25km of cobblestones, he set out with his colleague Jean Stablinski and the Friends of Paris-Roubaix to make a ferocious campaign to preserve the pavé.

## Resurrection
## 2000

Without the cobblestones there is no Paris-Roubaix. And so they refurbish them, protect them, and in this case exhume them. A covering of soil caused these "jewels" to disappear. A road crew works with passion and energy to dust them off like family heirlooms.

**The border**
**2004**

The most delicate part of
restoring a sector of pavé
is the gutter, or border. A
special cobblestone, longer
than usual, is needed to
achieve this exacting work.
It adjoins the clay and
so becomes a sort of
frontier between the
world of the spectators
and that of the racers.

**Chain reaction**
**1995**

The cobblestones are
neither one thing nor the
other. Some are hidden by
dust, some are slippery.
These are the worst because
you think they're easy, and
then—*bam!*—a chain
reaction as one goes down,
and two more follow.

# CHAPTER III

# FIVE STATIONS OF THE CROSS

The Hell of the North includes some sections of cobblestones that are even more infernal than others. Yesterday, it was the hill at Doullens. Today it's the pavé at Troisvilles, Wallers-Arenberg, Mons-en-Pévèle, and the Carrefour de l'Arbre. Among the numerous pitfalls of Hell, these five sections stand out. Here whistles the wind of legend.

**Wallers-Arenberg**
**1968**

The so-called trench of Wallers-Arenberg is only 2,400m long, but it's just as symbolic, challenging, and dramatic for Paris-Roubaix as l'Alpe d'Huez is for the Tour de France. Proof of its significance is the 30,000 spectators that show up religiously each year to line what are the cruelest cobblestones of the event. The fans can hear, see, and feel the riders as they tackle the section like penitents. It may not be a truly religious passion, but it resembles one.

**Mons-en-Pévèle
1965**

This small hill is only 107m—
about 350 feet—above sea
level, but it makes the racers
fight hard to conquer it. They
have to make a special effort
on this cobbled climb, much to
the delight of the spectators
who come here to see the
riders grimace, stagger,
struggle, and finally take off.

# The holy places

The countryside is unchanging, if a bit depressing. Stop here a second, and go up the hill. There's a good chance you'll hear the wind whisper. It comes from far away. You don't need much imagination to see them pass by, those racers of the heroic era, with their spare tires crossed over their shoulders, their goggles lowered as they prepare to push through the clouds of dust.

There was a time when the greatest challenge of Paris-Roubaix was not just a mucky cobblestone road, but rather a hill: Doullens. The very name of this small village in the Somme evokes old racing photos from the days of Henri Pélissier, Georges Ronsse, and Gaston Rebry. The champions have passed by, but the place hasn't changed. The two neat rows of trees heading off into the distance give witness to this history. Almost half a century ago (the last time the race came here was in 1965) the hill at Doullens was abandoned. That was when the start was moved from Saint-Denis to Chantilly, then to Compiègne, so that the route could be moved to the east, to seek out the obligatory cobblestones.

Yet for decades, the hill of Doullens was the high point of Paris-Roubaix, the first psychological barrier, the rendezvous you could not miss. Between the two world wars, it was here, on this straight road that splits the countryside, rising toward the plateau of Artois, that the race was most often decided. It was a make-or-break challenge, at least until the derailleur appeared in the second half of the 1930s. After that, even though it was less decisive, this climb remained daunting enough.

## At Doullens, the peloton splits

Of course, the hill at Doullens would seem almost laughable to today's pro cyclists. Yet it remains an object of respect. First of all, this dead-straight ramp rises sharply from the streets of Doullens, the capital of a canton that's nestled in the valley of the Authie, which flows through the Somme's green countryside.

At one time, the town's main street was covered with cobblestones, the only escape being a sidewalk on the right. The race, shaken up here, immediately tackled the climb. The first steep pitch ends at the hamlet of Beaurepaire, a large Picardy farmhouse surrounded by plowed fields. The road, still lined by trees, bears slightly to the left, and even from there you cannot see the end of this interminable false flat that's often exposed to crosswinds. It's the wind up here that grabs the peloton and splits it into small packs of fifteen to twenty racers, or even fewer. The race of the echelons—they knew how to do them back then—was under way. It was better to be in front, though it took a true free-for-all to arrive well-placed at the top. A race by elimination was in progress, sometimes without second chances—but not always. The year of his victory, in 1955, Jean Forestier found himself mired in the eighth echelon after Doullens!

In all, the climb stretches 2,500 meters, from leaving Doullens to a summit that leads to the wide expanses of Artois. After 30 more kilometers, on the distant horizon, you reach Arras, the last "station" before the entrance to the original "Hell" at Hénin-Liétard.

Doullens is halfway between Amiens and Arras, on the Route Nationale 25. It's been a long time since the racers last passed through this town. The wind has long since carried away the cheers of the crowds that once gathered here to see the race take shape. It would be very dangerous today to position oneself at the edge of the road here. At regular intervals, a hellish noise shakes the moroseness of the place. Alas, the hill at Doullens is now in the kingdom of the trucks.

## At Troisvilles, the race spins out of control

Troisvilles, the village on the front line, is where today's Paris-Roubaix racer leaves civilization behind. Since 1987, this is where he first puts his wheels on the pavé, whereas before it was at Neuvilly, a place where, one year, the entire race was blocked by a press car mired in the mud.

Troisvilles, the gate to Hell. Upon leaving the village, immediately on the left is the rue de la Sucrerie (Sugar House Street). A banner announces that this is pavé section number 26, listed in descending order from here to the finish.

Here are the first jolts, the first flat tires, the first confusion. The race becomes a machine that spins out of control. And there's nothing anyone can do to stop it. "If you arrive in front on the first cobblestones, it's as though you have won a stage," recalls 1969 winner Walter Godefroot. "From then on, you have no more time to think about anything."

Even the approach to Troisvilles is highly stressful. "I often watched videotapes of preceding editions," says two-time Paris-Roubaix winner

**Le pas Roland
1959**

For the second year, still in the neighborhood of Mons-en-Pévèle, the riders also have to climb le pas Roland, a kilometer of slimy cobbles that lead to the town's cemetery. Belgians Marcel Janssens and Noël Foré have taken the initiative here, and the section is so decisive that these two will fight out the victory in Roubaix.

Gilbert Duclos-Lassalle, "to look for markers like a house or a water tower, so that I could reach the pavé in good position." Troisvilles, a dreary place, makes the adrenaline rise. But the first cobblestones, at least as Duclos recalls them, "are a deliverance."

## At Wallers-Arenberg, a sudden rush of terror

There is no place that mixes so closely the legend of Paris-Roubaix with the traditions of the North.

The race becomes brutal once it bolts at top speed past the miners' cottages of Wallers, neatly lined up in all their modesty. On the left is the mineshaft tower. From up there a visitor, if not a victim of vertigo, lords it over the 11,000-acre Raismes-Saint-Amand state forest. In the distance, you can see as far as Tournai in Belgium. Many lives were lost in this mine. At the height of its activity, almost five thousand miners descended to the bottom of the pit every day. The Wallers mine, once worked by the Anzin company, is a carefully maintained reminder of the town's laborious past. In 1990 it became the last mine to close down in the North. It illustrates its slice of history so well that it served as the location for shooting *Germinal*, a movie by Claude Berri inspired by Émile Zola's novel.

When very young, Jean Stablinski knew that the bicycle was his means of escaping from the throat of that mine. He lived here, in the town of Belaing, rue de Verdun, in the family home. Every morning his mother cycled through the woods of Arenberg to her work in the pottery at Saint-Amand-les-Eaux. His stepfather toiled at the coal face. The young Jean, starting at 19 years of age, also descended into the stomach of the earth at Wallers, working as a carpenter. He didn't use a pickax, but he cleared away the coal, pushing the wagons and bringing timber for structural support. A foreman told him that this tunnel extended under the woods of Arenberg. Thus he was, no doubt, the only cyclist to ever race across the Arenberg "trench" and also work below it!

For the 1968 edition, which will forever mark a turning point in the race's itinerary, his friend Albert Bouvet enlisted his help to uncover new cobblestones. New cobblestones? Of course Stablinski knew where to find them. "At first I didn't dare show him Arenberg," Stablinski

recounts. "But then I relented. He was in awe, and brought along a photographer. When [race director] Jacques Goddet saw the shots, he said to Bouvet, 'But I asked you to find cobblestones, not ruts and potholes!' Having ridden over that section of pavé every day, I would never have dreamt that Paris-Roubaix would use it one day. I was extraordinarily emotional when I reached 'the trench' as a racer in my last Paris-Roubaix. Lots of fans were there waiting for me, dressed as miners."

Since that first crossing in 1968, the Arenberg woods have become the symbol of Paris-Roubaix. A mythology is now associated with this charming, even restful place during the 364 days of the year when it's not invaded by a bike race. "The Arenberg woods were the miners' lung," recalls Stablinski. "We hunted and fished there. We went looking for mushrooms and, during the month of May, we gathered lilies of the valley." The pond at Goriau is a marvelous body of water covering 275 acres. It was formed after the soil sunk due to the extraction of coal. The woods now serve as a bird sanctuary, and many species sing there.

The Paris-Roubaix racer, however, does not see Arenberg from such an idyllic perspective. Somber and disturbing, its straight road slices through the forest for 2,400 meters. The journalist Pierre Chany did not hesitate to give it a name more in line with the intensity of the battle: "the trench." Paris-Roubaix, as mentioned earlier, often borrows from the vocabulary of World War I.

The first 800 meters, slightly downhill, are the worst of the worst. The road is potholed, and even if you manage to stay on the ridge of the pavé, staying upright is a constant problem. Here, both Johan Museeuw and Philippe Gaumont were knocked down in accidents.

Entering Arenberg, the racers experience a sudden rush of terror. As soon as they catch sight of the barriers of the Paris-Valenciennes rail crossing, they know they are about to cross the frontier into another world. And it's a shocker. The earth is black. It's from the dust, the dust of coal. The abandoned footbridge, once used to clear waste from the mine to the dump at Sabatier, only adds to the sinister aura. It's as if the race had just entered a deep tunnel.

Monsieur Cardon, the forest ranger, holds the keys to Arenberg. The official name of the cobbled path through the forest is the "drève des Boules-d'Hérin." *Drève* is the name for a forest track. *Boules*, French for balls or bowls, has so many meanings they've been lost over time, but Hérin is a hamlet next to Arenberg.

A barrier blocks the passage to all motorized vehicles. Yet it does not prevent visitors, now and again, from entering and plucking a fat cobblestone from the pathway as a souvenir of the race. One less stone, one more pothole! Once a year, Cardon raises the barrier. The pulse of the race accelerates amid a crowd that usually numbers around 30,000. There was a time when, to avoid chaos on the pavé, the racers rode in single file, threading their way at top speed on the dirt footpath that runs to the right of the cobbles. A few years ago, however, the organizers found a solution. They installed some immovable barriers that stopped the riders opportunely using this rideable surface, and gave them no alternative but to ride on the cobblestones. That was a bad break for them, a very bad break.

That was especially true at the start of the section. Dew falls from the trees and makes the pavé slippery in every season. Out of concern for security, the National Office of Forestry banned the passage from 1974 to 1983. When the racers finally returned to Wallers-Arenberg, the public quickly recognized that this stretch was the most spectacular part of the race. Nevertheless, safety concerns persisted, especially after Museeuw suffered his severe fall in 1998, fracturing a kneecap and nar-

**Troisvilles**
**2004**

It's here, at Troisvilles, the start of the first sector of pavé—
number 26, because they are numbered in reverse order.
This is where things get serious, where the leaders put
their foot on the gas.

**Le Carrefour de l'Arbre**
**1991**

Marc Madiot has just attacked. It's the winning move. This
corner, on a strategic sector of cobblestones 14km from the
finish, is the Frenchman's back garden. It was here in 1985
that he took control of the race; now he has done it again.

rowly avoiding amputation when gangrene set in. As a result, for the following two editions, the organizers had the racers enter the forest from the opposite end, with a turn that slowed them down at the start of the section and the slight uphill at the end. It was Wallers in reverse.

But in 2001, the race returned to its traditional route, to this spot that no one hesitated to label a death trap. There was one exception in 2005, to allow roadwork that would prevent the pavé from deteriorating excessively. Several trees were sacrificed, while others were pruned, to let in some light and allow the sun to dry out the always damp cobblestones near the entry. Workers also scraped around the edges of the path, filled in holes created by wild boars, and removed the earth that covered parts of the pavé. They restored the section to its original width of 10 feet, whereas it had shrunk over time to just 8 feet in places.

Thus Arenberg was made safer, without toning down its essential character. "Arenberg fills the same role for Paris-Roubaix that l'Alpe d'Huez does for the Tour," asserts Jean-Marie Leblanc, the former race director. "It's a symbol. But it's also something of an island of cobblestones in that area. We don't want to deprive ourselves of other new sections of pavé, as we know there are some around Valenciennes, and so we don't have to go through Arenberg at any cost. As with l'Alpe d'Huez in the Tour, we are for alternating its inclusion."

Still, Paris-Roubaix does not want to renounce Arenberg. To be sure, this straightaway is rarely the decisive part of the race. In the reverse tally of twenty-six cobblestone sections, it's number 15 from the end. In other words, it's well before the area of Orchies, with its Chemin des Prières (Path of the Prayers) and Chemin des Abattoirs (Slaughterhouse Lane), prophetic names that traditionally open the door to the race's finale. After Arenberg, there are still 92 kilometers to go until the velodrome, easily two more hours of racing. So the peloton is a long way from the finish. "If a racer enters Arenberg in 24th position, he has already lost. But the winner-to-be isn't necessarily in the top ten either," explains Alain Bondue, a Northerner, who in 1984 had the great thrill of racing through the forest on a breakaway with his teammate Gregor Braun.

Over time, racers have learned to tame Arenberg. The fury of the first few years has given way to somewhat "softer" crossings, whereby racers try as hard as possible to avoid a free-for-all. "At Arenberg, the impor-

tant thing is not to eliminate yourself and to come out of it as close as possible to a group that can lead you to the front," explains two-time winner Marc Madiot, who generally counted on his teammates to ensure his safe passage.

The "trench" at Arenberg, on the other hand, is prominent in the sense that for the teams it determines the distribution of forces as they prepare for the finale. And everyone knows that the law of numbers is a decisive factor in this race. As Eddy Merckx says, "This isn't where you win Paris-Roubaix but it's where you can lose it." Arenberg remains the place where the wheat separates from the chaff. Jean Stablinski refers to it metaphorically: "In the mine, when the cage takes you five hundred meters underground, you don't know for sure if you'll ever come back up. Arenberg is like a descent into the coal mine. If you start to think of the danger you won't even go there."

## At Mons-en-Pévèle, the race disintegrates

Mons-en-Pévèle (Mound of Stones, roughly) is a village that carries its name well. Perched on a hill, 107 meters high, it's the highest point in the region. It's also a high point of the battle for Paris-Roubaix.

It was in 1955 that the race incorporated, for the first time, cobblestone climbs—namely, the hill at Moncheaux, followed by one at Mons. By including the new cobbled sections, Paris-Roubaix increased to almost 270 kilometers in total length, 20 more than the classic distance. This move was undertaken because the pavé had all but evaporated from the traditional finale after Hénin-Liétard. The race then took to exploring the Pévèle region to unearth some new sections.

In 1958, the main attraction was the Caouin: a short, tough climb adjacent to the village of Mons-en-Pévèle. But this chaotic stretch was soon tarred over. Hence the inauguration of le pas Roland (the Roland step), on another side of the same hill, a lane climbing to a cemetery for a short kilometer, followed by a cobbled descent. It was here, on a scouting mission with Jacques Anquetil, that Jean Graczyck, winner of the Critérium International but never Paris-Roubaix, followed a small footpath he spotted in anticipation of Sunday's race. It took him straight

**Wallers-Arenberg
2004**

In the trench, the wet cobbles see the peloton scattered like soldiers in a Napoleonic battle. They slip, skid, head out of control, and swerve to avoid the feet of the barriers.

into a farmyard, and, voilà, the famous "Popov" Graczyck ended up in a cesspool. True story!

In time, the cobblestones of the pas Roland were also tarred over. When the peloton passed here in 1967 as if riding on velvet, race director Jacques Goddet began to worry about the future of his race. Precisely because the Roland "step" was no longer what it used to be, Goddet enlisted his new collaborator, Albert Bouvet, and ordered him to find a new course for the following year.

Since then, the village of Mons-en-Pévèle has watched the race pass by with a haughty air. Up there, the cobblestones are but a memory. Paris-Roubaix now bypasses the hill on a section of pavé that is no less severe. In fact, in absolute terms, it's probably the most difficult section on the entire route, because of both its length, 3,000 meters, and its profile. It starts out on a slight downhill, descending at 2 percent for 300 meters, which, because the cobbles are badly cambered, makes balance precarious. Following this tricky part comes a gradual uphill for 800

### HELL'S "HIT PARADE"

No one today is better placed to judge Hell's worst cobblestone stretches than Jean-François Pescheux, the man responsible for mapping out the course. His personal inventory:

1. "For me, the worst is Mons-en-Pévèle. It's always windy and it's never flat. Plus there's a place where the pavé is a mess, and to ride there—watch out!"
2. "Wallers-Arenberg is legendary. It's the only section passing through a forest and it's entirely straight, as if you had entered a tunnel. The first 800 meters, on a slight downhill, are the most obnoxious. Once you pass the bottom, it gets better."
3. "The Carrefour de l'Arbre. You already have 200 kilometers in the legs. It's the last truly difficult section. This is where the race is played out."

meters, followed by a 90-degree turn to the right that follows a flattish section before climbing a final false flat for another 1,000 meters. This whole section is even more of a test when the wind sweeps across the open countryside. By now, we're on the threshold of the final hour. The race is disintegrating as never before.

## At the Carrefour de l'Arbre, it's time to give whatever's left in the tank

It's the last battlefield. Paris-Roubaix is decided here, precisely where the battle of Bouvines took place on July 27, 1214, when Philippe II united France by crushing a coalition of three powers, including the English troops of King John and the Germanic armies of Otto IV.

The Carrefour de l'Arbre (Crossroads of the Tree), invariably included since 1980, is where the race is often decided. The velodrome is only 14.5 kilometers away. And the last sections of pavé, at Gruson and Hem, are a piece of cake. There's no more reason for crashes. It's also practically the last chance for a rider to make a difference.

The Carrefour de l'Arbre sector follows the very difficult stretch at Camphin-en-Pévèle, where the pavé used by the racers is an ancient Roman way coming from Tournai. This is the heart of the final stretch. These are the 2,100 meters where you have to give it your all, emptying whatever you have left in your tank. The first 1,200 meters are flat until a right-angle left turn that's tough to negotiate. Finally, you come to this false flat that rises imperceptibly all the way to the bistro at the crossroads.

For many years, this shack lost in the middle of the Bouvines plain was run by Madame Jeanne, a personality from another time. There was neither running water nor electricity. Only a few local farmers drifted in for an occasional drink "chez la Jeannette." Besides, lacking a license, the café was open to the public only once a year: the day of Paris-Roubaix.

Madame Jeanne is no longer in this lowly world. Some have proposed that her miserable brick building, coated with white paint, be transformed into a Paris-Roubaix museum, but so far that proposal has gone nowhere. Happily, the new owners of this establishment put fresh life into the place. The seedy café has become charming, almost affluent. The food is good, the welcome excellent. Today, the Taverne de l'Arbre does as good a job tracing the history of France through the battle of Bouvines as it does depicting the epic history of Paris-Roubaix, to which the walls are dedicated. A series of colored frescoes collects all the big names of the cobblestones. It's a must-see for any cycling fan.

At the Carrefour de l'Arbre, one is simultaneously nowhere and at the very crux of the race. Mercifully, the racers will soon be finished with all these stations of the cross.

PHILIPPE BOUVET

**Doullens**
**1925**

The spectators have come
by car, motorcycle, and
bicycle—just look at their
shoes. They've all come to
see the Paris-Roubaix riders
climb the hill at Doullens. It's
a ritual. The leader, with his
goggles, long-sleeve jersey,
spare tire, and aluminum
water bottle, races between
two rows of caps. His name
suddenly spreads like
wildfire. It's the Italian
legend, Alfredo Binda.

**Doullens
1950**

The fans no longer wear caps, but they do have winter jackets and the excitement is just as intense. Fausto Coppi is pushing ahead, and the peloton explodes, much to the delight of the spectators and photographers. Doullens has again come up trumps for an Italian champion.

**Doullens**
**1965**

The trees still provide a
handsome guard of honor,
but not the spectators. The
peloton is still grouped on
the course's major climb.
Maybe it's time for the
organizers to change
direction.

**Mons-en-Pévèle**
**1967**

The trees are in blossom; the
peloton gets tipsy on le pas
Roland, which is as lethal as a
shot of hooch; but the crowd
is restrained. It's a lovely
Sunday for Paris-Roubaix.

**Mons-en-Pévèle**
**1967**

Le pas Roland is a kilometer that
never seems to end. It's even
tougher at the top, and the
applause becomes louder.
German ace Rudi Altig smashes
down on the pedals, not hearing
the fans, while Eddy Merckx sticks
close to the world champion.

**Troisvilles
2005**

This is where the racers lock
their helmet straps, tighten
their brakes, and take a sniff
of oxygen. This first sector of
cobblestones is only 2,200m
long, but it's dangerous
when the gravel gives way
to the pavé.

### Le Carrefour de l'Arbre
**1994**

The tavern is for sale, but former Soviet rider Andreï Tchmil doesn't see the sign. He hasn't yet recovered from the cobbles at Camphin, let alone those of the Carrefour, which he is already leaving. The sparks of Hell stick to his skin, he's boiling hot, but he pushes on. A promised victory soothes the spirit.

### Le Carrefour de l'Arbre
**1998**

The crowd is at fever pitch, a Belgian flag flies. We're not at Pamplona's running of the bulls, but it resembles a *corrida*. The survivors already have 250km in their legs, and now, besides the pavé they have to be wary of the fans and not even risk turning to see who's chasing. After all, the toughest is behind them.

### Le Carrefour de l'Arbre
**2001**

There's no buffet stop planned for this phantom express, but a shower is waiting at the end of the line, back in the civilized world. For the moment, the riders' weary arms can just about grip the handlebars. They stretch their fingers as they move a hand from the bars to the brake levers. That's what the Carrefour does to you.

**Wallers-Arenberg
1998**

An ambush, a death trap, a
bear trap, a snare, or even a
cement mixer? The trench
is a little bit of all those
things, and can even
resemble a full-scale battle,
with collisions, confusion,
and cannonades.

**Wallers-Arenberg**
**2000**

The heart of the forest at Wallers is also the heart of Paris-Roubaix. It's like a big steel mill where the peloton narrows, becomes two lines, and gets smashed to pieces. Photographers and cameramen don't miss the slightest sign of distress or suffering. The red flag is raised for a good reason.

**Wallers-Arenberg
2001**

The cobblestones, two
waves of spectators all
worked up, a golden brown
dust floating through the
gaps in the trees, and a
peloton that rushes through
at breakneck speed.
Compared with all this, the
charge of the light brigade
seems trivial.

# CHAPTER IV

# IN THE MUD, THE DUST, AND THE WIND

To have a good Paris-Roubaix, you need ample cobblestones and certain weather conditions. If it's dry, dust comes into play. But if it's wet, mud has pride of place. And if the weather is particularly harsh, the public is delighted. The wind and cold intensify the ordeal, making the race even more epic and relentless.

**_Homo roubaitus_**
**2001**

No, this is not the masked cartoon villain Fantômas, more likely the Ogre of Arenberg and far less Hitchcock's _Stranger on a Train_. No, it's _Homo roubaitus_. We know he gobbles up the cobbles, coats himself in mud, and he's spotted only once a year—when it rains in the Arenberg area. A sort of yeti that photographer Christian Biville, a former racer, miraculously captures through his lens in 2001.

**The echelon
1968**

Echelons form in the peloton
to fight against the wind. The
best riders, the pretenders
to victory, get in the first
echelon. Behind, there's a
desperate race, all or
nothing, to chase back or
jump forward. A flat tire often
leads to these forms of
acrobatics that gut a rider
of precious reserves.

# Storm warning

The magic of Paris-Roubaix is so powerful that it causes millions of spectators and television viewers to blurt out this most improbable remark on an Easter Sunday morning: "Wonderful, it's raining!" Of course, weather plays an important role in all cycling events. But it becomes a critical factor in an April race in northern France, when showers, cold, wind, and snow are in the forecast.

A dry Paris-Roubaix is a completely different affair from a wet one, even if, as the knowledgeable former racer Jean Stablinski maintains, the results are generally weatherproof. According to Frédéric Guesdon, the 1997 winner, dryness usually gets the better of rain this time of the year. In his own ten starts, he rode seven times in the dry and only three times in the wet. Of course, Jacques Goddet, when he was the race boss from 1959 to 1987, preferred the rain, which he felt made the race "tougher" and even more spectacular. But whatever the weather, says Marc Madiot, who won a wet edition in 1985 and a dry one in 1991, the rider who triumphs at Roubaix is a "survivor." Yes, a survivor. For having inevitably avoided or overcome cramps, aches, multiple flat tires, broken frames, saddles, wheels, or forks, and crashes caused by follow cars, press motorcycles, dogs, or even geese, the winner also has to contend with the wind, dust, rain, mud, cold, and their consequences.

## Like half a formation of flying geese

To win World War II, the British prime minister Winston Churchill warned his people there would be "blood, sweat, and tears." Barring a miracle, even under the best conditions, that's precisely what's in store for the participants of Paris-Roubaix.

Describing the strange sentiment that pervades the riders on the starting line, Pierre Chany wrote in *L'Équipe* in 1987, "More than fear, there's dread." Yes, dread, for here there's everything to be scared of—left and right, but also above and below. First, there's the wind. Capricious, it comes from unpredictable directions but it's almost always on the menu, whether the day is pleasant or damp. When it's a favorable wind, the pace is high, but the race is slightly less captivating. When it's the opposite, it adds the first spice to the contest, right from the start. To say nothing of the demoralizing changes of mood through the race.

Let's take the most interesting case, when the wind is unfavorable. Louison Bobet, the 1956 winner and an unlucky animator in many other editions, once observed, "The winds blow continually in Picardy." He advised racers to take advantage of that "by attacking early to air out the peloton." That is to say, race hard to make the peloton split into small echelons, each of which forms a sort of wedge to fight the wind, a practice that has been part of the charm of Paris-Roubaix since the roaring twenties. Typically, racers organize themselves into an echelon, similar to half a formation of flying geese, to fight and better penetrate the wind. The strongest riders go in front and, seen from an airplane, the race resembles "half a fish skeleton," as the journalist Raymond Huttier whimsically put it in 1938. For his part, sportswriter Pierre Chany, originally from the Allier valley, spoke of "salmon ladders." André Darrigade, who rode the classic fourteen times without winning, recalls, "In 1952, having flatted three times, I spent so much energy going from one echelon to the next that I had nothing left when I found myself in the front."

Yes, these strategic maneuvers "air out" the peloton all right. Albert Bouvet, another unlucky race hero from the 1950s, says, "The first echelons are formed between Creil and Amiens, but especially at Doullens, after the hill, where crosswinds blow. Those who aren't in the first three groups are out the window." Excellence starts here. Like bones stuck in their throat, the echelons block the progress of the weaker racers. And when the wind blows strong from the start, the race is even more likely to favor a true strongman. It takes some doing to race at the front while conserving enough ammunition for the finale. Those who don't make it may have been distracted, had a moment of weakness, or been feeble in the wind.

Having taken off early, the riders in the morning breakaway, with dreams of going the distance, inevitably ride in an echelon, their backs arched into the wind. They try to create their destiny. And even if they frequently fail, they always have the merit of shaking up the race. If it's dry, the wind blows the dust stirred up by the automobiles. If it's wet, it will scatter the showers. If it's cold, or even snows, as it did in 1908, it will accentuate the pinpricks of the snowflakes that go right through jerseys and shorts. And if it has rained, the wind will dry out the mud and transform the riders into zombies pedaling mechanically, robotically, toward the unlikely finish.

**Snow
1935**

The spectators have their hands in their pockets
and collars up, but the hardy racers aren't even
wearing tights.

**In the doghouse
1959**

This year everyone is wearing black masks, the
motorcyclists as well as these breakaways, Noël Foré,
Gilbert Desmet, and Angelo Conterno. No, they aren't
chimneysweeps, they've just had a severe beating-up
through the minefields. And it hasn't finished yet....

A harsh component in this pitiless race, the wind, despite creating endless echelons, remains the invisible guest, while dust and mud are the visible components—good for the spectators, bad for the racers. When one asks champions which is the lesser of these two evils, they invariably reply it's a bit like choosing between the plague and cholera. Three-time winner Rik Van Looy adds that "the weather is of no importance; what matters is to arrive first at the velodrome." To be sure, the Belgian champion belonged to that category of racers known as "the unsinkables," or "amphibians," to use the colorful term coined by Albert Baker d'Issy, the renowned columnist of the 1950s who loved to distinguish types of riders. In sum, for these great professionals, the weather conditions are neither hot nor cold. It's as if they simply have to go from one end of a tunnel to the other. Whatever difficulties lie in between are there to be overcome. So you might as well adjust to them and think no more of it.

## Cowboys dashing to the Wild West

A majority nonetheless seems to prefer dust to mud, especially nowadays, given that glasses are more efficient and less troublesome than they used to be. However disagreeable it might be, "the race is more predictable and less dangerous when it's dusty as opposed to muddy," Eddy Merckx admitted in 1973, himself a triple winner and the number one victim of the terribly muddy episode of 1975.

Dust, the curse of dry weather, transforms the racers into cowboys dashing toward the Wild West. Mud, in contrast, sends the last of the Mohicans on the warpath and gives the race its priceless air of an epic adventure that promises photographers a field day.

While the famed dust makes spectators and television viewers happy, it gives riders sore eyes and throats. To be sure, dust doesn't kill, but its unbearable burning sensation has, over the years, forced even top stars to quit the race. This was the case in 1910 with Louis Trousselier, and also in 1911 and 1912 with Maurice Broco, Julien Maîtron, and Lucien Petit-Breton. The first three-time winner, Octave Lapize, spurned glasses and won with courage, his eyes reddened as much by the dust as by the glare of sunlight from the baked clay road. Henri Cornet, the default winner of the 1904 Tour, said after winning Paris-Roubaix in 1906, "What a race! Never in my life have I swallowed so much dust!"

Dust reigned again in 1922 and 1923. "It is so dreadful that it burns the eyes," affirmed Constante Girardengo, Italy's first *Campionissimo*, who had to stop as early as Amiens to wash his face, a ritual racers usually put off until after the finish.

In 1929, it was Charles Meunier's mask of dust, accentuated by the white outline of his glasses around the eyes, that entered into race legend. The dust Bernard Hinault took "in the throat" in 1978 deeply impressed the writer Guy Lagorce. The special correspondent for *L'Équipe* observed in 1965 "blood mixing with dust," and, in 1971, he was struck by the "back roads choked in dust."

Yet, as the perceptive Cyrille Guimard has observed, riders who wear glasses seem more bothered by mud than by dust. The bespectacled Laurent Fignon, on his first muddy foray, abandoned the race after just 500 meters of mud-covered cobblestones. Then, in 1988, he rallied, losing only narrowly, in third place. On the other hand, Jan Janssen and Jan Raas, two other champions who wore glasses, managed to overcome what seemed an insurmountable handicap. Janssen wore his conventional specs when he beat out Rik Van Looy and Rudi Altig in a desperate sprint in 1967, whereas Raas wore special glasses when he prevailed in 1982 (with a hole in each lens that he could look through as a last resort).

## "The threshold of cruelty"

In his particular case, Janssen's methodical and philosophical approach to the race merits an aside. He did not carry a spare pair of glasses with him, having consigned one to his directeur sportif. But he did stuff four or five handkerchiefs in his pocket so that he could clean off his lenses. That was only as a last resort, however, for he was fearful of any unnecessary distractions, noting, "If I overlook even a fraction of the danger around me I'm taking a big risk."

Ironically, it was not the juddering of the cobblestones that caused the Dutchman to lose his famous glasses one day, but the smooth roads of Milan–San Remo. The Hell of the North so engrossed Janssen that, if he admits losing a race or two on account of his glasses, he does not include Paris-Roubaix on that list.

All this mud, rain, and havoc amount to what Jacques Goddet calls "a hardship approaching the threshold of cruelty." Given the rain

**Blizzard**
**1970**

Besides the pavé and the fatigue, here comes the
snow. It falls heavily, making the cobblestones slick,
numbing fingers despite their gloves, and stinging
their eyes, making it even more difficult to see
where to ride.

**Paddy field**
**1983**

Mud, cobbles, ruts, and pools of water. All the toxic charms
of Hell are there, along with the spectators who've come to
see how the champions cope with it—how they will juggle
with the devil's horns. Simple. They'll ride on the right, where
it's less infernal.

and, inevitably, the mud on the often earth-covered roads, the race
followers look for great performances and the racers struggle to meet
their expectations.

That's the lamentable weather that brings on superlatives, descrip-
tions of the apocalypse. When a eulogist affirms that "the 1947 edition
was the hardest of all times," another replies: "No way!" and cites the
1975 edition. "At Neuvilly," one reads in *L'Équipe*'s account of the latter, "Guy Santy and Simonetti and Rotta, carrying their bicycles over
their shoulders, even managed to lose their shoes. In the sector at Inchy,
some girls in light-colored dresses mistook the mud-covered survivors
for Martians. One of the racers burst out laughing. Had he lost his
mind? No, it was just Ferdinand Bracke, the onetime world hour record
holder, who was so caked in the molasses that he chose to laugh rather
than cry."

## "Passed through the drum of a cement mixer"

After looking over the course before the 1978 edition, future Italian ace
Giuseppe Saronni, then age 20, shuddered and admitted, "What I saw was
frightening. Water, mud—terrain at the extreme limit of practicability. I
would never have imagined that Paris-Roubaix would be as bad as this."

The normally reserved journalist Jacques Augendre agreed, describing the narrow alleyway at Neuvilly in *Le Monde* with these words: "At
this place, the most popular classic ceases to be a cycling competition and
becomes instead a super cyclo-cross, or maybe a championship of escape
artists, a tightrope act."

Abel Michéa, a sportswriter in *L'Humanité*, weighed in. "It's not an
inhuman race, but only a few—the greats—are truly cut out for it," he
wrote. As usual, the editor of *L'Équipe*, Jacques Goddet, had his own
take. "Paris-Roubaix is an uncivilized race," he decided, "but it is not
made for bullies." Writer Toussaint Bruscher raised the tone even more,
saying, "The ruts left by the tractors resemble the footprints of prehistoric monsters upon which the racers become fleeting fossils." An important detail that year was that the wind was light, and intermittent showers periodically flooded the course, rendering it even slicker than usual,
according to the specialists, because the combination of dry and sticky
pavé is fearsome. Launched into this molasses-like mud, Bernard

Hinault got bogged down three times. But like all true champions, he
sprang back, to prompt journalist and author Pierre Chany to quote
Russian anarchist Mikhail Bakunin: "You have to die many times to
become a man." Half in jest, racers spoke of Albert Bouvet, the architect
of this hellish sabbath, as a "murderer."

Thierry Bretagne, another attentive observer of the carnage, saw
very few smiles, especially on the faces of racers who had "passed through
the drum of a cement mixer." Between Valenciennes and Nomain, he
noted, "this infamous dust factory saw them leave the slimy alleyways
looking as black as chimneysweeps, almost inhuman, with the red eyes of
gun dogs." Meanwhile, he observed, the fans "yelled like they were
watching a wrestling match."

The writer Alphonse Boudard, a special correspondent for *L'Équipe*,
also had the good fortune to chance upon a rainy edition in 1984.
Indeed, the downpour was so severe during their pre-race reconnaissance
that some racers didn't even get out of their team cars. Witnessing the
bedlam, the joyous scribe was struck by the "tons of manure" and the
invisible cobblestones "lurking under dung, holes and puddles."

## "In the eyes and ears . . ."

Four-time winner Roger De Vlaeminck, a master at cyclocross, rode
even faster and more confidently in the rain, like Hennie Kuiper and
Marc Madiot in more recent years, yet in 1979 he, too, found himself
mired in mud, fell, and lost the race. In this his race was like that of
Walter Godefroot before him, another excellent cobblestone rider, who
said, "In a difficult stretch I took to the grassy shoulder to avoid the mud
and the slimy cobblestones. But, once back on my bike, 100 meters
farther on, another treacherous section of mud made me skid again."
This quicksand, which makes riding on the shoulders impracticable and
multiplies the number of punctures, forces the riders to follow the road's
centerline, on top of the pavé, where only the best racers can stay in control. Hence broadcaster Jean Bobet's clever remark, "*Quand le haut du
pavé se trouve sur le pavé du haut.*" (When the hierarchy of the pavé
arrives on top.)

One small consolation. According to Jean-Marie Leblanc, a former
pro racer who became a journalist and later director of the race, "The

Tights and long sleeves
don't stop the mud and the
icy rain from biting into
the body, and the racers
fight with all their might to
keep going, trying not to
succumb to the elements.

mud doesn't only get into the eyes, ears, hair, or teeth. The soil just gets everywhere."

At times, one has the impression of watching boys who have just played Eton College's famous and muddy Wall Game in England, or a rugby match fought in the trenches, or an unlikely and surreal round of polo. But these clay figurines reminiscent of the crèche in *Germinal* (Émile Zola's novel that takes place in Roubaix), these devilish men resembling beekeepers, are not delivered for all that. Here, their derailleurs are clogged, gears jammed, and brakes blocked. Everyone wins a "ticket to the stalls," as Jean Bobet put it, who himself graduated in the mud therapy of Roubaix.

Between two sections of pavé, a racer tries hard to free up his derailleurs, for whether he's Merckx or some unknown, no one is immune from dealing with mud on his drivetrain. But the exercise is almost pointless, since there's more mud to come. The racer is truly confused. He knows not where to direct his wheel as it sprays a volley of water from every puddle. A flat is not far off, nor a fall, leaving the racer so dirty and disoriented that he doesn't know anymore how to get through this mire. In 1973, a stultified Cyrille Guimard, covered part in mud, part in dust, admitted he did the last 20 kilometers on automatic pilot.

## Six falls in 1 kilometer

The Paris-Roubaix survivor no longer feels his fingers, or, at times, his bleeding toes—as happened to Louison Bobet before he fell in the treacly mess.

Through the mud, the whiteness of his teeth sometimes bursts through. No, the racers of Paris-Roubaix still don't wear mouth guards—that would make it make it hard for them to hold their rain jackets in their teeth, "before putting them back into the rear pockets of their jerseys and then putting them on again, because the showers follow one another at regular intervals," as Pierre Chany observed in 1987.

Today, for safety, all the racers are helmeted, so when a mud-caked Eddy Planckaert, Servais Knaven, or George Hincapie emerges from the Arenberg woods, he looks more and more like an infantryman from World War I—like the soldiers that Cyrille Guimard, having become a directeur sportif, compared to his own racers in the harsh edition of

1984: "Half of my men were lying on their backs and the other half were on their stomachs." The Great War or a small squabble, there's a bit of everything in this wild contest, especially when rain and mud thicken the plot.

The Spaniard Pello Ruiz-Cabestany, who fell six times in 1 kilometer on the wet cobblestones of 1983, told us, "You bump shoulders left and right. We're all friends here, but all of a sudden, nothing matters anymore. There's no safe haven. It's a full-blown war out there. Everyone becomes crazy. But I'll return."

Yes, Paris-Roubaix is the race of all races. Whether there's rain or wind or a combination of the two, whether it's a dry edition for the greyhounds and the gazelles, to use Jacques Goddet's terminology, or a rainy one for the crocodiles and the bulldogs. Like a ride on a ghost train, here the dangers abound, tension is always at its highest intensity, and the suspense is absolute. It's the last race that makes you shudder. Where the fear is dreadful, where the fear is a delight. Where there is wind, mud, dust, rain, and blood—and so much joy at the finish.

SERGE LAGET

**Pedaling in the rain
1939**

They prefer to put their
noses in the downpour
rather than use rainwear.
Is this attack just a token
gesture or a serious move?
The group behind is
assessing the situation:
the finish is still a long way
off, and on this long
straightaway it's easy to
keep the aggressors in sight
and under control.

**Raymond Poulidor
1965**

Poulidor's chain is tangled, his rear tire flat, but he doesn't panic as he awaits his team car. In the heat of the battle, he doesn't notice the mud and his drenched jersey. The rugged French hero was at home in Paris-Roubaix, in which he gave his best eighteen times, often the top home rider, and had four top-ten finishes.

**Rain clouds over Arras
1954**

Soaked to the skin, they grimace and arch their backs, just like the rest, but they try to ignore the rain. They know that the race has barely started; the real difficulties lie ahead.

**The tracks**
**1960**

They're not tram tracks though they look like them. Even so, you still have to avoid them so as not to get bogged down, trapped, or shackled. So they keep to the outside on the crest of the cobblestones. They follow each other's line to avoid the potholes . . . and never turn around.

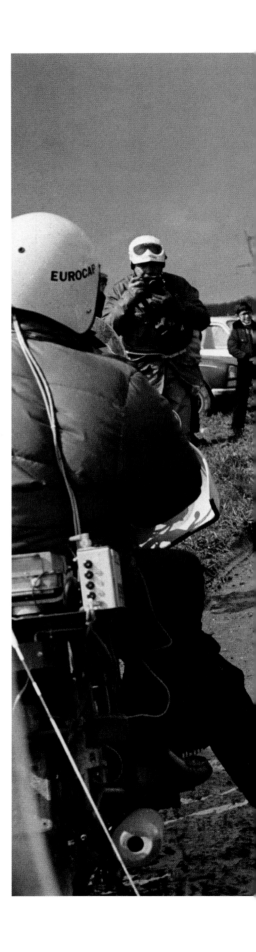

**About-turn**
**1977**

He has certainly stopped pedaling, but this rider in the middle of the road hasn't turned around to head back to Paris. He's simply fixing his handlebars that got mistreated by the pavé.

**Mud-caked Walter**
**1978**

No, this is not French rugby star Walter Spangero after a match with the All Blacks; it's the Belgian, Walter Godefroot, one of the best riders of the pavé in race history. The winner in 1969, he has since placed second, fifth, and eighth. He's unlucky and sad.

**Sideswiped**
**1979**

This is not the year for
Michel Pollentier. But did the
Belgian champion crash in
the mud to avoid the
motorcycle, or was it the

other way around? The
mysteries of Paris-Roubaix are
unfathomable, even for the
photographers.

**Puddle or mud?**
**1981**

As in a restaurant, you have to choose. Not cheese or dessert, but puddle or mud? Crash or rut? Pothole or puncture? The plague or cholera? The motorcyclists don't hesitate, but the cyclists are of two minds. Some riders head for the water, while the rest stay on the land, even though it's not that firm.

**The deep end**
**1981**

Even the stars do it with abandon. Roger De Vlaeminck is in the water, while Ferdi Van den Haute leads Ludo Peeters, Sean Kelly, Francesco Moser, and Bernard Hinault on the pavé. They splash around, make laps, cover themselves in mud, and grit their teeth. It's like a race for big kids.

**Ruts and potholes**
**1983**

The left side is rutted, impassable, so they go to the right. It's not as bad here, but will they fall? The spectators are so absorbed by the question that only one of them applauds, almost by reflex.

**Askew**
**1987**

Belgian star Éric Vanderaerden's legs are dead, his ears full of mud, his eyes coated, and his nose stuffed. He has trouble breathing. With his face a mess, he's drawn like a magnet to the north, like a lost soul emerging from a Rembrandt canvas.

**Under control**
**1990**

The rider in the red shorts juggles like a true devil. He looks for some help, maybe a cobblestone less slick. He sticks to the crest of the pavé, but danger is always present. He has avoided the motorcycle, but he's worried about the car just ahead.

**Some air, please**
**2001**

Over the kilometers, the puddles, and the pavé, the riders have donned another coat. And, from head to foot, they are now fully encrusted in the tradition of Roubaix. Only their mouths remain pink. No need to send an SOS; just a little air will suffice.

**On the deck**
**2002**

More scared than hurt. Between the Belgians Ludovic Capelle (on left) and Jo Planckaert, George Hincapie suddenly feels the ground give way. Back home in the States, there are quicksands and marshes, but he's never seen such a diabolical surface as this.

**Ghosts
2000**

On a dry day, there's lots of dust, and the riders are hidden or even invisible. It's like a mirage but we're not in the Sahara. It's more like Atlantis. You need to protect your eyes, throat, and lungs.

**In a cloud
2000**

The follow cars and motorcycles kick up clouds of dust through which the riders pass like circus performers...with a little bit of luck...

**Invisible**
**2003**

They're so covered in dust that it's hard to identify them. Their glasses protect their eyes from burning, but not from suffocation or crashing, the photographers hope.

**Tunnel ahead!**
**2000**

The clouds of dust surge and retract, depending on the state of the road and the presence of vehicles. And so the riders vanish and reappear. They say it's like entering a tunnel—without the warning lights.

**The Horsemen of
the Apocalypse
2004**

The spare wheels are ready;
the cavalrymen push on in near
blindness. The motorcycle
kicks up the dust, but happily
the riders can follow his rear
light. Surreal.

# CHAPTER V

# TO PUNCTURE AND SURVIVE

Flat tires, with their sinister hisses, don't necessarily stop a racer from winning Paris-Roubaix. But they can make him lose it.

**The alien**
**1978**

No, it's not an alien, Granny, it's just a Paris-Roubaix contestant who has flatted outside your house. Should the repair vehicles arrive quickly, you'll ask yourself if it wasn't just an apparition. They can surprise you, these heroes of the super-classic.

# The unavoidable epidemic

If flat tires still feed the legend, it's because, 110 years after the creation of this race, they are still an unforgiving and constant reality. The puncture-proof tire has yet to be invented.

And if this race remains the absolute reference point, the so-called classic of the classics, it's precisely because its prehistoric route, replete with cobblestones, ruts, and danger spots, never fails to produce punctures. Just when a racer thinks he has the race won, a tire suddenly betrays him. Conversely, just when the pursuer believes all is lost, his hopes rebound when he looks ahead and sees his opponent's tubular tire subside. Even if one can overcome a flat or two, it's far better to avoid them, as quadruple winner Roger De Vlaeminck knew so masterfully.

Perfectly blind and unjust, blowouts give this event an unparalleled suspense. They are the key to the gates—of paradise if you overcome them, of hell if you don't. They're the key to the jackpot in any case.

Paris-Roubaix thrives on its nuances and inevitabilities. During dry years, dust is at play. During the damp years, preferred by the public, the puddles become cursed ponds and the mud a sinister pitfall. But rain or shine, the Hell is always there because of the cobblestones, the crashes, the mechanical mishaps, the wind, and that disagreeable constant known as the puncture. It's the standard of rotten luck. Every spring, through some 110 years and 100 editions, flats are a flourishing part of the race whether it rains or stays dry. Throughout the dramatic, unforeseen turns in this race of obstacles, punctures perform their role—like a hangman with a thousand arms.

## Francis Pélissier and Speicher out of tires

But let's be fair; the cobblestones are not entirely to blame. With great dexterity, a racer can avoid squeezing his tires between two little blocks of stone, but chances are he'll still wind up flatting in Paris-Roubaix. It doesn't matter where it happens: on the asphalt, in a pothole, jumping a curb to ride on the sidewalk, or on the sidewalk itself. It could be caused by a stray nail—or perhaps carpet tacks deliberately strewn about, as was the terrible custom at the turn of the nineteenth century. But even if the racer believes he has escaped all the traps, chances are he's still not out of the woods. Hell is, after all, paved with bad intentions in these hostile places, where even a small piece of grit or an

insignificant flint can suddenly inject misfortune. They inspired the writer Robert Dieudonné to keenly observe in 1927, "A small stone in a bicycle tire can cause graver consequences than the one lodged in Cromwell's bladder." (English statesman Oliver Cromwell died from a kidney stone in 1658.)

There was a time when racers carried spare tires crossed over their shoulders, and repaired their own flats with fingers that were often frozen and always working shakily and feverishly. It took about a minute or so to change a tire and inflate it, assuming the rider still had a spare. For if one flatted for a third time, like Francis Pélissier in 1919 or Georges Speicher in 1939, victory was a lost cause. Indeed, after two punctures, a racer was simply riding on a razor's edge. That's why Octave Lapize, a triple winner, had to abandon the race in 1914 with the finish line in sight—and at his wit's end. Charles Crupelandt found himself in a similar situation in 1910, but, as a hometown hero, he gamely soldiered on to finish in fifth place.

Yet from the turn of the century through the roaring twenties, a few punctures did not automatically stop riders from finishing the race, placing respectably, or even winning it outright. The same holds true in modern times, especially since 1965, when organizers first authorized wheel changes between teammates. That major decision, along with the presence of following team cars and mechanics on motocross bikes close to the action, means it is no longer inconceivable that a racer who suffers two or more flats can still win.

And to think that before these fast fixes, the champions simply managed on their own! But regardless of the era, flats are the lot of the Paris-Roubaix racer. Learning to cope with punctures is truly the great secret to success in this race. Two-time winner Gilbert Duclos-Lassalle eventually came to this conclusion after riding the race many times. On reaching his maturity as a champion, he said, "I finally got around to admitting that, to reach Roubaix, and perhaps be the winner, I had to flat at least once and fall at least once."

## Leducq flew to victory thanks to a puncture

Duclos's destiny was accepted by 1904 Tour de France winner Henri Cornet in 1906, when he flatted in Paris-Roubaix . . . and still won. The

**Jacques Cadiou**
**1967**

He has a black look, does French rider
Cadiou. He's had a good start to the
year, was feeling good, but then,
crash, bang, wallop! A pothole. A
broken wheel. Race support doesn't
arrive, so, grumpy and in low spirits,
he walks back down the road. This
determined racer would like to reach
the end of the race, to show his
sponsor's colors, but it's not to be.

**Georges Speicher**
**1934**

There's familial compassion from the onlookers, but the reigning world champion and Tour de France winner makes his repair alone. He's not going to improve on his previous Roubaix results of 35th and 17th.

**André Leducq**
**1935**

He's flatted and the French heartthrob's hopes of another Roubaix victory slowly escape . . . like the air from his tire. You inflate the new tire, lose some time, just enough to make the difference between winning and losing. Gaston Rebry will win again this year.

same applied in 1910 to Octave Lapize, who not only flatted but also fell twice before he finally prevailed. Paradoxically, a puncture can bring some good. So it was in 1928, when André Leducq flatted 25 kilometers from Roubaix and changed his tire in less than a minute. At a time when racers were restricted to a single gear, Leducq took advantage of his enforced stop to switch to a higher gear (47x17) that was more suited to the finale. So, instead of losing momentum, he flew toward the victory.

Cyrille Van Hauwaert, the winner in 1908, was less fortunate. Having punctured on two separate occasions too close to the finish, in 1909 and 1911, he simply ran out of energy to challenge Lapize in 1910. But another Belgian, Émile Masson Jr., overcame the same snag as Leducq, flatting 25 kilometers from the end of the 1939 race. His rear tire deflated when he was alone in the lead. Masson's repair vehicle, stuck in a bottleneck, could not reach him to hand over a new wheel so he had to change the tire himself.

Passed by a group of fourteen chasers, Masson caught and repassed most of them by staying on top of the cobblestones, while the others rode on the bike path at the side. Georges Speicher, the 1936 winner, tried hard to stay on Masson's wheel, but he punctured when the Belgian, in order to drop Speicher, jumped his bike onto the sidewalk to avoid a difficult section of pavé. Masson's puncture became a passive defense weapon for him because he caught up with Jean Majerus and Roger Lapébie, and then took off alone toward the finish.

A year earlier, the outcome had been somewhat similar, because Lucien Storme, who had broken away with Louis Hardiquest after the rail crossing at Ascq, flatted 8 kilometers from the end. That snag could have been fatal for him, but his team car was on hand to pass him a new wheel and Storme quickly regained the lost 200 meters and then easily beat Hardiquest in the final sprint.

Of course, the best solution is never to puncture at all, or at least as rarely as possible. This requires a combination of luck and individual skill. Arguably, technical adjustments can also help. In the old days, racers used more supple bamboo rims on their front wheels. More recently, some have fitted hydraulic forks. This allows the bicycle, as Duclos-Lassalle puts it, "to roll more softly over the cobblestones," and thus reduces the chance of flats by not riding on the gritty sides of the road. Another old trick is to hang tires in the garage to dry out over an extended period before the race, which is said to make them less susceptible to punctures.

## Poulidor punctures five times in 1976

Then there's the phenomenon known as "great form," which is said to alleviate the hassle of a punctured tire. There's something to this, but it is by no means a surefire cure, as the case of Raymond Poulidor illustrates. A starter in eighteen editions of Paris-Roubaix, Poupou had never flatted when he was riding badly. On the day he had great form in 1976—"the year I should have prevailed," as he put it—he flatted no fewer than five times. With the benefit of hindsight, an older, wiser Poulidor noted that to win, "above all you must not flat before reaching the cobblestone sections," but "you can [flat] after the hierarchy is determined," provided there's a repair vehicle or a sympathetic teammate nearby. He also recalls that Rik Van Looy somehow found ways to win this race despite using silk tires, which are much lighter than regular tires and theoretically more likely to puncture.

How is that possible? Besides luck, the best explanation might well be the technique a racer uses to ride the pavé. The proof? In fourteen editions of Paris-Roubaix (from 1969 to 1982), and never finishing worse than seventh, Belgian champion Roger "the Gypsy" De Vlaeminck won the event four times, came in second four times, and suffered just a single puncture! Yes, he deliberately underinflated his tires for the cobblestones, as experts advise, contenting himself with a pressure of 65 psi rather than the more typical 100 psi, which considerably reduced the likelihood of his tires getting squeezed between the cobblestones (though slightly diminishing their performance on smooth pavement). But for Poulidor, the Gypsy's success hinged mainly on the fact that he had developed an admirable technique on the cobblestones. His ability might well have been unique and directly tied to his proficiency in cyclocross, a discipline in which he became world champion in 1975. "Roger always found the best trajectory," recalls Poulidor, "as if he were swaying to shelter his bike from the jolting" of the pavé.

A quick review of his four victories allows us to better appreciate the extraordinary talent of Mr. Paris-Roubaix. For his first victory, in 1972,

**Rolf Wolfshohl**
**1965**

Even a cyclocross specialist, like the German Wolfshohl, can flat. But he has some good fortune with his bad luck. The team car is just behind, and his mechanic is soon pushing him back into the action.

**Jan Janssen**
**1965**

There's absolute equality with a puncture. Here, Dutch world champion Janssen has to stop. To save time, he has already removed his defective wheel. He's not panicking. But after placing third and eighth the past two years, he'll finish 59th this time.

De Vlaeminck did not flat at all. In contrast, runner-up André Dierickx punctured three times, twice in the final stretch. The third-place finisher, Barry Hoban of Britain, flatted at Wallers-Arenberg.

## Even Merckx got stabbed

That same year, defending champion Roger Rosiers was going strong until he was waylaid by two blowouts. Eddy Merckx also flatted (and crashed), along with Willy Van Malderghem, who had made a long solo breakaway before being passed by De Vlaeminck. Yet, while his adversaries were suffering flats all around him, the master of the cobblestones remained unscathed.

The carnage was less pronounced in 1974. Still, Walter Godefroot, who had broken away with Francesco Moser, flatted with 36 kilometers to go—just when his superior sprint speed seemed to justify his dream of beating Moser at the finish. Left alone in the lead, Moser was soon caught by De Vlaeminck, and when the young Italian fell 7 kilometers farther on, the Gypsy easily grabbed his second win.

In the muddy 1975 edition, De Vlaeminck once again escaped with no punctures, and his rivals were punished once more. Eddy Merckx flatted 8 kilometers from the end, wore himself down in a 3-kilometer pursuit, and lost the victory to De Vlaeminck in the sprint. A third Belgian, Marc Demeyer, suffered the same fate when he flatted with 3 kilometers to go, and had to be satisfied with fourth place.

For the 75th edition in 1977, the year of his fourth win, De Vlaeminck was immersed in a squabble with Freddy Maertens, the world champion. Their rendezvous promised to be epic, like the showdown between Fausto Coppi and Rik Van Steenbergen at the 1952 Paris-Roubaix. The triple-winner of Paris-Roubaix had just won the Tour of Flanders, while his rival had prevailed in the Flèche Wallonne. But the duel was short-lived. On a course with "only" 46.5 kilometers of pavé, including the difficult section at Orchies, De Vlaeminck did not flat at all. His rival, however, had to stop twice to change wheels. Maertens still managed to make a go of it, after his teammates Michel Pollentier and Demeyer led him back to the front, but the majestic Gypsy raced the final 25 kilometers solo to collect his record fourth win.

## The dance of the damned for Janssen and Wolfshohl

Before De Vlaeminck, two other three-time winners just failed to add a record forth success: Eddy Merckx and Rik Van Looy. Van Looy started his march toward his eventual "title" as the Emperor of Herentals (his hometown) with his first Paris-Roubaix win in 1961. In fact, that was already his seventh try, but this time he did not figure in the seven lines of puncture victims listed in *L'Équipe* the next day. He thus avoided the fate that overcame the young British racer Tom Simpson, who flatted with 32 kilometers to go, and French veteran Bernard Gauthier, who was stopped by a puncture 10 kilometers from home.

In 1962, Van Looy was superior to three former winners, Noël Foré, Pino Cerami, and Jean Forestier, who all flatted or fell. In fact, the Frenchman Forestier, who had never ridden stronger, had his fate sealed by two successive punctures. Also hoping for glory that year was another French rider, Jean-Claude Annaert, who was plagued by three blowouts in 1959, two in 1960, and another in 1961. Annaert was convinced he would be logically and mathematically spared of any tire problems in the 1962 edition. And he was right—this time, it was his frame that broke.

Rik Van Looy's third victory, in 1965, was flat-free and ended with his racing the final 10 kilometers solo. His two most serious rivals, Rolf Wolfshohl of Germany and Jan Janssen of the Netherlands, would have been strong threats had they not met with terrible luck. In less than half an hour, the German flatted three times and fell. And in a span of only ten minutes, the Dutchman with the glasses suffered exactly the same plight. If that wasn't a dance of the damned, it was pretty close.

## Bernard Hinault and his pilot fish Poisson

In this race, neither the world champion's rainbow jersey nor the status of former winner offers a racer any protection from flats. Like Freddy Maertens, who finished third in 1977 after two flats, reigning world champion Bernard Hinault had bad luck in the 1981 edition. To be sure, the Breton did not care for this race, but he knew that the public would not consider him a true champion until he added Paris-Roubaix

**Henry Anglade**
**1960**

The gesture of a castaway in Paris-Roubaix. The road is dry, you can ride on the dirt, but there's always the risk of flatting. Holding his bike to the side, his wheel in the air, the champion of France isn't worked up. There's still a long way to go.

**Johan Museeuw**
**1996**

You can puncture and still win. The Lion of Flanders is proof of that as he flats here for the second time, just 8km from the finish. He decides to change his bike, not the wheel. That eliminates any chance of a mistake.

to his *palmarès*—his career record. Thanks to his teammates Yvon Bertin and Pascal Poisson, Hinault overcame two punctures to stay in contention, and he quickly recovered after a stray dog caused him to fall, before he outsprinted Roger De Vlaeminck and Francesco Moser on the Roubaix velodrome.

An example of a past winner overcome by flats is Frenchman André Leducq. He prevailed almost miraculously to win the 1928 edition, but that was not the case in 1935, when a slow-leaking tire stopped him 5 kilometers from the finish line and ruined his chances of a second win. Though less brutal than blowouts, such insidious slow leaks are just as unwelcome. In the same category of cursed former winners is the Italian Antonio Bevilacqua. The audacious victor of the 1951 edition lost his chance of repeating when he flatted at Wattignies. Two decades later, his compatriot Felice Gimondi, who had won the 1966 edition after a memorable 40-kilometer solo, flatted at the same place in 1971, and had two more blowouts that doomed his bid for a second victory.

In this race with an abundance of spirit but very little pity, many potential heroes have seen their hopes dashed within sight of the finish line. The long list includes François Faber and Gustave Garrigou in 1909, Louis Caput in 1948, Jacques Dupont in 1952, and Gilbert Scodeller in 1953 and 1955. Their sorrow contrasted sharply with the joy of the winners who overcame a similar predicament. Or predicaments, as was the case with Walter Godefroot in 1969. He flatted before Arenberg, returned to the front group, flatted again before Coutiches, then took off alone to ride the last 30 kilometers to victory on tires that weighed only 10 ounces apiece.

## Guesdon the first winner on clinchers

This account would not be complete if we failed to mention the match between clinchers and tubular tires as both vie to overcome the cobblestones and punctures. To date, only Frédéric Guesdon, in 1997, has won the race on clinchers. But tire manufacturer Michelin, committed to its slogan "The clincher soaks up difficulties," fully expects to find one day the ideal tire profile—the right claws, so to speak.

Today, even if a blowout can be overcome more easily than in the past, it can still produce the same dramatic consequences if it happens at the wrong time, far from race support. In 1958, for instance, Tour de France champion Jacques Anquetil made a heroic attack that was capsized by a simple puncture sustained in Baisieux, with just 13 kilometers to go. He fought to join three others, but they were overtaken 3 kilometers from the sacred goal. Anquetil, convinced he would have won, never again had such a great opportunity of winning at Roubaix.

Between a dream and a nightmare, Paris-Roubaix will never stop swaying to the rhythm of the riders' tires. But that unpredictability is just another element in the race to win this classic of classics.

SERGE LAGET

**Francis Pélissier**
**1920**

While his brother Henri won
Paris-Roubaix in 1919 and
1921, Francis Pélissier
played a big part in his
victories, despite having
three flats the first year, one
the other. This time,
Francis's chain has snapped.
He has tried to mend it but
has given up. No more help
for big brother today.

**Émile Masson**
**1939**

With 25km to go, when alone in the lead, the Belgian Masson's rear tire flats. With his team car nowhere in sight, he starts to make the repair himself. The chasing Roger Lapébie and Jean Majérus are about to pass him, but he'll get back to them and win the race. Masson is the strongest today.

**José Beyaert**
**1951**

It's raining and cold. Beyaert, the 1948 Olympic road champion, has numb fingers. The help of two spectators is invaluable. He manages to restart but can finish only 72nd, three minutes behind the winner, Antonio Bevilacqua.

**Disaster**
**Late 1940s**

A puncture has created a
crisis. One rider is on the
ground, another holds his
head, and two more make
repairs. A fifth victim seems
to ask what happened,
while a sixth asks if his bike
is still working.

**We were there
1959**

It's something they'll remember all their lives. In their Sunday best, they helped a champion, one holding his bike, the other his tire. Their calmness contrasts sharply with the agitation of the rider. Your friends will never believe it....

**Henry Anglade
1959**

It's kilometer 208. Two spectators in their best raincoats make temporary assistants. A mud-covered Anglade has not given up, but he will finish only 65th, 12 minutes behind winner Noël Foré.

**Down but not out**
**1991**

The leaders have already gone, and the team cars disappear into the dust, but this TVM rider's vehicle is delayed. Forewarned on the race radio, the team helpers won't be long and they'll have no trouble finding him; he'll soon be on his way.

**Christophe Laurent**
**2002**

Scattered by the worst cobblestone sectors, riders have trouble getting service after a puncture. They hold their defective wheels high like a distress signal, as if that will hasten the repair. Laurent still believes: isn't that the repair motorcycle's headlight in the distance?

# CHAPTER VI

# HELL'S DAMNED

Falls, flats, broken seats, broken wheels. No race is as cruel as Paris-Roubaix. Yet, in the end, it often renders justice to those who really love it.

**Jacques Anquetil**
**1958**

Anquetil, like every champion, dreams of victory in the Classic of Classics. He knows that the rider who wins, even if he has already won the Tour de France, earns his place in the legend of the sport, just like recent Tour champions Fausto Coppi and Louison Bobet. He wants to join them in the record books on this April 13. He has planned well and raced well. He made what looked like the winning break when, only 13km from the velodrome, a puncture undid all his good intentions. The win went in a sprint to Belgian Léon Van Daele. More than just beaten, Anquetil feels defeated, cursed.

# From love to hate

This bitch of a race never fails to arouse the most contradictory sentiments. One loves it to death, and one detests it. It is at once beautiful and cruel. Over some slight infraction, it is capable of denying victory to its most worthy contestants—and for that very reason it arouses an irresistible urge within champions to conquer it.

It also provokes passionate drama. Many an illusion has been destroyed here, victim of a fatal encounter. Many dreams of greatness have sadly slipped away along the course's shoulders of impure clay.

It is the eternal image of the hard-luck racer by the side of the road. He grasps a wheel in his hand and lifts it high, his eyes searching for the help that never comes. "It's awful when you have to wait for the wretched support car," says Gilbert Duclos-Lassalle, a back-to-back winner in 1992–1993. "You watch the others pass by, and you recognize them. You ask yourself if you can possibly get back in. That's why it's essential to have teammates nearby. I had Francis Moreau, who was always supposed to stay behind me on the cobblestone sections."

Duclos-Lassalle's knowledge is hard-earned. He paid his bad-luck dues for many years, entering Paris-Roubaix fourteen times before he finally exacted his revenge. It was a victory all the more sweet since by then he knew well the price of trying. "At that point she gives you back all that you gave to seduce her," muses this great lover of Paris-Roubaix, speaking of the race as if it were a demanding, fickle mistress.

There is no shortage in this race of brutal and devastating fallouts, of tragic setbacks to which nothing else compares. Hell's damned matter no longer. Jean-Marie Leblanc, the director of the race from 1988 to 2006, remarked, "I always think of the words of Jacques Goddet [his predecessor] who said that Paris-Roubaix is the last 'folly' that the sport of cycling offers. I have often pondered the meaning of folly here; it implies accepting the excess once a year. Nowadays we know how not to push things too far, but I'm convinced that Paris-Roubaix must remain—just a tad—over-the-top."

Jacques Goddet gave his own definition of this diabolical test. "Paris-Roubaix brings together the range of characteristics, including excess, that permit the complete expression of class in its purest state," he wrote. As he saw, this race with a thousand nicknames presents a striking paradox: more than any other, it is entirely subject to the whims of luck and yet, at the same time, it often favors the champion. Not always, of course; the cobblestones sometimes inflict the most flagrant injustice.

And so at the end of this trip through Hell, when the last judgment sounds, the results are sometimes shocking.

Take the case of poor Joseph Curtel, who had come up from Marseille in 1927. In the final sprint, he beat out Georges Ronsse, Charles Pélissier, and fifteen others. He was feted with the usual to-do—a bouquet of flowers, the national anthem, and so on. Suddenly the finish-line judge, Mr. Trialoux, changed his decision and Ronsse, who had sprinted along the railing, was declared the winner. Indeed, as the photos prove, the sprint was very close between the two. Of course, a decade of controversy followed. According to legend, Curtel became even more racked by doubt and bitterness two years later when his bike sponsor, Peugeot, bought out Ronsse's builder, Automoto. Along with the purchase came Automoto's accounting books, which allegedly showed the record of a check made out to the same Trialoux, dated April 18, 1927, the day after the race. Fact or fiction? The flow of time has washed away the truth.

## The scandals of the century

Paris-Roubaix certainly has its scandals, some of the best in cycling, in fact. . . .

The Frenchman Jean Maréchal was barely 20 years old for the 1930 edition of the race, when he arrived in Roubaix alone and in first place. He was already in the showers when he learned that Ludovic Feuiller, the all-powerful directeur sportif of the Alcyon team, had issued a protest. The Frenchman was accused of having provoked the spill of his fellow racer, the Belgian Julien Vervaecke, 5 kilometers from the finish line on one of the last cobblestone stretches. Here, too, it is difficult to establish the facts. According to some, Maréchal, frustrated that his rival would not cede more than a centimeter, delivered a blow to Vervaecke's shoulders, prompting his fall. Up until his death in 1995, the Frenchman defended himself vigorously. "I felt that Vervaecke, behind me, was about to attack by hopping onto the sidewalk," he said. "As I was a bit of an acrobat, I also jumped on the edge of the sidewalk. Our shoulders collided and he fell. . . ."

Maréchal was disqualified. But the backroom doings common to that time encourage other possible explanations. For example, Maréchal

**Joseph Curtel, Georges Ronsse**
**1927**

Misfortune, rotten luck, punctures, and crashes all afflict the accursed of Paris-Roubaix. If that's not enough, then you can add the finish-line judges. Here, in 1927, they decided that Belgium's Ronsse, sprinting in the center of the road, was the winner, whereas the Frenchman Curtel appeared clearly to cross the line first. The band started to play "La Marseillaise," the French national anthem, but quickly changed to Belgium's "Brabançonne" when the judges announced their decision. Curtel never got over it.

**Jean Maréchal
1930**

Whether he bumped into his breakaway partner Julien Vervaecke by accident or deliberately doesn't really matter because Jean Maréchal, who crossed the line first by 24 seconds, was disqualified. There was talk that the judges favored Vervaecke because his bike sponsor, Alcyon, bought huge advertisements in the organizer's newspaper, whereas Maréchal's bike supplier, the modest Colin company, bought none.

**Olimpio Bizzi
1947**

On this rainy April 6, he finished sixth at Roubaix, 56 seconds behind winner Georges Claes, but Italy's Bizzi has a hard time keeping his cool. While in the lead and apparently headed to victory he was first directed off course and then, with 17km to go, broke his wheel in a pothole. He was passed only 2km from the finish. He couldn't have had worse luck.

was sponsored by a Parisian dealer of bicycles named Colin, whose modest business probably would not have given him the means to place advertisements in *L'Auto*, Paris-Roubaix's sponsoring newspaper. In contrast, the richer Alcyon team was able to purchase numerous spots celebrating Vervaecke's victory. Makes you wonder where the truth really lies.

Equally painful was the lot in store for Roger Lapébie, who would be deprived of victory for an infraction of the rules. He was disqualified in 1934 for having exchanged bicycles with a spectator after he suffered a flat. The Belgian Gaston Rebry, who finished second, was declared the winner. Surprisingly, Lapébie, the moral victor, harbored no resentment. "I refused to make a federal case of it," he would later explain. "Rules are rules. Moreover, that disqualification game me an enormous amount of publicity!"

Olimpio Bizzi also merits a prominent place in this pantheon of the cursed. In 1947, after breaking away for 210 kilometers, he sabotaged his efforts by taking a wrong turn at the entrance of Wattignies. Compounding this blunder was the state of his rear wheel, damaged at the exit of Lesquin, 17 kilometers from the finish line. The Italian gamely carried on, but he was overtaken just 2 kilometers from the velodrome! For the hapless Bizzi, it was a black day indeed.

### A constable drives André Mahé to despair

But the most underhanded blow took place in 1949. Indeed, it was one of the greatest injustices in the history of the sport. That year, the handful of favorites (notably Fausto Coppi and Rik Van Steenbergen) allowed a group to precede them to the velodrome, consisting of the Frenchman André Mahé, the Franco-Spaniard Jésus Moujica, and the young Belgian Frans Leenen. Behind by at least 200 meters, the favorites seemed to have no chance of getting back into it.

But no! As the three breakaways entered the stadium, a policeman's gesticulations sent them on a detour created for the team cars! Moujica, seemingly the fastest, was also the first to realize the blunder. But he fell in the confusion, effectively losing any chance at winning.

Eventually, the three breakaways, joined by Georges Martin, who had just escaped the peloton, made their way onto the track by another entrance. Mahé crossed the line first, ahead of the other three. A few seconds later, Serse Coppi, the little brother of the Campionissimo, won the official sprint in his group, only to learn that it amounted to fifth place.

Coppi's team, Bianchi, filed a complaint based on article 156 of the rulebook, which stipulates, "the official itinerary must be regularly followed." Oddly enough, though, this same article states further on, "The racers must naturally conform to the indications given to them by agents of law enforcement," thus leaving the door open to another interpretation of the affair.

As it turned out, Jacques Goddet, the director of the race, arrived at the velodrome entrance by car, just behind the men in the lead. In an editorial for *L'Équipe*, he wrote, "I found myself just behind the three victims at the precise moment of the incident, and I can certify that the police agents placed at the intersection of the correct route did, by their obvious arm gestures, mislead Moujica, Mahé, and Leenen, thus taking away all meaning for this particular Paris-Roubaix." Regarding the officers, he icily added, "I will not go out of my way to compliment them."

Mahé had barely completed his lap of honor when Henri Boudard, on behalf of the officials, informed him that he was disqualified. "It felt like someone had just punched me in the face," recalled the hapless hero. "My ears were buzzing. I looked at people without seeing anyone."

The pill was even harder to swallow given that he had actually ridden a greater distance than the peloton! From the main entrance to the track, where he made a wrong turn, he should have had just 500 meters to go to the finish line. Instead, he and the other breakaways covered exactly 1 kilometer to get to the other gate. To be sure, at that point they were just 20 meters from the finish line, whereas the peloton had to go another 260 meters from the main entrance. Still, in total the errant breakaways covered an extra 220 meters.

But rules are rules. *L'Équipe*, the sponsor, justly condemned the decision that clearly defied good sportsmanship. Still, it had to abide by the official verdict rendered by an independent commission. In the guise of compensation, the sporting daily awarded Mahé, Moujica, and Leenen a

**André Darrigade
1959**

The French sprinter Darrigade seemed made for Paris-Roubaix. But his best finish in more than ten starts was only fourth, in 1957. His bad luck appeared to be over in 1959 when he looked to be headed for the win until, with 17km to go, a TV motorcycle knocked him over. Upset? You could say that.

**Rolf Wolfshohl, Noël Foré
1963**

With 20km to go, it looks as though victory can't escape them. But then Wolfshohl crashes, and Foré takes his chance to attack solo. Once recovered, Germany's Wolfshohl chases and passes his Belgian rival. But he has to put out too much energy and a chase group catches him near the end.

sum comparable to the earnings of the top three finishers, which they divvied up amongst themselves. But Mahé's true consolation came a few days later, when the sporting commission of the French Federation decided to reclassify him as first, in a shared victory with Serse Coppi. And so it is that the official list of Paris-Roubaix winners exceeds the number of races by one.

## Anquetil loses the lottery

Like all great champions, Jacques Anquetil wanted to add a victory in Paris-Roubaix to his palmarès, even though he knew his smooth style was at odds with the brute strength required to win this race. And so, in 1958, he was ready to give it his all. Early on, he had his teammates push him hard and, by the 70th kilometer, he was catapulted into the lead. When Anquetil and his fellow escapees approached the Gates of Hell, near Courcelles, they were fifteen in all, holding a lead of three minutes over the peloton.

The climb over Monchaux, followed by the ascent of Mons-en-Pévèle, claimed the group's first casualties, and that's when the former hour record holder took over. Anquetil led a train through Hell, devouring the kilometers and always pushing, pushing, pushing. Soon there were only four left in his lead group. Anquetil rode shoulder to shoulder with Nicolas Barone, with the Belgians Willy Truye and Roger Verplaetse close at hand, in a spirited race hurtling headlong into a bitter wind. Anquetil glided along. "He amazed us," wrote Jacques Goddet that same day.

But the Norman Baisieux suffered a flat on his rear wheel at just 13 kilometers from Roubaix. At that point, the peloton, presided over by the two Riks—Van Looy and Van Steenbergen—narrowed its gap to about a minute. The Norman's repair took twenty-five seconds. Anquetil took off again and caught up with his former companions in the space of 5 kilometers. But he had been deprived too long of his principal motor fuel, and he gave up at the climb over the Hem, four clicks from the velodrome. This day of *vent*—wind—turned into the day of Van—as in Léon Van Daele, the Flemish racer who surged ahead in the final sprint to claim a victory for the ages.

"That did not pay off," lamented Anquetil as he headed for the showers. "In the end I needed those precious seconds I lost after the flat. All I needed was to save enough energy to get to the final sprint. And I swear I would have won that sprint."

Anquetil's pride would never let him admit that he could have lost this race while still being the best in the field. And he never again started the race with the right attitude, that unshakable conviction that his talent would prevail. "Luck plays an overly important role in this race," he moaned. For him, racing in Paris-Roubaix was little better than entering a lottery.

## Graczyk and Darrigade, Foré and Wolfshohl—studies in futility

Tom Simpson no doubt shared Anquetil's bitterness. In 1960, after leading a solitary breakaway for 40 kilometers, the British star was overtaken 5 kilometers from the finish. He then lost the final sprint. It's safe to say that Jean Graczyk was no fan of the race, either. In 1961, his saddle broke at kilometer 215; the following year he fell, only to have fifteen comrades roll over his thigh. André Darrigade, the great sprinter, had equally hard luck, although one might have expected exactly the opposite. In fact, he completed the race only once in eleven tries, when he finished fourth in 1957. The other ten times he was a victim of crashes—the curse of Paris-Roubaix.

No luck either for Rolf Wolfshohl and Noël Foré in 1963. It's as if they went to Rome without seeing the Pope. Both took turns believing they had won the race during one of the most exciting—and bewildering—final stretches of all time, only to falter at the gates of the velodrome.

The German and the Belgian had broken away 20 kilometers from the finish, when Wolfshohl suddenly suffered a flat. That left Foré alone in the lead, and he gave the distinct impression that he could reach the end unchallenged. Five kilometers from the finish, he led Wolfshohl by 25 seconds and the rest of the pursuers by over a minute. But Brik Schotte, his directeur sportif with Flandria, asked him nevertheless to let Wolfshohl catch up, believing that the German would give Foré valuable reinforcement down the stretch while posing no threat in the final sprint (Foré, after all, had already won this event in 1959). But the Belgian refused. He would later explain, "I felt strong enough to win on my own, so why should I take such a risk?" As a result, the two leaders were condemned to an exhausting pursuit. Wolfshohl managed to come back and catch Foré at the Lys-lez-Lannoy square, 1.5 kilometers from the velodrome. In the meantime, however, Rik Van Looy's group, given up for dead, had caught up. Just as the leading pair reached the gates of the velodrome, Van Looy's group dashed by. First place went to Emile Daems, who stunned Van Looy in the sprint. Jan Janssen finished third. Foré and Wolfshohl divided the remains. In the long list of Hell's damned, their names will always be inscribed.

## A wheel, a wheel!

Besides its history with a big "H," Paris-Roubaix has many smaller tales to tell. These anecdotes too are replete with pain and injustice, and at times pose moral dilemmas. Take, for example, Agnès Gougeat. In 1994, she was the communications director for the Gan group, whose cycling team was led by the two-time winner and defending champion, Gilbert Duclos-Lassalle. His main rival that year was Franco Ballerini, whom he had beaten at the wire the year before. Gougeat, for her part, was not content merely to shuffle her guests from one cobblestone stretch to another. Immersed in her team's sporting adventure, she and other colleagues unofficially helped out at her team's repair stations spaced along the course.

"We would hop along the route," she recalls. "To help the racers recognize us without the organizers catching on, we wore distinct Coca-Cola hats. At one point, I hid my two spare wheels behind a Mercedes that happened to be nearby. There was a large crowd on the left side of the road, but I was the only one on the right. Then the racers arrived, and all of a sudden some guy approached me, as black as a coal miner, yelling 'A wheel, a wheel!' Everything happened in a flash. I could see he wasn't one of ours, but I immediately thought if this were our Duclos who had flatted, and someone refused to give him a wheel, I would have shot that person on the spot! So I scampered behind the Mercedes and retrieved my two wheels. He took the rear one and did his thing. When he took off I looked at the number on his back and saw an '11.' I still didn't know who he was, but I had a gnawing feeling I had just made a bone-headed move."

Confirmation was not long in coming. When Michel Laurent, one of the members of the team, saw her return with just one wheel he interrogated her:

"You helped someone out?" he asked.

"Yes," she replied meekly.

"Who was that?" he persisted.

"Number 11," she replied.

"You didn't help Ballerini, I hope!" he gasped.

There may well be an angel who looks after good-hearted women. Ballerini did not win; he finished third (Andreï Tchmil took first) and, in any event, Duclos-Lassalle, the leader of the team, fell out of contention with a flat. Ms. Gougeat nonetheless felt lingering pangs of guilt. "I waited until Duclos retired from cycling before I admitted to him that I had given Ballerini a wheel," she said.

Gougeat's infraction was a serious roll of the dice. But who can say if all racers are equal before the god of bad luck? "You have to know how to factor in luck," states the great Eddy Merckx, "even if it is always the same ones who seem to escape unscathed."

## A formidable love affair

At heart, is Paris-Roubaix unjust? "There are times when it is," allows Duclos-Lassalle, who was nonetheless too well treated by fate to harbor any ill will. "It's true that one sacrifices a great deal to the race. Whenever I started off I would think of all the eight-hour, nine-hour training rides I had been through. I told myself that in the race I would get a flat, and I would fall once, but I also told myself I would win anyway. Sometimes, it's true, you resent the injustice of it all. There were times when I told myself, 'I am for this race, but does she want me?' And yet, I always adored her. You have to be strong with her. I was so fixated on her one year that I did not say hello to my own son, Hervé, when I left the hotel that morning. He was hurt by that. But I knew that I was facing a monumental race, that it would not give me any gifts, and that I shouldn't give it any, either."

Get a flat, change the wheel, and get back in it. Get another flat, and still believe. To find paradise at Roubaix, you need faith. "In 1993, when I won it for the second time," adds Duclos-Lassalle, "I had seen it all: two flats on the tarmac, another after the first cobblestones, a fall at Arenberg. I fell way behind. If at that moment I had not found the strength to tell myself that I could still win, I would have lost that Paris-Roubaix." Never give up.

And yet one must acknowledge that this fickle race dispenses a form of rough justice. After all, the majority of great champions have managed to register their names, sooner or later, in its roster of heroes. Names like Van Steenbergen, Coppi, Van Looy, Bobet, Gimondi, Merckx, Tchmil, Museeuw, Van Petegem, and Boonen. In the final analysis, few classics can claim a record as rich as that.

Nor is Paris-Roubaix insensitive to those who have shed tears over it. It's impossible to forget Ballerini's terrible letdown after he was beaten at the wire by Duclos-Lassalle in 1993. He swore then that he would never return. Yet he came back to win the event twice, in 1995 and 1998.

"Those who have the qualities to win it one day or another will get there," vouches Duclos-Lassalle. "You will suffer blows, but, in the course of years, you must analyze all your mistakes so as not to repeat them. And when you love the race the way I did, sooner or later you will prevail."

PHILIPPE BOUVET

**Gilbert Duclos-Lassalle**
**1980**

Asked whether this race really likes him, Frenchman Duclos-Lassalle has fallen madly in love with the event. He picks himself up after every fall, saying they're a necessary evil, and he continues trying to win despite his setbacks. In 1980, he crashes, flats twice, and still places second, behind Francesco Moser. He knows he can win, but has to wait another twelve years before finding the key to the Hell of the North.

**Roger Lapébie**
**1934**

French star Lapébie knows he has won the race on merit, and it is only an antiquated rule that has taken away his victory. Yes, after flatting with no repair vehicle in sight, he grabbed a female spectator's bike, then changed it for one with racing bars, and he still managed to catch and pass the two leaders. Changing bikes is against the rules in 1934, but he smiles for the cameras, and he knows that he crossed the line first. That memory can't be taken away from him.

## Gaston Rebry
### 1934

Has he really won, Gaston Rebry? He hopes so, because the rules are in his favor. It doesn't matter that he crossed the line in second place, as Roger Lapébie is sure to be disqualified. But he has a hard time celebrating. A technical victory is not something the Belgian Bulldog appreciates. But he already won in 1931... and he'll do it again in 1935.

## Romain Maës,
## Georges Speicher
### 1936

It seems indisputable that the Belgian Maës (left) has crossed the line ahead of Frenchman Speicher. The judge and his assistants see it otherwise. The finish is on a horse racetrack this year; perhaps that influences the poor decision. Or is it because, of these two Tour de France winners, Speicher carries more weight in terms of popularity and charisma?

**André Mahé**
**1949**

Still emotional moments after crossing the line, his bouquet still in hand, Frenchman Mahé is congratulated by his directeur sportif, Paul Le Drogo. A victory at Paris-Roubaix is immense.

**Serse Coppi**
**1949**

On either side of the great Fausto Coppi, his entourage confers and waits. They all know his brother Serse (far left) crossed the line after Mahé, but the group he outsprinted followed the correct course. It's a problem for the race commissaires.

**André Mahé**
**1949**

Mahé feels the restlessness in the velodrome. He's also feeling skeptical. He knows that he crossed the line first, but he also knows that a commissaire directed him off course in the final kilometer, and he risks being disqualified. He also realizes the influence of Fausto Coppi. In the end, being given equal first place with Serse Coppi is not quite the same as an outright victory.

**Jacques Anquetil
1958**

The defending Tour de France champion is in the good move, the one that looks like winning, when at Baisieux, with 13km to go, he gets a stupid, banal, fatal puncture. The seconds are ticking by: 20 ... 30 ... the time it takes to get a new wheel. To chase back to his former three companions he digs deep, and just after catching them, they're absorbed by the peloton. It ends in a sprint, with Anquetil not even in the top ten.

**Jean Graczyck**
**1963**

The two-time points champion at the Tour, Popov Graczyck doesn't shine as expected on the pavé of Paris-Roubaix. Partly because when he doesn't flat, as in 1960 and here in 1963, he breaks his forks (1961) or crashes (1962). One consolation is that the spectators are sympathetic.

**Tom Simpson**
**1960**

On a solo break for the past 40km, English newcomer Tom Simpson can almost feel the victory. He's less than 5km from the line in the gloomy suburbs of Roubaix. But, fading fast in his first taste of the Hell of the North, Simpson is passed by eventual winner Pino Cerami and seven others before the velodrome. He's left with the crumbs after glimpsing the feast.

**Rolf Wolfshohl
1963**

The German rider has just flatted less than 20km from the finish, after being in the lead with 1959 winner Noël Foré. Wolfshohl sets off again and chases after Foré, who despite the advice of his directeur sportif refuses to wait for his former companion. Together, they might have made it to the finish, but Wolfshohl expends lots of energy (bottom photo) in catching the Belgian. He even has the strength to drop Foré, but he's caught within sight of the velodrome and doesn't even make the top ten.

**Alain Bondue
1983**

For his first participation in Paris-Roubaix, the local rider Alain Bondue says he is "super happy, even though I fell eight times. I flatted a first time at Neuvilly, then again. I left there in second-to-last position, and despite another wheel change I reached [Wallers-Arenberg] in second place. After the pileup at Orchies, it was hard. I've finished 10th but one day I'll be here for the win."

**Alain Bondue,
Gregor Braun
1984**

After breaking clear with Gregor Braun in the Arenberg "trench," Bondue and his German teammate stay ahead for 80km. Their lead plateaus at 1 minute, 48 seconds, and then shrinks after the German flats twice, despite the young Frenchman's efforts to push on. Chasing them are the Irishman Sean Kelly, having a strong day, and the Belgian Rudy Rogiers, who catch Bondue and Braun on a section of pavé called la Vache Bleue (the Blue Cow), with 20km to go. Kelly's immediate acceleration sees Braun drop back, leaving Bondue with the new leaders.

**Alain Bondue**
**1984**

Bondue skids on the greasy cobblestones and falls behind. Helped back into the saddle by the fans, he starts to chase ferociously after Kelly and Rogiers, but he has already lost a minute. Despite a heroic pursuit, he can't get closer than 36 seconds behind the winner. He finishes third, and afterward realizes that even if he had caught the two in front, he wouldn't have been able to sprint: his forks were cracked.

**Francis Moreau,
Gilbert Duclos-Lassalle
1994**

As in 1993, when he won for
the second consecutive time,
Gilbert Duclos-Lassalle (at
right) flats in the Wallers-
Arenberg forest. And once
again, his team plan works to
perfection: his teammate
Francis Moreau, who has
ridden right behind Duclos on
the cobblestone sections, is
there to help. He gives his
team leader his front wheel
immediately....

...and helps him to get going again. This wasn't enough for Duclos to score his hat trick at Roubaix, but helps him finish in an honorable seventh place. Duclos wouldn't win again, but in his seventeen starts he proved that with hard work, passion, and good organization it's possible to alleviate some of the race's inevitable setbacks.

# CHAPTER VII

# THE RACE OF MIRACLES

A victory in the Queen of the Classics is a dream for anyone, from the great champions to the lesser-known hopefuls. Among the many names in the victory books are those of a few who got there by dropping their anonymity on the cobblestones. These include the Belgians Charles Meunier, Lucien Storme; and Dirk Demol; the Italian Antonio Bevilacqua; and the Frenchman Frédéric Guesdon.

**Dirk Demol**
**1988**

At the party organized in his honor by his family, friends, and supporters the day after the race, he's starting to believe he really did it. Yes, that's him, Dirk Demol, who's just won the Queen of the Classics. He, the modest, unknown racer who has joined the ranks of Paris-Roubaix winners like Sean Kelly, Hennie Kuiper, Jan Raas, Bernard Hinault, and Francesco Moser. That's him on the newspaper's front page, crowned with a hat.

# Impossible winners

You only have to look at their faces on race morning to understand that this is an event like no other. The favorites are so intent on their objective that they have taken great pains to prepare. They toe the start line exuding confidence, about to confront the most hazardous route of all. And then there are the others, who have no reason to hold out any hope for victory. Yet they, too, go forward, these adventurers of the "why not?" school of thought who dare to fancy a small dream of victory.

"If you have a number on your back, you have a prayer," attests Marc Madiot. "Whoever you are, if you have that number, you can find your El Dorado. Sometimes, I see obscure racers and I know that, in their heads, they are thinking the pace might slow down, giving them an opportunity to burst ahead. There are a lot of maybes in this race, but there is always hope. It may be miniscule, but they live their race on that basis. And I have the utmost respect for them."

The palmarès of Paris-Roubaix is a roll call of sacred idols: Merckx, De Vlaeminck, Moser, Van Looy, Van Steenbergen, Coppi, Bobet, Lapize, Hinault. And yet, from time to time, some illustrious unknown comes out of nowhere to claim his day of glory. He's one of a handful of champions no one expected; indeed, he himself probably didn't anticipate his own victory.

## Meunier, a miner in the mud

The first of these party-spoilers was no doubt Charles Meunier, a Belgian from the Hainaut region who, after toiling a bit in the mines, showed so much promise on his bicycle that at the age of 20 he was signed as an independent racer. He dutifully served out his four-year apprenticeship before becoming a professional in 1926, when he was 23 years old. He was focused, serious, and tough. Though not particularly ambitious, he always fulfilled his contract. In fact, that's just what he did in the Paris-Roubaix of 1927 when he finished 75th. Meunier lagged so far behind the leaders that by the time he crossed the finish line, he had missed all the excitement. The winner, Joseph Curtel, had been disqualified, to the benefit of Meunier's compatriot Georges Ronsse.

In the 1928 edition, however, he found himself at the head of the race, alongside André Leducq and Ronsse. His foes were perplexed. If Meunier was up there, they reasoned, he must not be too bad. But no one really knew anything about him, much less his sprinting abilities. Ronsse jumped the gun, fearing that Meunier would prove formidable in the final stretch. His premature attack, however, benefited only Leducq, who finished first in front of Ronsse and . . . the surprising Meunier.

This honorable mention gave Meunier the opportunity the following season to join the formidable Alcyon team, in support of its two Belgian stars, Ronsse and Aimé Déolet. Meunier's duty was to help one of his compatriots bring the great classic's bouquet back to Belgium. Meunier's orders were simple: stay shoulder to shoulder with Ronsse, the leader, until Ronsse and Déolet could take off together for the final sprint.

But Paris-Roubaix has a catch: it is a race like no other. Everything was going according to plan for the Alcyon team as the leaders approached the Prouvost stadium, where the finish was to be judged. Better, in fact. For Ronsse was flanked not only by Déolet (the Redhead) but also by . . . Meunier.

Raymond Huttier, the special correspondent for the *Miroir des Sports*, was most impressed by Ronsse, who he felt "had the best form of the three." He said, "His rhythm is magnificent; much purer, less jerky, and more graceful than in previous years." Obviously enchanted with the Alcyon leader, the journalist added, "The silk stockings with which he has covered his knees and lower legs reflect regular glimmers of light, hiding his muscles at work; the ensemble makes you think of perfectly adjusted connecting rods."

Ronsse's victory seemed all the more inevitable given that Déolet "trailed with great difficulty" and Meunier "was hunched over on his bike." Summing up his impression, Huttier wrote, "Everyone figured the final order would be Ronsse first, Meunier second, and Déolet third."

But a stadium is not a velodrome. The track at this time was composed of dirt, an unknown world to Ronsse. He entered the track with great caution, riding tentatively on its crumbly surface. But Meunier, who followed him, knew perfectly well what a cinder path was all about. After all, he had not spent all that time in a mine for nothing. Naturally, he was better able to control his machine. Fifty meters from the finish line, Huttier witnessed a catastrophe. "Ronsse skids and sprawls out on the ground, taking down Déolet with him." By the time Ronsse got up, discovered a damaged front wheel, and draped his bicycle over his shoulder, it was too late. Meunier had passed his teammates and won almost in spite of himself. But he had been good enough to figure among the

**Charles Meunier**
**1929**

He has won, the former coal
miner who once worked at the
pit face. His happiness is
discreet, held within, like all
the great joys of life. Around
him, the journalists, officials,
and race followers have a hard
time believing Meunier has
won Paris-Roubaix. He has
dignity, this Charles. Someday
he could even return to the
mine without losing face.

**Lucien Storme**
**1938**

Just an unknown rookie with no results to speak of, Storme rides like a champion in his first Paris-Roubaix. He wins in style, charging through this railway crossing, not concerned about the reputation of the stars, and goes on the attack.

**Roger Rosiers**
**1971**

Eddy Merckx, Roger De Vlaeminck, and Jan Janssen are perhaps marking each other too closely, and an audacious Rosiers takes advantage of the situation. Even so, to win here you have to have power, skill, and panache, and know when to grab your chance. Bravo, Roger!

finalists, and experienced enough to avoid a fatal fall. Charles the obscure, who wore a thick mask of dust punctuated by his sparkling teeth, was the indisputable winner of the 13th Paris-Roubaix. The surprise victor will never for an instant leave his eternal niche of glory. Back on the field, tears streaked the black faces of Ronsse and Déolet.

Did Meunier dare crack a smile? The answer has been lost in time. In any event, he had done his job. Over time, no doubt, he would have wanted to do a little more than that. But an uncooperative knee forced him into early retirement. He had just enough time in between to snag a few more honorable mentions and to make one final appearance in the Hell of the North. That was in 1931, when he was 31 years old. Shortly thereafter, he returned to the shadows of the mine. He could count just one—though highly memorable—victory in his professional career: the Paris-Roubaix of March 31, 1929.

## Storme like a hurricane

In this race of miracles, it was another Belgian, Lucien Storme, who made the news in the late 1930s. At that time, the stars were named Gaston Rebry, Romain and Sylvère Maës, Gustave Danneels, Éloi Meulenberg, Jules Lowie, Georges Speicher, Edgar De Caluwé, and Robert Wierinckx. But the 1938 edition was particularly unpredictable. A fierce storm blew, the hill of Doullens did its usual job weeding out the weaker racers, and, after Amiens, the echelons acted as guillotines, making away with the last big stars still in the running.

At Seclin, Robert Oubron and Constant Lauwers surged ahead. For 10 kilometers, they maintained control. That was just enough time to burn out or get a flat. Just after Lesquin, only 17 kilometers from the finish, two unexpected breakaways burst into the lead: Louis Hardiquest, a veteran nicknamed the Belgian Binda, and Lucien Storme, a newly turned professional who had only fourteen elite races under his belt.

Storme was but 22 years old, but he had a good feel for the race. At Carvin, he had already started to break before he changed his mind: 35 kilometers was too far to ride alone. With Hardiquest, however, he sensed the time was right to break away. He was so much at ease, this man from Poperinge, that he not only overcame a blowout 8 kilome-

ters from Roubaix, he also promptly settled matters with his accomplice, who was nonetheless no slouch, having won the Tour of Flanders two years earlier.

The career of this Paris-Roubaix winner, a former unknown, was about to take off. The following year, 1939, Storme finished second in Paris-Tours, third in Paris-Brussels, and third in Paris–Saint-Étienne. But the outbreak of war put an end to his hopes. Taken prisoner at the start of hostilities, Storme was held in Germany until the liberation of the Sieburg camp, on April 10, 1945. That was two days after Paul Maye triumphed in the first postwar edition of Paris-Roubaix.

## Bevilacqua and Rosiers, the prize to the attackers

The Italian Antonio Bevilacqua was by no means an unknown in 1951. But truth be told, he had earned his fame primarily on the track as a pursuit racer—an excellent one, in fact. In 1947 and 1948, he reached the lower levels of the podium at the world championships, before standing on the highest in the 1950 edition. On the road, he wasn't bad either, but he was far from being a great captain. If he made anyone's list of favorites to win Paris-Roubaix in 1951, it was truly on the second tier, far below Ferdi Kübler, Bobet, Van Steenbergen, Pierre Barbotin, Loretto Petrucci, André Declerck, and Fiorenzo Magni.

The weather for this edition was dry and dusty, just as it had been when Meunier and Storme claimed their surprising upsets. Those conditions were generally in Bevilacqua's favor, for a pursuit specialist cannot easily slip into high gear when the cobblestones are wet. And since this time around, the race was not shaping up to be a long cyclocross competition, Bevilacqua was eager to exploit the opportunity to register a win. After Doullens, he was the one who launched the decisive attack, along with Bernard Gauthier, Attilio Redolfi, and Guido De Santi. Their echelon soon absorbed Raymond Impanis and Lionel Van Brabant, who had broken away from the peloton at the ninth kilometer. So they all arrived together at Lesquin, just 17 kilometers from the finish, the same place where Storme and Hardiquest had lost their anonymity back in 1938. At that point, Gauthier went on the attack, provoking a fierce response from Bevilacqua. He slipped into his 50x14 gear on the cobblestones, pedaled like the devil, and took the lead.

Behind him, Bobet was doing his own acrobatics. But he was handicapped by a blowout and forced to mount a long, crazy pursuit. He could not make up the difference. "Tonio," wearing number 177, looked behind over his shoulder. His lead was solid. There was nothing left for him to do other than crush his pedals. And this he knew how to do better than anyone—his average speed would be over 40 kilometers an hour. At Roubaix, he led the favorites, Bobet and Van Steenbergen, by more than a minute and a half. Crossing the finish line, Bevilacqua was so dazed he forgot to smile.

Paris-Roubaix loves, from time to time, to thumb its nose at the greats. Twenty years later, in 1971, Roger Rosiers was riding alongside the heavy favorites when he had the audacity to attack. After all, he had nothing to lose and everything to gain! Neither Merckx nor De Vlaeminck, Éric Leman nor Jan Janssen, wanted to assume responsibility for leading a pursuit. The unranked Belgian thus acceded to glory that day.

That was also the case with his compatriot Jean-Marie Wampers. In the rainy 1989 edition, he found himself in a good breakaway accompanied by numerous wet-weather specialists, including Marc Madiot, Gilbert Duclos-Lassalle, Edwig Van Hooydonck, Eddy Planckaert, and Dirk De Wolf. But Wampers was in command, and one by one he dropped them all, with the sole exception of De Wolf, who accompanied Wampers as far as the velodrome before bowing out.

On occasion, a team can also reward a faithful servant with a victory. Such was the case in 2001, when the Dutchman Servais Knaven skillfully exploited the numerical superiority of his team, Domo, directed by Patrick Lefévere. And from time to time there are true surprise winners, like the Swedish giant Magnus Bäckstedt, who in 2004 mastered a breakaway composed of secondary racers whom the French like to call "second knives."

## The triumph of the criterium racer

In this contemporary era, the legend of Paris-Roubaix values above all the "triumph of a *manneke*" (a "small man," in Flemish), as Jean-Marie Leblanc wrote in *L'Équipe* in 1988, when the modest Dirk Demol enjoyed his day of glory.

Demol was the eighth and last man selected by his team, ADR. The previous Thursday, however, at the Grand Prix de Denain—his type of race—he showed signs of good form. Still, when he glided into the breakaway that Sunday morning of Paris-Roubaix, he entertained no illusions. He was simply trying to fulfill his team duties. Moreover, the favorites were not about to panic. Most of Demol's dozen companions were as unknown as he. To name a few: Corné Van Rijen, Eddy Schurer, Franck Boucanville, Loïc Le Flohic, Michel Cornelisse, and Yves Van Steenwinkel. "I was hustling for Eddy Planckaert," Demol later explained, but he was in for a big surprise. "I waited for him to come back and he never did. So I said to myself, 'Just stay in the lead, you never know.'"

Though Demol was a relative unknown, he was a solid road racer from the region of Courtrai in the Netherlands. And what few observers appreciated during the race was that he had already finished second in Paris-Roubaix, in the amateur race of 1980. But this promising performance was quickly overshadowed by the imposing personality of the winner, the Irishman Stephen Roche, who would go on to become a major star. It was entirely predictable, nonetheless, that the racer from

**Jean-Marie Wampers
1989**

He leads the pack so strongly on the cobblestones that race followers think that this lanky Belgian, Jean-Marie Wampers, can cause an upset. And in the record books, his name does follow that of Dirk Demol. One "unknown" after the other; that's never happened before.

Kermis would turn professional. In his native land, he compiled an extensive win list: Wielsbeke, Izegem, Rummen, Geraardsbergen, and Desselgem—not a bad résumé, all told. But through it all he mainly felt that he was just earning a living. This brave young man who generally fed the soft belly of the peloton was already 28 years old in the spring of 1988. And he never expected to change his destiny when he joined those early breakaways at kilometer 44, near the border of the regions of Aisne and Somme. He was then in the barren countryside, on local road 932, stretching endlessly toward the horizon. It was so straight and long, in fact, it seemed the horizon kept pushing back the end of the road. Finally, 222 milestones later, Demol and his coconspirator had accomplished the longest victorious breakaway in the entire history of the Queen of the Classics.

"Honestly, no one thought they would go the distance," admitted the Frenchman Thierry Casas, the instigator of the breakaway who was simply trying to show off his jersey. In fact, the group of thirteen had barely taken off when, according to a tacit agreement, half the pack stopped to pee. All of a sudden, the lead rose to eight minutes, even though the breakaway had only been initiated 11 kilometers before. Though the peloton seemed to have little to worry about in the long run, the race gods favored the breakaways. It was a spring Sunday, without a hint of wind, and a host of other factors helped set the stage for a miracle. For example, in this year, 1988, a reform was enacted limiting to eight the number of racers a team could enter in a major race. Consequently, the leaders were worried about prematurely burning out their support racers, and the coaches had not yet come to terms with this new policy. As a result, the pace of the peloton was slower than usual. To be sure, by cobblestone section 11, the gap had fallen to three minutes. But then the pace of the peloton slackened again and the lead reexpanded, reaching considerable proportions. By kilometer 200 it was back up to five minutes. But as the French proverb states, it's a long way from the cup to the lips. . . .

## What would those guys have done in the peloton?

Meanwhile, the favorites were tangled up in a dangerous waiting game. After Wallers-Arenberg, Sean Kelly and Adrie Van der Poel were about the only ones to show any desire to intensify the pursuit. But the Irishman soon fell, and he lagged too far behind to put any real pressure on the peloton to pick up the pace.

Ahead, on his lucky day, Demol was still light on his feet. He was visibly the freshest of the breakaways. What's more, he fell on the right horse, once he found himself alone with Thomas Wegmüller, a Swiss racer who was holding nothing back. "When we found ourselves in the lead approaching the next-to-last section, I began to believe I could win," Demol recounted. He was not, after all, expending as much energy as the generous Wegmüller. Moreover, the Belgian was quick to seize the extraordinary opportunity given him. "At the end, I kept telling myself, 'You must win, you must win.' Wegmüller was still leading on the cobblestones, but I was holding something back, and I knew the strongman in the sprint would turn out to be me."

In fact, once on the track, Demol had no problem dispensing with his rival. His good luck that day was equivalent to winning the lottery. In third place, about two minutes behind the two lone survivors of the breakaway, was Laurent Fignon. The Parisian was in excellent form that day, but he took off too late, just 7 kilometers from the end. "I was truly very strong," he lamented. "This was certainly a good opportunity for me to win, but that's easy to say after the fact."

"Those two guys, what would they have done all day long if they had remained in the peloton?" wondered the northerner Bruno Wojtinek, who had finished second in 1985. "They would have yielded to their leaders. They are nonetheless strongmen themselves, who had never really understood their own capabilities."

Following a stop in Bruges where his team held banquet in his honor, Demol returned just after midnight to Bavikhove, his village in western Flanders, to find his name painted in loud colors on the sidewalk. A local artist had also decorated the windows of Demol's little house, in praise of his newfound glory. The hero went over to café Villa to meet his fans, where pints of beer flowed freely. This was the same place where he had once collected 1,000 Belgian francs (about 25 euros) and a meal after winning a race early in his career. Demol, from a working-class family with five children, was from such a humble background that he had not even seen a modern bathroom until he traveled with the national team. Demol will forever remain a hero of Paris-Roubaix, but his head did not spin for long. As it turned out, his glory proved as ephemeral as it was sudden. His career quickly resumed along familiar lines, and Paris-Roubaix was but a short tour in paradise.

"Mark the day of Paris-Roubaix in your agenda," Madiot advised the young racer from Brittany when he joined the team. "This should be your top priority."

Madiot certainly possesses the power of persuasion. That Sunday, Guesdon tore along within a group of counterattackers that chased breakaways Andreï Tchmil and Frédéric Moncassin to the very gates of the velodrome. Along the way, destiny accorded Guesdon a stroke of luck. Johan Museeuw, the heavy favorite, punctured at the hill of Gruson, 15 kilometers from the finish. Museeuw's flat provoked a last-minute regrouping, and Guesdon now found himself in good company. "When the big boys hit the cobblestones, I never stopped telling myself, 'You've got to let yourself go like a vagabond,'" Guesdon said. "So I didn't budge from my position. It wasn't up to me to attack, even if I had a great urge to go all out two milestones from the finish." Indeed, the man from Brittany wisely eschewed the temptation, and was content to keep his legs churning steadily in his elegant style. His pedaling was so easy he made himself inconspicuous as the race came to its climax. Once Tchmil and Moncassin were caught, the total of eight racers entered the track together. Guesdon thought he was dreaming. "It's not possible, Fred," he told himself. "You're poised to win!"

He was almost afraid to believe in his own chances. When the sprint took off, he was attracted to the opposite right line. "Let's go over there," he said to himself. "I had to accelerate the machine. I went as far to the right as possible [with the chain on the smallest rear sprocket] and gave it my all." Museeuw was slow to respond, a hesitation that proved fatal. Guesdon recounted this final sprint, which made him the winner of Paris-Roubaix: "I took the lead, but I fully expected to be passed. At the last straight I snuck a peek under my arm, and I saw that I was about 10 meters ahead. It didn't seem possible. Then, I figured someone would pass me on the right. I didn't know until after I crossed the line that I had actually won."

Guesdon was indeed the strongest man in this final stretch, or at least the freshest. "On television, I had seen Hinault, Madiot, and Duclos-Lassalle hoist their cobblestone trophies high in the air. And now I had one, too. I thought to myself, 'Am I dreaming or what?'"

No, Guesdon was not dreaming. His name is forever inscribed in the palmarès of Paris-Roubaix, between the victories of Museeuw (1996) and Franco Ballerini (1998).

PHILIPPE BOUVET AND SERGE LAGET

## "It's not possible, Fred. You're poised to win!"

Frédéric Guesdon, like Demol, finished second in a Paris-Roubaix for amateurs (1994), which may have given him some ideas later on. He finished his first pro Paris-Roubaix far behind the leader, but did well enough to earn the right to make a ceremonial lap around the track—something he considered a bountiful reward. "I thought there would still be a few people lingering at the velodrome," he recalled, "but there was hardly anyone left and I was very disappointed." Still, what was more important was his upbeat conclusion: "I like this race." He was further encouraged when he finished a respectable 14th in the 1996 edition.

But when he returned the next year, he was still far from being counted among the favorites. All the same, Marc Madiot, his directeur sportif at Française des Jeux, adopted him as a kind of spiritual son.

**Charles Meunier**
**1929**

Until 1967, the race always took shape on the hill at Doullens.
Here, goggles on top of his head, Charles Meunier rides with
the best. He knows that to be competitive at the end, you
have to save yourself—unlike the two men attacking to his
left, Maurice Geldhof and Alfred Hamerlinck, neither of whom
will make it into the winning move.

**Antonio Bevilacqua
1951**

The Italian's completely
spent after his long solo
break. He just played his
strongest card, that of a
world champion track
pursuiter—and he won.
He finished more than 90
seconds ahead of two race
specialists, Louison Bobet
and Rik Van Steenbergen.
Seeing the smiles of the
spectators, you know he's
a great winner.

**Jean-Marie Wampers
1989**

Wampers is overcome with joy at his good fortune. He really needed this major win to bolster his rather thin palmarès. And he did it on courage, perseverance, and not a little talent. In the final sprint, he's just beaten Dirk De Wolf, who's also an expert on the pavé.

**Dirk Demol,
Thomas Wegmüller
1988**

In the suburbs of Roubaix, the day's two heroes near the end of their epic breakaway. The Belgian Demol in front and the Swiss Wegmüller behind know that the victory of their lives will be played out in a few minutes. They can feel the tension.

**Marc Madiot,
Frédéric Guesdon
1997**

The win by Frenchman Frédéric Guesdon is also that of his directeur sportif, Marc Madiot (at left), whose joy is just as intense as that of his rider. It was the former two-time winner who persuaded Guesdon that in the final sprint on the velodrome he could beat the intrinsically faster Eddy Planckaert and Johan Museeuw. And he did.

# CHAPTER VIII

# THE VELODROME IS A CATHEDRAL

To arrive at the famous velodrome of Roubaix, after traversing Hell, is an unmatched blessing in the sport of cycling. It's one of the strongest emotions a racer can experience.

**A regal sprint**
**1967**

Rain, wind, mud, punctures, and crashes have shredded the peloton. The leading half-dozen survivors fight out the victory on the velodrome's concrete track. The final sprint is magnificent. There are still five men racing for the win, its glory, and its paradise. Only one can take it all, and it's the Dutchman Jan Janssen who ferociously throws his bike across the line ahead of Rik Van Looy, Rudi Altig, Georges Vandenberghe, and Ward Sels.

**Émile Idée,
Rik Van Steenbergen
1948**
Approaching the Roubaix velodrome, the Frenchman Émile Idée seems to have the race in his pocket. Then, as if shot from a cannon, Rik Van Steenbergen catches him as he races onto the track. It's a terrible blow to Idée's morale because he knows he doesn't stand a chance in the sprint against the powerful Belgian.

# The gates of paradise

How do you get to paradise? Over there, at the exit of Hell, just follow avenue Alfred-Motte, and it's at the end, to the right. A great clamor arises. The entire velodrome stands up like one man welcoming another man who has just returned from the underworld. A great chill runs throughout the crowd and makes everyone share in the winner's emotion, as well as the losers' despair, for naturally they all have good reasons to bemoan the outcome.

In a flash, the racer passes from one world to the other, from shadows into light. Some go from the galleys to glory, others from suffering to recognition.

They were all prepared to soldier on for hours over roads no one would ever have thought fit for a bicycle race, just so they could savor this magical and even unique moment when they feel their pride surging from within. Arriving in the velodrome of Roubaix is one of the strongest emotions a racer can experience. "It's pure ecstasy," agrees Marc Madiot, who arrived twice alone in first place (in 1985 and 1991). "You hear the roar of the crowd, it's an explosion."

They will all tell you about the sensations that ripple through their skin, from hairs that stand on end to goose bumps.

The railings of the Roubaix velodrome are the gates of paradise. Jean-Pierre Danguillaume found them closed in his face, early on in his career, until he finally completed his first Paris-Roubaix despite numerous delays that placed him almost an hour behind the winner.

"Someone—an official, no doubt—told me that I could stop then and there and be counted anyway," he recalls. "But I said to hell with that. I want to enter that velodrome no matter what, with my noisy derailleur and my bike as out of whack as I was. The others headed immediately to the showers, but I balked and went into the velodrome instead. A track meet had already begun, and there was a motor-paced race going on and I found myself at the base, along the ropes, while those guys were flying all around me. As wiped out as I was, I wasn't bothering them as much as they were me! But I was absolutely determined to finish Paris-Roubaix on the track."

Later on, after he became a road captain, Danguillaume frequently told the anecdote to youngsters who were just starting out on their racing careers. A kind of initiation rite, a story intended to strike fear in their hearts. That's what Gilbert Duclos-Lassalle heard, as a very young professional, on the eve of his first Paris-Roubaix. Proclaimed Danguillaume to the freshman, "If you arrive before the closing of the gates, then you're a real racer." The latter was proud to announce that Sunday evening, "I finished Paris-Roubaix." He had just one burning ambition left, to go back and do it again.

## Cordang's mad pursuit of Garin

The velodrome. Everything started here, at this track in Roubaix that opened in 1895, originally built in Barbieux park, at the edge of Roubaix near Croix, about 5,000 meters from the present Parc des Sports where the race ends today. At the end of the nineteenth century, the velodrome in Roubaix was the only French track outside Paris that could compete in popularity with the famous venues in the capital city. It was built by two textile magnates from Roubaix, Maurice Perez and Théophile Vienne. They went on to create this race as a means to enhance the reputation of their track. The survivors of Paris-Roubaix were expected to complete six laps around the velodrome to conclude the race.

As it turned out, that distance gave rise to a fierce pursuit in just the second edition in 1897. The Dutchman Mathieu Cordang arrived at the velodrome sharing the lead with Maurice Garin, only to fall and lose some 200 meters. Cordang, however, refused to give up, and by the end of the six laps he trailed by only two lengths. "I won the race, but Cordang was stronger," admitted Garin, showing an abundance of good sportsmanship.

The velodrome at Barbieux park was also the setting for smaller incidents. In the 1904 edition, for example, the stands were still empty and the officials were still eating their lunch when Hyppolite Aucouturier streaked in alone, an hour ahead of expectations. Everyone was caught off guard! Not to mention Georges Passerieu's misadventure three years later. The first racer to enter the velodrome, he was immediately stopped by an overzealous policeman. The officer demanded to see the racer's fiscal license plate as proof that he had paid the annual tax imposed on bicycle owners during the Golden Age. Drat! Passerieu triumphed anyway, but he had little time for discussion, not with Cyrille Van Hauwaert suddenly roaring in barely a minute behind!

When officials surveyed the route before the 1919 edition, the one slated to end the five-year hiatus caused by World War I, they discovered, alas, that the wooden track at the velodrome in Roubaix had been

**Refreshments
1954**

When it's hot and dusty rather than wet and muddy, the velodrome takes on the air of July's Tour de France ... and the finishers soon guzzle their bottles of mineral water.

dismantled. Only its concrete substructure remained. The planking had no doubt been converted to firewood during the conflict. The organizers thus improvised a new arrival point, along the avenue de Jussieu, near Barbieux park. But it proved unsatisfactory. Consequently, the Paris-Roubaix finish line moved several times in subsequent years as organizers searched for an ideal locale.

The first choice was the Jean-Dubrulle stadium, less than one kilometer from the present velodrome. Then the finish line visited various arteries within the City of Threads. From 1922 through 1928, it faced 37 avenue des Villas (today Gustave-Delory). In 1929, it was moved to Amédée-Prouvost de Wattrelos stadium. But this dirt track did not permit an acceptable sprint to the finish—Georges Ronsse, for one, lost a race when he wiped out while trying to make a turn. Ironically, the previous winter, the organizers had rebuilt the track to their satisfaction. They had determined that the turns were not sufficiently steep, but the ensuing work probably loosened the soil to the point that it gave way under the whirling wheels of the Belgian champion. In any event, the finish line soon shifted back to the avenue des Villas (1930–1934), then to the hippodrome of Flanders, the famous Croisé-Laroche in Marcq-en-Baroeul (1935–1936). Finally, the last editions before World War II (1937–1939) ended once again along the avenue des Villas. When the race resumed in 1943, the survivors arrived for the first time at the present Parc des Sports.

## Jean-Marie Leblanc's defense

At last the organizers had discovered the right setting. To be sure, the décor was out-of-date and the stands, supported by concrete pillars, were a bit worn out. Moreover, only the side near the finish line was sheltered. "If you go there on an ordinary day," says Marc Madiot, "it seems extremely small and insignificant. It almost looks sinister, as if this place gets light just once a year." It's nonetheless this velodrome that has given posterity the unforgettable images of winners who arrive in glorious solitude (Fausto Coppi, Felice Gimondi, Walter Godefroot, Eddy Merckx, Roger De Vlaeminck, Francesco Moser . . .) or who prevail in a wild sprint (Rick Van Steenbergen, Louison Bobet, Rik Van Looy, Émile Daems, Jan Janssen, Bernard Hinault . . .).

And this velodrome will continue to generate memories until the day Paris-Roubaix sells its soul to the devil. It almost did. Bowing to the whims of its financial sponsor, La Redoute, the giant French mail-order house synonymous with Roubaix itself, the finish line migrated to the doorstep of the firm's downtown headquarters, on the avenue des États-Unis, for three editions from 1986 to 1988. This setting witnessed the successive triumphs of Sean Kelly, Éric Vanderaerden, and Dirk Demol, but it was impersonal.

It fell to Jean-Marie Leblanc to mount a strong protest. In September 1988, after a stage in the Tour de la Communauté Européenne (European Community) ended in Roubaix, he published an article in *L'Équipe* entitled "Nostalgia for the Velodrome." "For about half an hour," he reported, "a nostalgic racer went all around the velodrome . . . and he expressed to us a thousand regrets. He was saddened to see how this place—once the ideal theatre to end a classic race—had practically fallen into disuse. True, the amateur version of Paris-Roubaix continues to end here, but the professionals have abandoned it now for three years. Commercial imperatives offered no alternative—or so we're told."

A bit further on, Leblanc continued, "Nothing compares to the setting of the old velodrome. It was so much more symbolic (compared with a corporate headquarters), and so much more dignified. Anyone who ever saw the greats arrive in this locale knows what I mean. Just think of them: Van Looy, Merckx, De Vlaeminck, Moser, Hinault, and—no less superb—Marc Madiot, the last winner here in 1985. Paris-Roubaix is one of the great monuments of cycling, but that structure requires a tradition worthy of dreams."

A happy coincidence: one month later, the journalist from the North was named the director of the Société du Tour de France, the organizing body of Paris-Roubaix. And one of his first major decisions was to return the finish line of this Classic of Classics to the velodrome. A giant screen was soon erected there as well, for the benefit of the five thousand or so nonpaying spectators who arrive every year at an early hour to sit under the open sky, on the exterior steps, or along the entry ramps at the turns. The finish of Paris-Roubaix became, once again, an emotional affair.

A hero emerges every time a solitary racer is the first to reach the salmon-colored cement track, triggering a wild ovation in the stands. And when the contest comes down to a final sprint, the outcome is never a given. Even the best can falter after a ride through Hell. Take Rik Van Looy, for example, in the 1963 edition. He was no doubt exhausted when he made the fatal error of rising too high on the final turn before starting his final sprint. His compatriot, Émile Daems, was more prudent on that occasion and took advantage of the situation to steal a victory.

## Bernard Hinault's mad dash

It's not so much pure speed that counts at the end of Paris-Roubaix but rather the relative freshness of the contestants. That is, the brutal force a racer has retained after an extravagant outpouring of energy. When Roger De Vlaeminck stormed onto the track in the middle of the leading pack in 1981, he was the odds-on favorite to beat out Moser, Hinault, Hennie Kuiper, Guido Van Calster, and Marc Demeyer. "When I entered the track, I was sure I would win," confessed the Gypsy, already a four-time winner. "What cost me the race was that Bernard Hinault took off in front. I was not able to catch up with him, given that the track is a ring where one can fly around in high gear. That said, Hinault was as strong as a beast."

The Breton, who thumbed his nose at conventional tactics, nonetheless entered the velodrome with a certain degree of lucidity. "I looked at the flags," he explained, "and I knew I would finish with the wind at my back."

Yes, Hinault's sprint was an insult to prevailing tactical wisdom. Although Kuiper was the first to enter the track, Hinault took the lead early on, 400 meters from the finish line, a folly with such a strong lineup on his tail! He slipped into his enormous 53x13 gear, which was so hard to push it almost seemed that the sprint started off in slow motion. The man from Brittany had taken care, however, to activate his enormous gear fairly far from the end, so that he would have enough time to wind it up. Despite the time needed to accelerate up to speed, Hinault nonetheless repulsed an initial attack by the immense Demeyer, who gave it his all to catch up, only to slip back into the row of followers. Now it was De Vlaeminck's turn to try to pass Hinault on the outside at the last turn. In such a perfect position the Belgian would surely win . . . but no! Hinault got the upper hand. "I was confident, and I felt very strong," the Breton explained. "When De Vlaeminck tried to pass I gave all I had left."

There have even been closer finishes that that—as little as one centimeter! That's all that separated Eddy Planckaert and Steve Bauer in 1990, after 265 kilometers of the worst kind. The Belgian and the Canadian battled it out to the end, side by side, in the far right lane. When the two crossed the line, the fans in the stands of Roubaix collectively held their breath. No one knew who had won. Neither the racers, nor the public, not even the finish-line judge, Joël Ménard. The latter consulted an enlarged photo of the finish and awarded the victory to Planckaert. And to think that the organizers had just borrowed a system belonging to the Fédération Française de Cyclisme for use that Sunday! Bah, the critics had said, there's no need for a photo-finish in a contest like Paris-Roubaix. But its use was approved in the final preparatory meeting prior to the contest. Albert Bouvet, the chief of services, wanted it installed in time for the race as a precaution. He had to insist vigorously to prevail. Well done, Albert!

## The shudders of Duclos and Madiot

If one needs another example of a super-tight finish, there's Gilbert Duclos-Lassalle's second straight victory in 1993. "If I win, it will be by a nose. If I lose, it will also be by a nose," he said to his trainer when he finally came to a stop at the other side of the track. Meanwhile, Franco Ballerini raised his arms in victory as he pedaled on to the next turn. "Neither he nor I could be sure who had won," recounted Duclos. "We were not elbow to elbow. I was along the rope; he was on the outside. I was familiar with track riding, and I told myself that the guy would never dare climb during the turn; that he would remain at the rope. I climbed and then plunged. He reappeared at the other edge of the track the very moment I threw my bicycle across the line."

The verdict: Duclos-Lassalle, by 8 centimeters. The narrow loss would haunt Ballerini for a long time. "I would often hear that bell sounding at the final lap," he revealed. "I should have taken off right then and there so as not to lose such a beautiful race in such an ugly man-

**Bernard Hinault**
**1981**

The Badger is the strongest, the most motivated. He leads the winning group into the velodrome—and stays there. After preparing as never before, Hinault wants to honor his rainbow jersey of world champion by winning a race he respects but doesn't really like. And winning it ahead of specialists Roger De Vlaeminck and Francesco Moser makes it even sweeter.

ner." Indeed, the Italian's disappointment that day was acute, even pathetic. His face showed his immense distress as he bolted out of the velodrome to make his way by foot to the showers. "That was the longest 100 meters of my life," he would say.

Duclos-Lassalle, who had entered the track alone the previous year, knew that he was fortunate to have won. "When I arrived with Ballerini, he was stronger than I was. I had to listen to the fans as they chanted my name just as they did the year before: 'Du-clos, Du-clos, Du-clos.' I lost my concentration from the entry to the first turn, but I needed to hear the fans. That really reinvigorates you! You don't even feel the pedals after that. It's a huge boost!"

"It's like finishing a stage with four climbs including the Tourmalet or the Galibier," observes Jean-Pierre Danguillaume. "In fact, it's even better than that, because you get many hilly days in the Tour, but you get only one chance a year to finish Paris-Roubaix. And when you leave this track to go to the showers, you can see from the looks of the fans that they regard you as a giant of the road."

The emotion at the velodrome is an incomparable experience. Marc Madiot thrived on it. "The first time, I was in a hurry to get it over with," he recalls. "Once I entered the track I thought about not slipping, and I stayed concentrated, making sure that I didn't screw up. I certainly deprived myself of a little pleasure but, happily, I won it twice. The second time, I made a point not to waste a single drop of happiness.

"On the avenue, I could already hear Mangeas [the stadium announcer] who was warming up the crowd. That day, he was at his absolute best because he has that ability to rise to the occasion. Just hearing his voice gave me chills. Strangely, the images from my youth of Moser and De Vlaeminck popped into my head. But the super moment for me, the greatest of them all, was that last turn, when I entered the track. That's when you feel safe; you think nothing more can happen to you. I had entered into the temple, and then all the people stood up in unison. They'd been waiting there for three hours, and now they finally got to see the winner in all his glory. I still get goose bumps when I think of the moment, as if I had been watching myself from the stands. It's was just like the Olympic Games, when the marathoner arrives in the stadium. . . ."

PHILIPPE BOUVET

### Maurice De Simpelaere
### 1944

The second finish at the new velodrome is for many a breath of fresh air. In a stadium packed with spectators, Belgium's Maurice De Simpelaere outsprints the 1937 winner, Jules Rossi, and Louis Thiétard, who's third for the second year running.

### Jean Forestier
### 1955

Perhaps he has profited from the tight marking between favorites Fausto Coppi and Louison Bobet, but Jean Forestier earns his victory all alone by taking a gamble. His childhood in Lyons prepared him for rain and cobblestones, and he races to his win in Roubaix without having looked over the course beforehand. He knows that the finish is in this velodrome, and that's what matters most.

**Noël Foré**
**1959**

These three Belgians—winner Noël Foré and runners-up Gilbert Desmet and Marcel Janssens—are in seventh heaven after conquering the Hell of the North. By riding in unison and surviving what Jean Stablinski calls "my toughest ever edition," the trio destroy a myth: that long-distance breakaways can't succeed. This trio was part of a seventeen-man break that started at La Folie Bonneuil, no less than 166.5km from the velodrome. Quite a triumph!

**Peter Post**
**1964**

A jubilant Peter Post is the first Dutchman to conquer the cobblestones of Paris-Roubaix. He also displaces Belgium's Rik Van Steenbergen of the Yellow Ribbon as the fastest winner of a classic longer than 200km; his speed for the 265km is 45.129kph.

**Broom wagon at the velodrome
1967**

With bikes piled on the roof, the broom wagon comes home. The race finished a long time ago for its crammed-in passengers, who before heading to the showers wait to collect their broken, mud-caked machines. But they'll be back.

**Rik Van Looy
1961**

After crossing the line in triumph, Rik Van Looy confronts another melee. Not the dangerous one he faced on the cobblestones, but a more irritating one composed of officials, journalists, gendarmes, and a hostess. It's a necessary evil for a star who'll go on to win this classic three times.

### The suspense
### 1975

There's not much danger for a breakaway made up of four Belgian stars, Eddy Merckx, Roger De Vlaeminck, Marc Demeyer, and André Dierickx. But in the final kilometer through the crowd-lined streets of Roubaix, an unsure Merckx looks back to see whether chasers Freddy Maertens and Francesco Moser are in sight. They're not, so Merckx (top right) slots onto the end of the line as the quartet turns into the velodrome. On the track, Demeyer knows he doesn't have the finishing speed of the others, and he makes an early charge for the line.

### The outcome
### 1975

Demeyer fades and the race comes down to a fierce sprint between Merckx and De Vlaeminck. If Merckx wins, he will become the absolute record holder with four Roubaix victories, while a De Vlaeminck success will give him a third career win in the Hell of the North. After De Vlaeminck comes from behind to take Merckx at the line, their faces reveal their contrasting post-race emotions.

**Servais Knaven
2001**

When the race is diabolical, as in 2001 when only 55 of the 190 starters finished, just to reach the velodrome is an achievement. And then to cross the line as the winner, as Servais Knaven does, is too much to believe. The Dutchman owes much to his Domo teammates in the group behind, former winner Johan Museeuw and reigning world champion Romain Vainsteins. Knaven is walking on water.

**Fair play
2004**

The Hell of the North sometimes doesn't treat riders that well, but the stars never lose their panache. The proof here is with former winner Peter Van Petegem (at left) as he honors three-time champion Johan Museeuw; both were in the winning move until they flatted in the final 10km. So Museeuw, in his final season, won't equal De Vlaeminck's record four victories. Seventeen seconds ahead of them, Magnus Bäckstedt won the race ahead of the remaining breakaway riders.

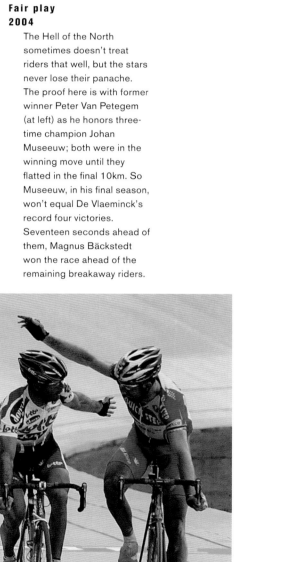

# CHAPTER IX

# THE ULTIMATE REFUGE

At the very end of a day in the Hell of the North come the showers of the velodrome. Only here can the racers' black-and-blue bodies and their battered souls recover.

**It's over**
**2002**

No, he's not dreaming. The nightmare is finally over. Our hero is dry at last. But he's so battered that it's difficult just to sit down. He recovers alone in his cubicle. In silence. Then he'll be ready to shower. But for now his head's still spinning. Does he have the strength to do the race again? He doesn't care anymore. The race is over.

**Like a battered child
1992**

Clobbered by the cobbles,
he's taking his time to
recover. Quietly, slowly.
He doesn't even have the
energy to take off his filthy
gloves. He sips a drink,
pecks at some food . . .
like a bird fallen from its nest.

# The water of resurrection

It's like a confessional in a church or the Wailing Wall, a place where you go to cleanse your soul. It's also a rehydration laboratory for the body, a memorial to restored muscles. These are the same showers that champions and also-rans alike have frequented for generations at the conclusion of Paris-Roubaix, whether they won, abandoned, or simply finished. After having shared cobblestones, pain, and suffering, tradition dictates that they also share the same place of purification, the same water. Then and only then is this classic truly over. Yet this great ritual and this sacred place stand today in peril.

Inside the shower room, a silence prevails—at least superficially. For on the walls are enamel plaques on which are engraved the names of past winners. And those walls talk.

It's deserted—but again only in appearance. For while the eyes may see nothing, the soul observes everything.

Today is an ordinary day. This means it isn't the second Sunday of April. The hour of Paris-Roubaix has yet to strike.

Nevertheless, in the immense shower room of the velodrome, one senses the presence of the champions of this race without equal, a contest that ennobles the winners and elevates the vanquished.

Behind the entry door appears the face of Josef Fischer, sporting a thick moustache. This German won the inaugural contest, in 1896. He seems to be saying, "I've been waiting for more than a century for another German to win this thing. Why does Jan Ullrich only care about the Tour de France?"

In a moving virtual dialogue, a passionate conversation unites two gentlemen of the cobblestones, Felice Gimondi and Marc Madiot.

"Signore, in 1966 I was still too young to watch you triumph in Roubaix, and besides, we had no TV at home at that time. But how beautiful you looked in all your suffering, on page one of *Miroir*."

"Thanks for the compliment, Marco. In 1991, I loved your tenacity. To win six years after your first victory, that's incredible."

The Dutchman Jan Janssen cleans off his glasses to get a good look at a prestigious neighbor, the imperial Fausto Coppi of 1950, who is trying to catch Eddy Merckx's attention.

Francesco Moser asks Octave Lapize about the cycling equipment prevalent in the early twentieth century. In 1980 the Italian became the equal to Curly Hair himself when he, too, notched three victories in a row.

And there's Rik Van Looy, adjusting his bottle-green tie in 1961. As elegant in the countryside as he is in the city, he exchanges his rainbow jersey splattered with mud for a becoming suit of bronze color.

Still infused with competitive spirit, Roger De Vlaeminck proposes swapping his title of "Mr. Paris-Roubaix," earned by his record four wins in the 1970s, for a second youth.

Sitting between Georges Passerieu (1907) and Paul Maye (1945) is Bernard Hinault (1981). He takes advantage of his knowledgeable audience to repeat his view that this race, this interminable cyclocross match masquerading as a great classic, is in truth nothing but a glorified "pig fest."

Marcel Kint turns toward Louison Bobet, victorious in 1956, and gushes, "You, you never gave up, you wanted victory at all costs."

Nicknamed the Black Eagle, a professional until the age of 47, the Belgian Kint was the first winner to use the showers of the boys' school at Roubaix. The scene unfolded in 1943. After three years of interruption, the northern population, set in its Sunday habits, saw the renaissance of the race as a small break from the misery of war, as marvelous as it was brief. That's because any distractions were extremely rare in this troubled period. The finish took place for the first time in the new velodrome. A pleasant surprise awaited the racers upon their arrival. Gone were the water basins and the precarious toilets. Now they had the luxury of true showers. Washed and dried, Kint returned to his home in Belgium by bicycle.

## Virtual ghosts, the excommunicated return from Hell

One of *L'Auto*'s special correspondents, Georges Février, edited a retrospective column. Among his many small stories, he told one that ended with the remark "this last scene took place behind the curtain, in the showers." To our knowledge, what follows is the first anecdote collected in the showers of Roubaix and published in the press.

Listen, but don't look, for our actors are sporting their most basic costumes—that is, what they wear when they try to get rid of sweat and mud.

**Enough, already**
**2002**

The journalists have invaded the showers; chaos
reigns. After living through Hell, the racer would
like to have a little peace. But it's not possible.
He won't be back.

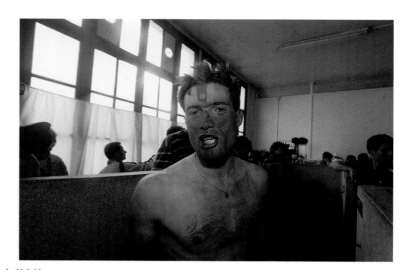

**I did it**
**2002**

He's been eating mud, and he still has some in his eyes,
his ears, and his hair. But that's no big deal. He's done it;
he has finished the race, and it took willpower. Just
getting to the velodrome gives him a certain pride.

Émile Idée: "It's your fault that I flatted."

Fernand Mithouard: "My fault? That's a good one!"

Idée: "Yes, I wanted to take off and you told me to wait. If I had
gone, I might not have flatted."

"This good mother hen Mithouard had eyes full of water. Yes, that's
right, he was taking a shower!" concluded the writer.

Sixty-three years later, the décor has not changed much. Facing the
entrance to the velodrome, the doors of the shower room open onto
small cabins, ninety-five in all. Some of the wooden benches are original.
At the far end of the room (now divided in two by a partition) are thirty
showers, a kind of earthly paradise for those who have just passed
through the Hell of the North.

The conditions here are quite rudimentary, at least for those living
in the early twenty-first century. But not for the Paris-Roubaix racer who
feeds off the legend of the cobblestones, who has been pounded all day
long by their sharp edges. To him this place is on a par with those fancy
marble showers at the great palace of Doha, where fortunate racers head
at the conclusion of the Tour du Qatar.

The place holds captive the echoes of past eras. By activating the old
taps that allow the water to flow through the showerhead, our heroes
dust off the living museum that is Paris-Roubaix, a timeless spectacle
hundreds of nostalgic fans from around the world visit every year.

Unrecognizable when they enter the room, the racers leave as good
as new—at least on the surface. When Cyrille Guimard first saw the
showers in the late 1960s, they brought back childhood memories. The
sight of the racers heading toward their narrow cubicles made him think
of cattle being herded into the stalls at Châteaubriant. The same miscel-
laneous mingling, the same misty environment. The racers, after their
long animal struggle in the jungle of Paris-Roubaix, even seemed to produce the same vapors as those cows on the move.

The lives of several generations of racing cyclists have unfolded
here, and continue to play out in this classy place that gives Paris-
Roubaix so much of its mystique. True, the notion of mystical showers
may seem far-fetched, but in truth they are indeed an integral part of
this great tradition.

What other place associated with competitive sports compares to
this scene of removal and cleansing, where aches from head to foot are
soothed, along with physical and psychological wounds? Only pain and
regrets evaporate here, behind these low walls.

The traces of Paris-Roubaix's heroes remain indelible in this austere
place, built from sandstone workers extracted from quarries in 1935
specifically for this building. It appears to have more to do with destitu-
tion than with disrobing.

The exhausted racers seem to carry all the weight of the cobblestones
they devoured for hours on end. Their silhouettes are gray and emaci-
ated. Their haggard faces reveal small eyes sunken to the bottom of their
cavities, gazing blankly at the aisles.

On the cobblestones, they were men, harboring fears as well as
courage. The race is now over—if it can even be called a race. It's a horri-
fying grinder, an energy-zapper, a consciousness anesthetic. They've been
turned into virtual ghosts, who were excommunicated but who have
now returned from Hell.

They had pedaled to the breaking point, flirting with disaster and
annihilation. The Belgians had tried to escape from "the man with a
hammer"—that was how they used to allude to a total breakdown. And
the small French racers were devoured by the "witch with green
teeth"—a reference to a traditional tale that gives children nightmares.
These are just a few of the characters in cycling mythology that can
strike racers when they are climbing mountains; they also appear on the
cobblestones.

The racers' prolonged struggle has numbed their muscles and gradually deprived them of consciousness. Suddenly, they find themselves
alone. They have gone adrift, carried away by an unknown current,
handed over by some obscure force. And there, under those timeless
showers, slowly, their paralyzed reflexes start to function again. Their
halting breath is at last back to normal. A miracle of life!

## One worries about those who look out of it

When the injustice of the race becomes overwhelming, the shower con-
versations unleash their own tide of thick mud. The 1968 edition was
truly terrible. Along with all the usual marshland new difficulties were
added, including the trench at Arenberg. The northerner Jean Stablinski
was the target of his enraged peers. Had he not suggested to the organizers, who were searching for new cobblestone sections, that they incorpo-
rate into the route that local road near his house? "I arrived at the showers

**In his corner**
**2002**

Like a boxer from Hell he has suffered a technical knockout, but he's recovering in his corner. He hasn't been knocked down. It's just the accumulation of blows that he took. Too many. He's all chewed up, so much so that he can barely comprehend what he has achieved.

**Debutant**
**1993**

A young Laurent Jalabert is slowly coming back to life, though his eyes are not truly focusing. He looks around. Who are these boys who've thrown off their helmets and are cleaning off the grime in slow motion? They're survivors, just like him.

feeling very small," Stablinski admits. "Inside, curses directed at me were flying in all directions."

"In the showers, we often discussed our misery," recalls Jean-Pierre Danguillaume, an eternal street urchin who finished eighth in 1976. "I vented like crazy, but I would also talk to guys in the neighboring stalls, asking things like, 'Hey, I didn't see you during the day, where were you?' At times you were next to a Flemish racer who didn't speak any French. So you said nothing. We were pretty wiped out, anyway, so there wasn't much to say at that point. We were certainly not in the mood for long speeches. But then you started to feel better. You felt sorry looking at a wounded Italian, and you said to yourself, 'Man, he's in bad shape. I got off easy.'"

In the shower-room talk, you worry about those who appear completely out of it. Words are inseparable from feelings, passions, and urges. Sharing a story can stir the soul if it is not already destroyed. Such was the case with the American George Hincapie in 2002. The New Yorker, who was among the heavy favorites, finished back in sixth place. He remained prostrate for long minutes on a bench, hiding his grubby face, his hands resting on his head, his elbows bent on his knees, and his forearms extending the profile, in near-perfect symmetry, of his slender legs.

A quarter of a century earlier, in 1978, the reporter for *L'Équipe*, Michel Séassau, wove a discreet veil when he recounted Roger De Vlaeminck's immense despair. "Standing naked in a shower stall, he was just about to towel off when two television technicians, unknown to us, suddenly presented themselves. One of them aimed a powerful spotlight on him, while the other began to film. At that point De Vlaeminck made a gesture to show his irritation, to make them understand that certain body parts were off limits to the public and that he considered their presence an intrusion. You did not have to know Flemish to understand his courteous but firm reaction. He did not raise his voice. He simply wanted to be alone for a few minutes, the time to regain a human appearance, to get his spirits in order and to brace himself for a second assault—by journalists."

Racers are rarely trained in the dramatic arts. Yet they are genuine actors. "It's a theater of suffering, or perhaps more accurately, of complaining," says Guimard, who finished seventh in 1969. "The race produces a strong mixture of sentiments, ranging from the satisfaction of having finished to the regret, among some, that their results did not reflect their potential. I have often observed disappointment but never distress. Even if the race went badly, everyone is proud just to be there. Under the shower, you hear the swearing. 'This shitty race, I'll never come back.' But once they've left that room, it becomes, 'Wow, what a race!'"

"It was an apocalyptic vision, seeing all those wounded men who sit down but can't get up," recalls Danguillaume, who descended into Hell eight times from 1971 to 1978. "That steam everywhere. It's extraordinary. It's something to see—you could make a movie about it."

"Those faces could certainly serve as movie images," adds Guimard. "Country bumpkins, encrusted with mud, who have taken a beating but who are proud to have fought to the bitter end."

In this place, pride is a common link. At the finish in the 1970 edition, Michele Dancelli, who had won Milan-San Remo a few weeks earlier, could not muster enough strength to shower. "My kidneys and hands are killing me," he lamented. "I wanted to finish as a matter of pride, but it seemed interminable."

"You tell yourself proudly that day that you belong to a noble race, without forgetting that there are giants above you," stresses Danguillaume. "The racer who finished 15th doesn't make fun of the guy who was 60th—assuming there were sixty finishers—or the guy who abandoned 30 kilometers from the end. After all, it wasn't fun and games even for those who had to finish in a support vehicle. If you didn't arrive in the top 25—and I was usually after the 30th—there was not much hot water left. And whenever there was some room in the showers, you knew the hot water had run out. So you finish the shower with eau de cologne. The ordeal of Paris-Roubaix was still not over." Danguillaume, in his old age, thrives on humor and fresh water.

## Competition from comfortable buses

In 1973, *L'Équipe* entitled its chat column "At the Office of Tears." It had instructed its journalists to gather the regrets of Paris-Roubaix survivors. The article began, "In this immense shower room, even sadder and grayer than usual, it was difficult to sort out who was who, so numerous were the casualties on this most unusual day."

Joop Zoetemelk, who had a spectacular fall at Arenberg, was "scraped up like a boxer who had taken a beating over fifteen rounds."

**Shedding skin**
**2002**

Having passed through Hell, overcome the pavé, and survived the mud, rain, and dust, No. 18 has thrown down all his gear to take a shower. It's as if he is changing his skin. And it's urgent.

His back aching, Yves Hézard recalled that, after falling down, he was almost crushed by the Peugeot team car. "I saw its wheels approaching me. It was a scary moment to endure. You have to believe that sometimes miracles do happen."

"I found myself on the ground five times, and that's a lot for one man," remarked Sylvain Vasseur. His complaint was received with nods of agreement. José Catieau showed his bruised shoulders; he also had scrapes almost everywhere. He made an inventory of the day: "Two falls, one blowout, a broken brake cable, and I forget what else."

"I don't even know how I finished and I don't really care," observed Alain Santy. "The essential thing is that I got the hell out of this without severe cuts. I sometimes think you have to be crazy to propel yourself over these roads at breakneck speeds," he added with a common sense sharpened by the jagged cobblestones.

How many others think the same, under the purifying water, after they have arrived at the confessional?

All the racers of Paris-Roubaix have earned a place in the hearts of the fans. Here's a case in point: The directors of the bicycle club of Roubaix and metropolitan Lille installed a small plaque in a cubicle to humor member Philippe Crépel, who had finished 43rd and dead last in the epic edition of 1968. To their surprise, "He shed a tear. So we didn't dare remove the plaque, once we saw what it meant to him," recounts the secretary of the club, Daniel Verbrackel, whose grandmother used to mend the jerseys of Tour riders when they stopped at Roubaix. And thereafter Crépel proudly declared himself "the representative of all those who have finished Paris-Roubaix."

In recent years, the teams have acquired luxury buses featuring leather seats, video monitors, bars, and... showers. This has dealt a harsh blow to the last episode in the Paris-Roubaix saga. As the race enters the twenty-first century, the showers of the old communal school are no longer an obligatory rite of passage. They remain, however, an essential experience for those who value tradition. And, fortunately, they are still numerous. In 2005, in his farewell to his beloved Queen of the Classics, which he had won six years earlier, the Italian Andrea Tafi insisted on changing in his own cubicle. A swarm of photographers encircled him to immortalize the scene. Tafi cried.

That same year, 90-year-old Émile Masson, the oldest living Paris-Roubaix winner, returned to the city of his exploit. He prevailed in the 1939 edition, before the velodrome served as the finish and before the showers were installed. He was nonetheless gratified to discover "his" cubicle. He wore a checkered sweater over a white shirt, a brown tie, and a hat. His eyes sparkled behind thick glasses. A cane helped him to keep his balance. He put his left hand on the cubicle slab. He was visibly happy, declaring, "Sixty-six years later, I had a wonderful day."

JEAN-LUC GATELLIER

**Red and black**
**1995**

No, he hasn't won the jackpot at Roubaix roulette, but he has survived his ride on cycling's ghost train... and the ghosts seem to have followed him.

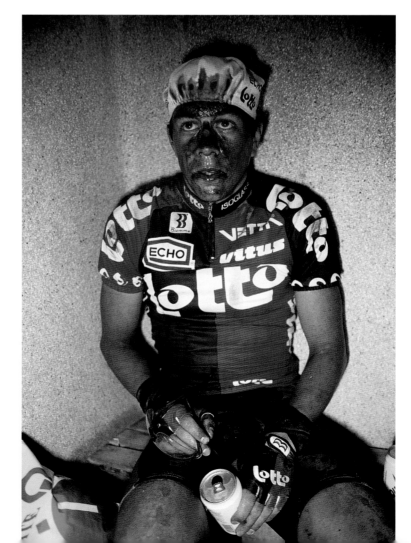

**Statuesque**
**2001**

Don't ask him where he was this afternoon, what he has done. He went for a trip and he came back. He doesn't know how. His body certainly made it, but part of him is still back there. It wasn't hard, it was infernal.

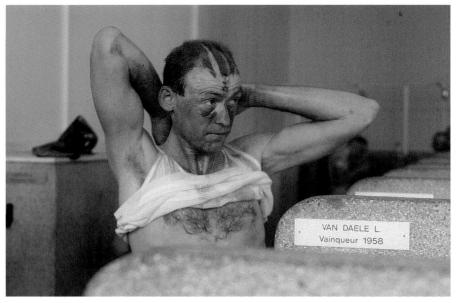

### In Van Daele's cell
### 2002

No, he's not a Mohican with his mud tattoo, but his face has absorbed some blows, and his arms feel heavy. Has he been tortured? No, he's still a free man despite standing in the cell dedicated to the 1958 champion.

### To the bitter end
### 2002

Looking sidelong, this mud-clad soldier seems to ask if someone is going to put him back on the road. Those glasses haven't served much purpose. He saw nothing, or perhaps everything, but he no longer remembers.

### Mano a mano
### 2001

Have they experienced the same race? Perhaps. One at the front, one at the back? One who abandoned, one who made it through? Paris-Roubaix is thus written in black and white. One has recovered, the other one has not. In any case, they're sharing memories of their different rides.

**At last**
**1966**

Those shoes were burning,
too tight. He no longer has
any need for them; he has
pushed too hard and he
needs to freshen up. He'll
take off his clothes later.
When he gets his spirit back.

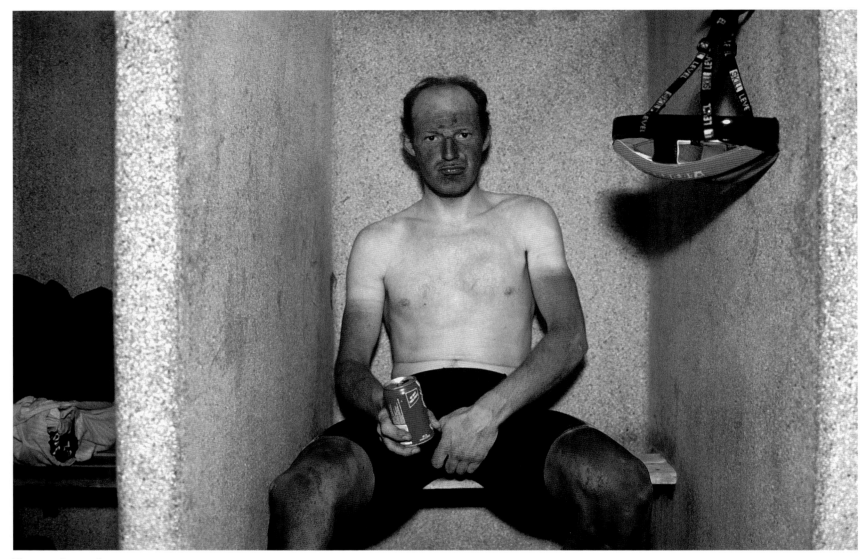

**The warrior rests**
**1993**

He's hung up his helmet.
It's over, and he's returning
to the land of the living. Just
about. Hell has crushed his
thighs and his arms. And his
head too was caught in the
vise . . . but his helmet saved
him. He's a true warrior.

**Coming and going
2002**

For an instant, those who are
as clean as a new pin brush
by those who've barely
arrived, still covered in their
armor of mud. Their fingers
are numb and have a hard
time undoing the helmet
straps. Some know that
they'll come back, the others
are not quite sure.

# CHAPTER X

# A PORTRAIT
## GALLERY

Every winner of Paris-Roubaix is an outstanding racer
who deserves to be remembered. Here, however, we
will limit our lineup to the greatest of the greats, the
most indisputable champions as well as those who played
an important role in the legacy of this classic. We have
selected eighteen winners in all, presented in chronological
order. Their stories allow us to survey this epic saga from
a unique perspective.

**Demeyer, Moser, and De Vlaeminck
1974**

Between them, these three riders won Paris-Roubaix eight
times. They were the best in the years 1970–1980, claiming
sixteen podium spots in ten years. But places in our Hall of
Fame come at such a premium that Demeyer (here raising
his arm after flatting) didn't make it.

# Josef Fischer
**(1896)**

## First for all eternity

At 31, Josef Fischer, a German with a heavy beard and moustache, was one of the oldest and most experienced racers favored to win the first Paris-Roubaix, held on Easter Sunday, April 19, 1896. Truly a man of the classics, he had already won numerous important city-to-city races, including Vienna-Trieste in 1892, Vienna-Berlin and Moscow-Saint Petersburg in 1893, Milan-Munich in 1894, and Trieste-Vienna in 1895. Were it not for a mechanical mishap, he would even have won the 1895 Bordeaux-Paris.

During the first Paris-Roubaix, Fischer relied heavily on his vast experience to prevail. First, he had to catch up with Arthur Linton, who had broken away. Then, after Amiens, when a dog knocked down his adversary, Fischer got behind his bicycle pacers and took off alone in the lead. At the velodrome in Roubaix, he came in 26 minutes ahead of the runner-up, the Dane Charles Meyer, 28 minutes ahead of the Italian and future Frenchman Maurice Garin, and 43 minutes ahead of Linton, the unlucky Welshman. A very international inaugural race this was, and one that Fischer had orchestrated perfectly. Not satisfied with rolling along at a good clip over the final 40 kilometers of cobblestones, the German champion barely avoided getting spilled himself, first by a horse and then by a herd of cows! Those frightening scrapes made him fully appreciate the glass of champagne he received as the winner. He had covered the 279 kilometers at more than 30 kilometers an hour.

Fischer came back to the race in the 1897 edition, but dropped out. He took a solid second place (auto-paced) in 1900, the year he finally won Bordeaux-Paris. But he would "only" finish 15th in the first Tour de France of 1903. He thus retired at age 38.

He went on to become a taxi driver, and he excelled at that activity, amazing people with his eagle eyes and uncanny ability to avoid obstacles and ruts. And cows, one presumes.

He is the only German to figure in the palmarès of Paris-Roubaix. According to legend, his would-be successors all failed because none wore his trademark long socks. Josef Fischer died in Munich in 1959.   S.L.

Until April 19, 1896, he has won most of his races in Germany, Russia, and Switzerland. But with the experience and maturity, Josef Fischer races with distinction in France and is brilliant in the very first Paris-Roubaix. At 31, his handlebar moustache is his signature, which seems to say, "I'm a bike racer, one with class, one that wins."

# Cyrille Van Hauwaert

**(1908)**

## The Lion of Flanders

In the early twentieth century, Belgian cycling was relatively unknown to the outside world, apart from a few classics. Consequently, at the start of Paris-Roubaix in 1907, no one paid much attention to this 23-year-old from Flanders, a farmhand turned brick maker, who nonetheless knew what he wanted. Although he did not speak a word of French, Cyrille Van Hauwaert managed to talk the company La Française into lending him a bicycle. To the surprise of all, he finished in second place at the velodrome of Roubaix. As the first Belgian to mount the winners' podium, he was the first to unleash the enthusiasm of his compatriots for this event.

To accomplish this feat, Van Hauwaert showed himself to be nothing less than courageous. He overcame a fall at Arras and quashed hunger pangs thanks to eight eggs and a bottle of lemonade. He was unable to take advantage of the pacers provided by La Française until the Georget brothers, the champions of the brand, withdrew.

From this point on, the career of this audacious challenger took off. He asserted himself by winning a rain-drenched Bordeaux-Paris in stride. Van Hauwaert, who could absorb anything in his stomach without wincing, was affectionately nicknamed by his fans "Iron Guts." At the start of the 1908 season, the young ogre overcame a snowstorm to claim an apocalyptic Milan-San Remo. Then he cut loose in a mad Paris-Roubaix, without pacers after Beauvais, without pursuers, and without even a support vehicle. Just cold, rain, and more snow. He dealt with hard luck with serenity and faith, encouraged by his motto "The bicycle is my god." Near Forest, he was five minutes behind the leader, François Faber. He gritted his teeth and nibbled away at the lead of the man from Luxembourg, who was at that time a novice bothered by snow.

1908. Impeded by a spectator at the entry to the track, Cyrille Van Hauwaert falls. The man who was leading, François Faber, has suffered the same fate in the moments before reaching the velodrome, and his fall was even harder after colliding with a child. The courageous Van Hauwaert picks himself up, rides the six laps of the track, and wins the race, to spark a new interest in cycling in Belgium. As for Faber, his bad luck continues, and he's beaten into second place by Georges Lorgeou.

### "We're on your tail"

At Hemponpont, a suburb of Roubaix, Van Hauwaert still trailed Faber by two minutes. His compatriots cheered him on, and he crushed his pedals. Ahead, Faber fell while trying to avoid a child. Van Hauwaert passed him and entered the velodrome in the lead. The clamor of the Belgian contingent made his blood rush. But just then an errant spectator made him suffer a spill of his own. No problem. He got up and took off again. He completed the necessary six laps around the track, shaken but untouchable. Behind him, Faber suffered a flat and was overtaken by Georges Lorgeou. The Belgian won out at last. Van Hauwaert, whose sky-blue Alcyon jersey was entirely covered by dirt, exulted.

Twenty years after this exploit, as a businessman and a renowned bike builder in Brussels, he reminisced in good French to the journalist Gaston Bénac, "I was embraced everywhere I went. Compatriots cried out 'Keep at it, Cyrille! We're on your tail!' That day was a milestone for the numerous workers and peasants on hand from Flanders. I showed them that a Flemish man with passionate ardor and professional dedication could compete with a Frenchman, who often lacks sufficient energy, being somewhat spoiled by an easy and opulent life."

Falls, blowouts, and above all the dominant Octave Lapize would conspire to deny him another victory in Paris-Roubaix. As consolation, however, he compiled an impressive collection of top finishes (fourth in 1909, second in 1910, third in 1911, and sixth in 1914). He also had the satisfaction of knowing that his double victories in Milan-San Remo and Paris-Roubaix will never be matched. In Bordeaux-Paris of 1909, he renewed his success by finishing 26 minutes ahead of his nearest rival.

A succession of Belgian kings—Léopold II, Albert I, Léopold III, and Baudouin I—received this veritable icon of Belgian cycling, dubbed the Lion of Flanders. He did not succumb until 1974, at the age of 91, following a great career as a champion, sponsor, and manager.  S.L.

# Octave Lapize
**(1909, 1910, 1911)**

## An open ticket

Paris-Roubaix was the private hunting ground for the smiling Octave "Tatave" Lapize. He won it three times in a row, each in different conditions and for different teams. Neither dust, mud, flats, nor crashes could stop him.

On April 11, 1909, Octave Lapize (nicknamed Tatave) competed in his first Paris-Roubaix. The 21-year-old newly turned professional was facing an ultimatum from his father: either finish the race in the top ten or else start a position in Paris with the Jackson firm delivering coal. Their storage facilities, near the Saint-Martin canal, were conveniently located next door to where daddy Lapize himself stocked beer. But Tatave had no intention of spending the rest of his existence there. He had already had his fill of loading and unloading coal, an activity that had helped him develop into a mass of muscle, 1.65 meters tall and weighing just 65 kilos! Moreover, as his buddies freely asserted, he was as sharp as a tack. In the peloton, he always seemed to be where there was neither flint nor wind. Which is not to say that Lapize was a cheat or a wheel sucker. He simply made his rounds carrying a few trump cards. He was a master of both cyclocross and track racing, and he was equally strong whether racing on his own or behind a pacer (in 1908 he won the Bol d'Or and set an hour record). Yet despite a few victories here and there (in 1907 he won the road championship of France and Paris-Chartres), he had had his share of bad luck. One moment a tire would blow, the next his adversaries would gang up against him. But he never complained. A graduate of the school of hard knocks, he was tough—a perfect candidate to win Paris-Roubaix.

At the start, at Chatou, he lined up with Trousselier, the brothers Georget, Passerieu, Beaugendre, Cornet, Wattelier, and Van Hauwaert, the 1908 winner. As a member of the modest Biguet team, he was in the thick of the 104 starters who took off at 6:45 in the morning. Riding in the dust, number 23 recalled that in 1905 he had already taken this road to Pontoise. He had failed in that effort, falling asleep on the hill of Ennery. This time, Lapize was not going to fool around. He was even carrying along a good-luck charm: a paper pig that a child spectator had stuck to his bottle bag.

Although he fell behind at the hill at Doullens, along with Charpiot, Passerieu, Léonard, and Alavoine, he felt at least some consolation: he had successfully avoided the nails, deliberately strewn about there.

## A star rises

Van Hauwaert, Masselis, and Trousselier took the lead at the summit. Without panicking, Tatave, whose thick curly hair was already blanched by dust, caught up with the trio. Georges Passerieu did as well, but fell in Arras after colliding with a pedestrian. The remaining quartet seemed destined to separate only by a final sprint at the Barbieux track. But then it was Cyrille Van Hauwaert's turn to fall. At the velodrome, the outgoing champion had to watch from afar as the debutant Lapize edged out the veteran Louis Trousselier. The headline in L'Auto was not mistaken: "A Star Rises." Indeed, Lapize was about to become the North's first great cyclist. Meanwhile, at the quai de Jemmapes, daddy Lapize exulted. The winner's 1,000 francs was twenty times the annual salary of a typical Jackson employee. Tatave had hit the jackpot. Good or bad luck notwithstanding, his future was now an open ticket.

Lapize's return to Roubaix the following year, on March 27, was highly anticipated. He was now racing for Alcyon, having been recruited by that firm. This time around, without being dropped at Doullens, he had to overcome two falls, a blowout, a broken saddle, and a twisted handlebar. After changing bikes, he broke away, before seven pursuers caught up with him. Approaching the Roubaix track, they were down to four, including Tatave. He easily won his second straight victory.

Insatiable, "Curly" was already dreaming of three consecutive victories, a historic feat befitting the star. On Easter Sunday, April 16, 1911, he succeeded in doing just that, though he was now racing for La Française and had only recently whipped through Paris-Tours. This time, with cinematographers rolling their film, and despite the ever-present nails, he took the lead at Doullens. Then, near Carvin, he broke away with his teammates Charpiot and Van Hauwaert. At Lesquin, the latter punctured, to the chagrin of the thousands of Belgians who had come to cheer him on. After a solitary romp of 15 kilometers, Lapize collected his record third straight victory.

The journalist Alphonse Steines, who was also the president of the Union des Cyclistes de Paris, remarked, "One can win Paris-Roubaix once by luck, maybe even twice at the most, but three lucky wins are impossible." And while Lapize remained the star of Paris-Roubaix, he also won the 1910 Tour de France and achieved two other triplets from 1911 to 1913, the Championship of France and Paris-Brussels. Enlisting as a volunteer in 1914, despite his objector status, Lapize died in aerial combat over eastern France on July 14, 1917—Bastille Day. **S.L.**

# Charles Crupelandt
## (1912, 1914)

## The man from Roubaix

Because he was the first true Roubaix resident to make the palmarès of Paris-Roubaix, and on two occasions at that, and because his name was given to the last stretch of cobblestones just before the velodrome, we must include him in our portrait gallery. In fact, this champion from heroic times deserves to be there anyway, almost as much for his defeats as for his victories. After all, in 1904 when he was only 17 years old, he finished a remarkable 13th. And so was born a beautiful love affair. And a lofty career as well, enhanced by superb victories (Paris-Tours 1913, Championship of France 1914) and impressive showings (second in Paris-Brussels 1907, third in 1911 and 1913, third in Milan-San Remo 1914). He even did well in the Tour de France, finishing sixth in 1910 and fourth in 1911.

In the Tour, he made a specialty out of winning the first stage. His motivation was clear: in 1910 it went from Paris to Roubaix and, in 1912, from Paris to Dunkerque. There, on his own turf, in his own backyard, the hometown boy was so confident of victory that he was virtually in cruise control. The cobblestones, wind, and dust constituted a natural environment for this solid and courageous young man who was fast in the sprint and fiercely determined.

could not escape the charge of trafficking in rationed goods, a common practice on the front to escape economic misery. Rumor had it that the Pélissier brothers, victims of Crupelandt's wrath and speed, denounced him. In any case, after the war, he could no longer pedal competitively except within his small dissident federation. His meager consolation was the memory of his two great Paris-Roubaix victories.

No doubt it was written somewhere that the son of a guesthouse keeper had no right to expect anything more out of life than enduring hardship—punctuated, perhaps, by fleeting moments of glory. And once both his legs were amputated, life did indeed get even harder before he finally reached the end of the road in 1955.

Those same legs had served him well as a cyclist. Even that one Easter Sunday when he fell in the trenches, scraped his knees, and gamely pushed off again toward the velodrome. He had lost any chance to win but, as he put it, "One must never abandon a Paris-Roubaix."  s.l.

## He never abandoned

When it came to Paris-Roubaix, he knew he could give it his all, for there was no stage the next day. And he gave so much of himself that he never once abandoned the race. In 1913, after falling at Beauvais, he got up and caught up on his own with the breakaways despite suffering a flat, only to fall victim to a mechanical mishap in the final stretch. That did not, however, prevent him from participating in the final sprint and finishing third behind the dominant François Faber of Luxembourg and the Belgian Charles Deruyter.

But his victories in 1912 and 1914 were what really propelled him to the threshold of greatness. During those years, he so easily outpaced the pack that he found himself both times in a small peloton of seven that vied for victory. The first time, he drafted Octave Lapize so skillfully that he eventually caught and passed the leader, Gustave Garrigou. In the second win, he unleashed the enthusiasm of 12,000 spectators in the velodrome by blowing past Louis Luguet, Louis Mottiat, Oscar Egg, Jean Rossius, Cyrille Van Hauwaert, and Pierre Vandevelde. The willingness of this little man to take on the big ones—be they Parisian, Swiss, or Flemish—delighted his fans. Crupelandt also gave the North something to crow about. This region, known for drowning the drudgery of daily life in rivers of beer, had finally asserted itself on the national stage and earned a measure of respect.

When the Great War broke out, the "Bull from the North" was only 28 years old. His career was nonetheless at an end. He did not fall on the front, like Faber or Lapize, but in the halls of justice. Although he fulfilled his military duty, he

Crupelandt is the first rider of northern stock to win at Roubaix, beating all the champions from Belgium and Paris. The one they call the Bull of the North, thanks to his spirit, gives a foundation for the race and confidence to his people. No longer just an event that Roubaix citizens organize and watch, it's also one they can win.

# Georges Ronsse

**(1927)**

It's a fact: some racers are built to win Paris-Roubaix, and Georges Ronsse, the son of a car mechanic from Antwerp, was one of those. Why? For starters, this solid and strapping chap (1.73 meters tall, 72 kilos in weight), as pale as he was nervous, proved a resilient and skillful racer who was adept at climbing. This tough guy, who also excelled at cyclocross and track, quickly compiled an enviable record. It was a harvest that became even more bountiful in 1925, after he overcame miserable weather to win the Grand Prix of Verwint, finishing fifteen minutes ahead of the pack. He also registered honorable finishes in the Tour of Flanders (fourth) and Paris-Menin (a race he would have won after an imperial performance at Doullens, had he not taken a wrong turn).

He was therefore the heir apparent to Octave Lapize. Indeed, he prevailed in the very dry and dusty edition of 1927 at the age of 21, after another impressive performance in Doullens and a gratifying sprint at the expense of his last fifteen adversaries, notably Joseph Curtel. This Paris-Roubaix, which he won going away on a machine equipped with a small fender on the front wheel, marked the start of an impressive series of outstanding performances. That year, he won

## The scout

Bordeaux-Paris and finished well in the race for the rainbow jersey. He went on to win two more editions of the former, in 1929 and 1930, and became world champion in 1928 and 1929. Only the heroics of Alfredo Binda in 1930 prevented Ronsse from winning the title for a third straight time.

## Three times second

Ronsse also continued to be a factor in Paris-Roubaix, but he was dogged by bad luck. On three separate occasions he barely missed registering a second victory on the grounds of the Amédée-Prouvost stadium. In 1929, following a sprint, it was André Leducq who came out on top. A year later, Ronsse slid, fell, and bowed out to Charles Meunier. Finally, in 1932, after a hotly contested race, it was Romain Gijssels who overtook him. Second three times! As a result, he had to cede the title Mr. Paris-Roubaix, which at first seemed his destiny, to his compatriot Gaston Rebry, one year his senior. A captain of the Belgian team in the Tours of 1960 and 1961, Georges Ronsse died in 1969. S.L.

The very happy winner over Joseph Curtel in 1927, Georges Ronsse (leading here) also becomes an unlucky loser on three occasions, which results in his becoming an epic figure in Paris-Roubaix history.

# Gaston Rebry

**(1931, 1934, 1935)**

## The Bulldog

In fourteen starts, Gaston Rebry wins three times, and so becomes the second Mr. Paris-Roubaix after Octave Lapize. His most memorable victory is this first one, in 1931, in torrential rain and cloying mud—weather that even a bulldog has a hard time in.

He was nicknamed Tonton, or the Bulldog, due to his powerful torso, short limbs, and feisty demeanor. And Paris-Roubaix was his backyard. In fact, Gaston Rebry got such a kick out of riding on cobblestones and braving the mud, wind, and other hardships that he never missed an edition once he turned professional in 1926 at the age of 21. He would eventually tie a record for participation: fourteen entries! Before 1939, only Eugène Christophe, the Old Frenchman, had started the race the same number of times. But whereas the latter never won the event, despite being a master of cyclocross, Rebry was a true powerhouse, taking three firsts. He thus joined Octave Lapize in the record books, becoming the first Belgian Mr. Paris-Roubaix. And, like Lapize, he achieved each of his victories under very different circumstances.

Rebry did not win his first Paris-Roubaix until his sixth try, in 1931, when he was 26 years old. Present at Doullens despite the wind, he successively dropped his last escorts, Georges Ronsse, Charles Pélissier, and Émile Decroix. Only Émile Joly remained on his tail, but he fell behind after a puncture in Lesquin. The Bulldog, wearing the sky blue of Alcyon, thus broke away alone in the rain with nothing left to fear.

Rebry was again among the finalists in 1934, in the company of Roger Lapébie and Jean Wauters. The former, who flatted twice and changed his bicycle each time, somehow managed to catch up with his companions and ultimately prevailed. But he was automatically disqualified when the judges determined that he had not arrived on his original machine. The ever-present Rebry, who had finished second, thus collected his second win thanks to a technicality.

A year later, in 1935, Rebry approached Paris-Roubaix like a kid on his way to a country fair. And once again the race

smiled back at him. This time, after Wattignies, he and André Leducq took the lead, reminiscent of the 1928 edition when the latter prevailed in a sprint. Would history repeat itself? No, because this time Leducq punctured his rear tire. While he tended to the matter, *L'Auto* kept its focus on Rebry: "Tonton turned up his nose, put his hair to the wind, and churned his short legs in victorious rhythm. He did not relinquish his impish schoolboy face until he crossed that white finish line. Then he smiled at the world he found so pleasing, revealing his own naïve candor." Very well done indeed. What's more, he had covered 262 kilometers in just 6 hours and 40 minutes, an average rate of 37.263 kilometers an hour. That was a new record for the course.

## The sprint, his principal weakness

In 1936 Rebry finished third after losing out in the sprint, his principal weakness. He participated again in 1937, 1938, and 1939, but by then the man from Menin had already gathered his harvest. That included, in addition to his Paris-Roubaix victories, a solid fourth-place finish in the 1931 Tour, in which he gave the winner, Antonin Magne, a good scare. In 1934, he registered two strong finishes in the Tours of Flanders and Paris-Nice. His earnings over the years enabled him to buy houses and invest in his linen business. But he would not live long enough to meet the next Mr. Paris-Roubaix, his compatriot Rik Van Looy. Illness carried him away in 1953, when he was only 48 years old. S.L.

# Rik Van Steenbergen

**(1948, 1952)**

## The man of stone

A professional for twenty-three years, from 1943 to 1966, the Belgian champion Rik Van Steenbergen (1924–2003), dubbed "the Boss" or "the Great One," on account of his unusual height in the peloton (1.86 meters, 83 kilos), won 1,656 races while covering 2 million kilometers on road and track. He excelled in both disciplines his entire career, a division of energy that prevented him from becoming the best in the world in either field and, perhaps, from winning a Tour. Choosing one type of racing was all but impossible for him, for he claimed that his "indifference was the source of his strength." He also maintained that he had to pedal every which way in order to provide a good life for his five children.

His improbable lifetime record is perhaps the most eclectic in all of cycling history, save that of Eddy Merckx. It ranges from forty victories in Six-Day races to three world championships, and includes victories in the Tour of Flanders of 1944 and 1946, the Flèche Wallonne in 1949 and 1958, Milan–San Remo in 1954, a Tour of Argentina, six stages in the Vuelta, fifteen in the Giro, in which he wore the pink jersey, and four in the Tour, in which the Yellow Jersey suited him beautifully on numerous occasions. Not to mention two victories in Paris-Roubaix—two one-of-a-kind gems, one that set a new speed record and the other an unforgettable victory over Fausto Coppi at his best.

His detractors charged that he chased money above all else. He was reportedly tight with cash yet also a chronic gambler. According to his friend and adversary Fred De Bruyne, "He would cut a franc in two to save money, yet he was also capable of betting his entire fortune on one ace of spades." Yes, Rik gambled like a champion. Over card games, horse races, anything—even bicycle racing. Even Paris-Roubaix, with its cobblestones and ruts, was something like a lottery for this man, whose name translates as the man of stone. It was a game he played continually from 1944 to 1959. He lost a lot, espe-

cially at the beginning and end of his career. But from 1948 to 1952, on two occasions, he hit the jackpot. Both times he had to fight fiercely to prevail, and both times he desperately needed a victory to rejuvenate his sagging career and depleted finances.

For once, he left behind his velodrome and Six-Day jerseys. It was not so much the money that he sought in Roubaix but rather glory. As restless as he was, he needed these wins for the sake of himself and his loved ones.

Even before he became a famous racer, a "perpetual cyclist" who juggled airline flights to fulfill two or three contracts in a single day, he was a proven champion. Quirky, yes—he was so frugal some predicted he would wind up living under a bridge and subsiding on hard-boiled eggs. Yet there was no denying his extraordinary power and class. His track training made him dangerous in road events, too, for he could mount a final sprint at breakneck speed.

## Scurrilous or just cunning?

Still, Van Steenbergen had to learn over time when best to unleash his great speed. Roubaix and its final stretch of track offered him an ideal opportunity—provided he could just get to the velodrome in one piece! That was not the case in 1944, when he was 20 years old. He fell near Amiens and had to abandon. Nor was it the case in 1946, for he flatted twice. Or even in 1947, when he fell at the start. Finally, in 1948, he got to the velodrome. Of course, having recently competed in three Six-Day races, his preparation for the Classic of Classics was not ideal. But a race of unusual character calls for a champion of unusual character, and the Belgian fit the bill. He also benefited from the beautifully dry weather and the soft wind at his back.

This time, Van Steenbergen deftly avoided falls, blowouts, and ruts. After Hem, less than 6 kilometers from the end, he surged from behind, accompanied by Marcel Hendrickx, Georges Claes, and Gildo Monari. The quartet then caught the leaders, Émile Idée, Fiorenzo Magni, and Adolf Verschuren, who were already imagining themselves standing at the podium. To avoid a sprint on terms he knew he would lose, Idée took off in the lead, and entered the track alone. Van Steenbergen wisely let Idée toil, then came within two lengths of the leader. That prompted Idée to start his final sprint prematurely, and Van Steenbergen easily overtook him down the stretch.

The victory was not without controversy, however. Some charged that number 117 in the violet jersey had drafted automobiles to get back into the race. That seems doubtful, though, since Jacques Goddet, in his scathing editorial in *L'Équipe*, would surely have included that charge in his litany had it any validity. Rather, the race organizer was content to label the Belgian an "exploiter" and a "shirker" for not going all-out.

To be fair, one could also argue that Van Steenbergen had simply been cunning. Indeed, he insisted that he "had never suffered so much to win a race." He had made a heroic effort, he maintained, to make right with his fans after a disappointing

Rik Van Steenbergen saw everything on the pavé, including this crash in 1953 on the bridge at Courrières, which prevented him from defending his title. His distant look sums up his high hopes, which are slowly receding. It's taking too long for help to arrive.

1952. After a ferocious chase, Van Steenbergen catches the three breakaways: Fausto Coppi (with whom he's talking), Ferdi Kübler (at left), and Jacques Dupont. Coppi will accelerate, but not fast enough to drop Rik, who will take the sprint victory in Roubaix.

Milan-San Remo in which he suffered two flats. This redeeming victory in Paris-Roubaix was in any event a historic achievement, for he had set a new course record of 43.612 kilometers an hour. The proud winner wore the symbolic yellow ribbon of the road, which distinguishes the fastest average speed in a race over 200 kilometers. Not until 1964 would the Dutchman Peter Post eclipse that mark (45.129 kilometers an hour).

In 1949 Van Steenbergen was again eliminated from the race by a fall. In 1950, Fausto Coppi tore up the course and the Belgian lagged behind, finishing a distant 16th. In 1951, Antonio Bevilacqua broke away and Louison Bobet ceded second place to the man from Flanders.

On the eve of the 1952 edition, the 50th, the public eagerly anticipated a showdown between Coppi and Van Steenbergen. In the Italian's first two appearances in Roubaix (he finished 10th in 1949), the Belgian star had not been a factor. The latter had regained his old form in 1951, but Coppi was absent that year. Now, at last, the two appeared to be in top form. The Belgian in particular needed this win in a big way. In the Tour of Flanders he had been so mediocre that a comeback was essential to dispel the critics' charges that he had squandered all his talent on track racing. Moreover, he had started to build a new house and he badly needed the prize money. For three days, the man in high demand avoided his café de Malines in order to prepare assiduously for this race.

On this particular Sunday, the weather was sunny and dry, just as it had been in 1948. Jean Baldassari, Jacques Dupont, and Ferdi Kübler quickly took the lead, but were overtaken near Carvin by an ever-imperial Coppi. The race seemed all but over for Van Steenbergen. At the famous turn at Wattignies, escorted by Bernard Gauthier, Maurice Blomme, and Loretto Petrucci, the Belgian fell a full 50 seconds behind Coppi.

But then the hardened gambler decided to go for broke. At Lesquin, he made a mad sprint for 5 kilometers, facilitated by Baldassari's exit following a flat. Coppi, who perhaps should have surged ahead once he had caught the breakaways, soon found himself alone with the Belgian. Dupont had suffered a blowout, and Kubler had given up. To avoid what he knew would be a fatal duel in the sprint, the Italian gave it his all on the hill of Hem. He pushed ahead relentlessly, but the stubborn Belgian resisted each time, and drafted Coppi as he had never done before. All the while he dreaded Coppi's next surge, but the latter, stunned by his rival's resistance, refrained for fear of a counterattack. In the final sprint, Van Steenbergen was unstoppable. By beating the Campionissimo at his best, the fantastic Belgian registered his most beautiful victory and signed a new lease on glory.

But as the years progressed, his trajectories toward the velodrome of Roubaix became increasingly less gratifying. In 1958, he lost out to Léon Van Daele, Miguel Poblet, and Rik Van Looy. By then he was forced to admit that, at the age of 33, he was no longer the fastest in this race. Rik I had passed the baton to Van Looy, Rik II.

Still, Van Steenbergen continued to skim the tracks for some time, even racing with his son-in-law, Palle Lykke. In 1966, he finally bade farewell to cycling. What followed was a painful decline. Reverses of fortune, ongoing problems with gambling, and family relations conspired to lead him down the wrong path. Illness finally took him away in 2003, at the age of 79.

The man of stone had been used up for some time. The great journalist Roger Bastide aptly summed up Van Steenbergen's checkered racing career when he wrote, "Here was a Paganini who chose to play every day in the bowels of the Métro rather than put on a glorious festival at La Scala."

Yet happily, on two occasions at least, Van Steenbergen turned Paris-Roubaix into unforgettable performances.  S . L .

# Fausto Coppi
**(1950)**

## Unique and sublime

1950. Wearing the jersey of Italian national champion, Fausto Coppi (at left) hides his emotions after winning at Roubaix. A year earlier his brother Serse shared the victory with André Mahé after a technical mix-up. This time, Fausto, the Campionissimo, champion of champions, has won emphatically, beating runner-up Maurice Diot by 2 minutes, 40 seconds.

**(1)** See Chapter 6, "Hell's Damned."

In the spring of 1949, Fausto Coppi was livid. He emphatically rejected the judgment of Solomon—reasonably fair, in the final analysis—as issued by the disciplinary commission of the French Cycling Federation following that year's flawed Paris-Roubaix. Accordingly, the Frenchman André Mahé was reclassified as first, finishing in a virtual dead heat with Serse Coppi, the Campionissimo's brother. To be sure, that race had given rise to one of the stormiest controversies in the history of the bicycle.[1]

Initially, Coppi vowed that he would never again cross the Alps to race in France—though in fact he wound up winning the Tour the following July. Nor did he, in fact, renounce the 1950 Paris-Roubaix. On the contrary, he opted to avenge his family's honor. He also sought to erase his own sour memory of the previous edition. A conspiracy to box him in enabled the breakaway by the said Mahé, in company with Jacques Moujica and Frans Leenen. This trio arrived first at the velodrome, only to be shown the wrong door. . . .

Of this Paris-Roubaix 1950, Fausto Coppi would later explain, at the twilight of his career, "I absolutely had to win that one. If one wants to make the list of great champions, a win in Roubaix is a must." To achieve as much, he prepared meticulously, modifying his training methods, which ordinarily did not put him in top form until the Giro. That the result would prove worthy of his extraordinary efforts is the least one can say.

### Fausto became "sublime"

From the start, Coppi demanded that his teammates set a furious pace. Then he personally led a ravaging attack near the storage facilities in Arras. From there on, he put on one of his great performances. Only the courageous Maurice Diot, on the Mercier team with Rik Van Steenbergen, managed to stay in his wake. But Antonin Magne immediately forbade any collab-

1950. Coppi has taken off on a solo breakaway at Carvin with 34km to go. Race director and *L'Équipe* editor Jacques Goddet later writes that his "sublime" escapade overcomes a "detestable surface . . . as if he had invisible shock absorbers helping him ride away." By playing with the opposition, and the cobblestones, on a gear of 52x15, Coppi was simply beyond the others.

oration with the Italian champ. Although that reflected typical team strategy, it doomed poor Diot. The great Fausto accelerated on the cobblestone sections in order to drop the intruder, and then took off alone on a bicycle-friendly sidewalk near Carvin. Equipped with a Campagnolo derailleur without jockey wheels, a design the Italian company pioneered, the Campionissimo pushed what was an enormous gear at that time, 52x15. The Frenchman, in contrast, cranked a 50x17 combination, a difference in gear ratio of more than a meter. Blazing through the final 34 kilometers, Coppi ultimately beat out Diot, his nearest competitor, by 2 minutes, 40 seconds. Fiorenzo Magni trailed by 5 minutes, 30 seconds and Rik Van Steenbergen by a full 9 minutes!

After his hard-won second-place finish, Diot famously remarked, "I'm thrilled to have won." Facing a stunned audience, he left this thought for posterity: "Coppi is beyond contention." That was indeed the opinion of Jacques Goddet, the director of the event, who wrote of the Campionissimo, "Coppi devoured this detestable terrain as if he were protected by invisible shock absorbers. For over twenty years here I've seen the greatest champions slow down on cobblestones like steamships approaching barrier reefs. Fausto was simply sublime."

## Coppi and Bobet offset each other

When the Italian returned to visit the Hell of the North in 1952, the contention for prestige between himself and Van Steenbergen was at a high point. Repeatedly embarrassed in his own backyard, whether over cobblestones or local hills, Van Steenbergen implemented an anti-Coppi plan: neutralize him in order to beat him in the final sprint. This clash of styles, between the slender man from Piedmont and the powerfully built man from Antwerp, gave rise to a fierce battle. Only by summoning all his extraordinary courage did Van Steenbergen finally succeed, alone, in shadowing Coppi, who gave yet another virtuoso recital on the cobblestones. The Italian repeatedly surged forward only to have the Belgian catch up. At last, the two men arrived together on the track. The result was predictable. In the sprint, Van Steenbergen easily surpassed an exhausted Coppi.[2]

To make life difficult for Louison Bobet, Coppi presented himself again in 1955, setting the stage for another prodigious duel. "If I don't come, he'll win," Coppi said of the world champion Frenchman. For his part, Bobet attacked again and again, after Arras, in order to make the race even harder for Coppi. But at the hill of Mons-en-Pévèle, it was Jean Forestier, the puncher from Lyon, who broke away. Behind him, Coppi and Bobet were among a group in pursuit. Coppi knew that if he tried to neutralize Forestier's attack, both he and Forestier would lose out in a sprint to Bobet. So he stayed put and let Forestier triumph. Bobet was outraged: "Fausto's conduct was unworthy of a great champion," he huffed. His unflattering remarks were relayed to Coppi in the shower. The Italian merely shrugged his shoulders. What did it matter? As always, Coppi had left his own indelible mark on the cobblestones of the north.   P . B .

**(2)** See the profile of Rik Van Steenbergen in this chapter

In 1955, Coppi comes to the race more to stop world champion Louison Bobet (at right) from winning than to win himself. Coppi marks his rival so closely that

Frenchman Jean Forestier is able to jump away from them to take the victory. In the showers, the quarrel between the two champions will be stormy.

# Rik Van Looy

**(1961, 1962, 1965)**

## The emperor's long march

Rik Van Looy won the first of his three Paris-Roubaix victories in 1961, at the age of 27, after six fruitless tries. He was a man who had learned how to be patient. As an adolescent in post-war Flanders, he started his cycling career on a sour note one Sunday in 1948. Circling around the little bell tower in his small village of Herenthout, he was lapped five times by the peloton and finished dead last!

The last shall be first, it is written. From the humiliation of a foot soldier burst the pride of an emperor, with his straight chest, pronounced chin, piercing eyes, a sleek nose shaped like an eagle's beak, and a serious expression revealing an imperial sense of duty.

He founded the famous "red guard," a reference to the color of the jersey worn by the Italian team Faema. He was a fearsome scout for the Great Army, whose readiness to serve him in the classics campaign was something to behold during the 1950s and 1960s. In his head, Van Looy never stopped seeking to extend his reign with the help of his teammates. And he remains, nearly a half-century later, the only racer ever to have won all the great single-day races.

The red guard was composed of *domestiques*, a Belgian term signifying teammates who are devoted to their star racer to the point of being truly servile. Van Looy and his mates are

considered a precursor of today's highly structured team. They rolled along in concert for the benefit of their leader simply to earn his gratitude and, above all, the perks offered by the team's commercial sponsor. In praising what was then considered "the world's greatest team," Edgar Sorgeloos, Van Looy's faithful lieutenant, remarked, "We train very hard with Van Looy, leaving at 8 A.M. sharp, not 8:01. The group never finishes together, and we only wait for someone if he has to repair a flat. Our biggest thrill is to get behind a truck and get our speed up to 70 kilometers an hour."

The recently retired Louison Bobet, for one, conceded his admiration for Faema's profound attachment to its leader. After Van Looy's second victory in Paris-Roubaix in 1962, he declared, "He has inculcated his team with an extraordinary submissive spirit in the service of his great class." Nicknamed the Emperor of Herentals after the village in Flanders where he had always lived, Van Looy clearly inspired reverence. And Herentals certainly sounded like a good place for this cycling star to reign supreme—if not nearly as compelling as Roubaix.

As the 1961 season got under way, Van Looy was in torment. His classics campaign was off to a miserable start. He had fared poorly in Milan-San Remo, then suffered a traumatic fall in the Tour of Flanders. On the eve of Paris-Roubaix, he personally removed the cast that had been set a few days before to heal a crack in his wrist. But despite these setbacks he felt in good physical shape. Indeed, he had ridden 1,200 kilometers during the two weeks separating "La Ronde" from Paris-Roubaix.

Van Looy was also called Rik II to affirm his worthiness as a successor to the great former champion Rik Van Steenbergen. Rik II was stouter than his glorious predecessor, but he was developing similar power. He, too, was built to crush both the cobblestones and his opposition. "Win it just this once, but win it well," he told himself before the race, hoping to wipe out all the frustration built up from his recent setbacks. This mason's son, though he had already secured himself a comfortable future, still exulted at the prospect of winning the northern classic. Wrote Pierre Chany in *L'Équipe*, "He forgot about all his worries as a millionaire and became once again the young Turk of old."

### "It wasn't the race that killed me— it was my nerves..."

On April 9, 1961, Van Looy lined up wearing the jersey of the world champion. His red guard soon unfurled a carpet of the same color to get him the lead. That is, until Henry Anglade of Lyon mounted an attack. That's when Faema's leader decided to take full control of the operation. He forced the powerful Dutchman Albertus Geldermans, who had made his move, back to reality. At the velodrome, Émile Daems tried in vain to surprise Van Looy. The final sprint was but a mere formality

In the 1963 Paris-Roubaix, Rik Van Looy believes he can win for a third consecutive time and so join Octave Lapize in the record books. The one snag is that Émile Daems, who made Van Looy dig deep to win in 1962, will save his strength for the final sprint. The two-time champion gives too much of himself on the pavé.

for this authentic finisher, who flirted nonetheless with an 11th-hour disaster. His rear tire had developed a slow leak, a frightening fact he discovered with about a kilometer to go. Anxiety accompanied him until the very last turn of the track. He opted not to swing high on the bankings so as not to risk losing his tire. At the end, even without the added speed he would have gained from sweeping down from the turn, he somehow managed to produce a powerful acceleration. He felt not only the thrill of victory but also a tremendous sense of relief!

"I'm dead!" he admitted. "But it wasn't the race that killed me—it was my nerves. They were on the verge of betraying me. I keep telling myself that I won Paris-Roubaix, but it probably won't dawn on me until tomorrow that it's not just a dream. This is just too beautiful. I'm even happier than the day I became world champion."

Jacques Goddet, the race organizer, was likewise thrilled with the outcome. "The gods agreed to demonstrate that the great athletes of today must overcome extraordinary obstacles to prove their merit," he wrote. The following year, 1962, Van Looy delivered an absolute triumph, elating the race director once again. Summed up Goddet, "He's the greatest racer in the greatest race." He then conducted a virtual autopsy of this "shining cyclist, who is as firm and cold as marble, and remarkably cool and lucid. He is a human being endowed with such fabulous physical qualities that medical authorities should dissect and examine him as the epitome of the modern athlete."

## Eaten up by the Cannibal

In snatching his second victory in the cold of Roubaix, Van Looy had been nothing short of imperial—just as he had been in the Tour of Flanders, when he easily crushed the competition. And once again he was wearing the rainbow jersey, having successfully defended his title in 1961. He dropped his last adversaries in the final kilometer. Yet despite his vastly superior speed, he conceded, "I broke away without attacking."

In 1965, his most loyal minions, Edgar Sorgeloos and Armand Desmet, followed the Emperor of Herentals to a new team, Solo-Superia. Van Looy had not won the slightest classic since his victory in Roubaix three years before. Rumor had already announced his demise. That's why, on the evening after the race, he would savor his sweet revenge. "That was the most beautiful victory of my career," he exclaimed.

The author of a break 10 kilometers from the end, he entered the velodrome alone, whereupon some 5,000 spectators gave him a standing ovation. He thus tied the record for wins held jointly at that time by the Frenchman Octave Lapize (1909, 1910, 1911) and the Belgian Gaston Rebry (1931, 1934, 1935).

Afterwards, a violent generational conflict, which grew more intense with numerous clashes and controversies, pitted him against Eddy Merckx, the rising star of international cycling. In 1968, handicapped by three blowouts, Van Looy opted not to enter the track a full eight minutes behind Eddy Merckx, to escape the future Cannibal's triumphant glare. Van Looy's fans preferred to put their own spin on the outcome: that day, Rik II finished a respectable ninth. But it would have been undignified for an emperor, particularly an aging one, to finish with a sprint unless victory had been at stake.   J.-L. G.

Van Looy absolutely wants this classic. It slipped from his fingers in 1958, but here in 1961, motivated by his world champion's rainbow jersey, he ignores a cracked wrist to win with supercharged energy.

1961. Van Looy is so overcome that he has a hard time realizing that this win has brought him a greater sense of accomplishment than winning the world title. That's saying something.

# Eddy Merckx
**(1968, 1970, 1973)**

## The extraterrestrial

Are we watching a human being or a page of bicycle history?

That question arose at the sight of Eddy Merckx entering the velodrome in Roubaix in magnificent solitude, one dark Sunday in April 1970. The enigma grew even more pressing as time appeared to stand still. At last, five minutes later (or, more precisely, 5 minutes, 21 seconds), the first of his victims arrived. They were Roger De Vlaeminck, Érik Leman, and André Dierickx, all from the Mars-Flandria team. This trio was not just defeated—it was annihilated! Not to mention Walter Godefroot and Jan Janssen, who approached the main grandstand more than seven minutes behind Merckx. Tack on another four minutes and there was Raymond Poulidor completing what he would shortly label "this amazing race."

The Merckx of this era was, as Jacques Goddet wrote from the press box at Roubaix, "a racer without peer, one who even prevails over injustice." He was indeed in a class all his own, the leader of the pack, a veritable "Merckxedes" on cobblestones. Again the nagging question: was this a human being or a page of bicycle history?

Merckx would eventually win three Paris-Roubaix in 1968, 1970, and 1973, and all under terrible—even abominable—weather conditions. Yet these successes were just a slice, if one dares to think it, of the extraordinarily thick palmarès he would compile as the greatest cyclist of all time. Merckx, as everyone knows, threw himself into all his races. He chose neither his victories nor his rivals.

### "I don't cycle anymore—I fly."

He was always the man to beat, because he was the man who won everything throughout the entire season, from Milan-San Remo (seven times!) to the Tour of Lombardy. Typically, Merckx would win the Giro in late spring, then triumph in the Tour a few months later.

During ten years of classics, he took on a host of rivals: Van Looy, Sels, Altig, Basso, Dancelli, Post, Janssen, Maertens, Moser, and a blooming Hinault. In the great tours, he battled Adorni, Pingeon, Ocana, Thévenet, Van Impe, Zoetemelk, Agostinho, Fuente, and Baronchelli. On both fronts, there was Poulidor (all the time!), Gimondi, and Van Springel. Yet, despite this intense competition he would win, in the final count, more major tours than Anquetil and more classics than Van Looy. The terrain changed, the climate changed, the foes changed—but Merckx remained Merckx.

He first entered Paris-Roubaix in 1966, placing 15th. He was already on the verge of being discovered. The next season, he finished an impressive 7th. His victory in 1968, an edition that strengthened the race's unique reliance on cobblestones, thus completed a mathematical progression. "I don't cycle anymore—I fly," he confessed, in the midst of a historic season during which he would transform himself into the Cannibal. His former Peugeot teammate, Christian Raymond, coined that

1968. The joy of a first win in Paris-Roubaix is immense, especially for the young Eddy Merckx, who's on course to acquiring his moniker, the Cannibal. On this day, he gives his opponents no chance.

term to allude to Merckx's astonishing ability to eat up the competition.

Nevertheless, at the start of this edition, the young Cannibal felt less like a hunter and more like prey. "If Paris-Roubaix plays out like the other classics of late, I have no chance at victory," he complained. "Some racers have only one objective in this race: to make me lose rather than try to win it themselves. My supporters always tell me, 'You're young, don't fret about it. You're among the best and eventually you'll win some great races, once your foes understand that they're going to lose more often than you at this game.' But even so. . . ."

Merckx, an impatient youth, had no time to wait. At only 22, he was itching to break out of his chains and transform his superiority into sovereignty over all of cycling's theatres. The

harder the terrain, the more he could develop his remarkable power and energy and the easier it would be for him to impose his regime. Now, three types of racing terrain favor the affirmation of individual talent: mountains, time trials, and Paris-Roubaix. And Merckx was not about to pass on the latter.

This Paris-Roubaix of 1968, designed by all the devils on earth and in the sky, was simply "Hell" for his foes. But the world champion traversed the viscous mud without getting bogged down by details. He made one small concession, to allow Herman Van Springel the privilege of accompanying him as far as the velodrome, during a magisterial breakaway gallop covering 52 kilometers. After the victory, he expressed intense satisfaction. It was his first season in Italy, riding for Faema, and he had salvaged his classics campaign. "This victory is most gratifying," Merckx declared. "I desperately wanted to win a

good race while wearing the world championship jersey. I took pains to study the course. The cobblestones were plentiful—far more than I had imagined."

Indeed, the venerable ritual had just received a facelift. To breathe new life into the race, the organizers had designed a much more rugged route, including new and previously unexploited sections of cobblestone. It was only fitting that a rising superstar should triumph in a rejuvenated Paris-Roubaix.

The Belgian expressed his fraternal gratitude to the former French champion Jean Stablinski, who had introduced Albert Bouvet, the great cobblestone searcher, to the trench at Wallers. At the entrance to the showers, Merckx hustled over to the northerner, then placed a friendly hand on his shoulder. "Thanks a lot, Jean, that was a great route."

1970. He needed to use his sprint to win in 1968, but two years later he is called "an extraterrestrial" by Mars-Flandria team director Brik Schotte, whose four stars, Éric Leman, André Dierickx, and the De Vlaeminck brothers, are smashed to pieces. The Martian finishes more than five minutes ahead of second-place Roger De Vlaeminck. These are extraordinary years for Merckx.

1968. Before beating Herman Van Springel on the Roubaix track, the world champion has to overcome Ward Sels (in second place here) and the Arenberg section of pavé, which is included for the first time.

## Poulidor never saw anything like that

His second Paris-Roubaix win, registered in 1970, commands even greater praise. Having won the first of his five Tours the previous summer, Merckx was knocking very loudly at the door of greatness. In outdistancing his top rivals—all superb racers—by 5 minutes, 21 seconds over the last 35 kilometers, he unknowingly set a new course record. And it was the greatest margin of victory since World War II. Indeed, to find a greater gap between the winner and runner-up, one must delve deep into the record book—all the way back to 1922, when Albert Dejonghe blew away Jean Rossius.

But what was most striking at the time was the way Merckx had scattered all the foes that had banded together for no other purpose than to defeat him. In particular, he did away with the quartet from Mars-Flandria composed of the brothers De Vlaeminck, Leman, and Dierickx.

Rather than lament this fact, Brik Schotte, their directeur sportif, explained that there was nothing anyone could do to stop an extraterrestrial. "In all the years I've been in this sport, I've seen many champions come and go. I've witnessed many great exploits. I've even participated in a few myself [he won the Tour of Flanders in 1942 and 1948]. But frankly, I haven't seen anything like this since Fausto Coppi [the 1950 winner]."

The humans could do nothing more than console themselves.

"I'm a true martyr—my kidneys and fists are killing me," moaned Michele Dancelli, the winner of Milan-San Remo, who was so overcome with pain that he could not even make it to the shower.

"Who won?" asked Raymond Poulidor after he got off his bike.

"Merckx," came the response.

"By much?" asked Poulidor innocently.

"By over five minutes."

"Holy smokes!" gushed Poulidor, shaking his head. After a few moments of silence he stammered, "Incredible! That's just unfathomable to build up such a lead at the end of a race like this. You'd have to be a real superstar to do that. Since I've been racing I've never seen anything like that. And I've seen some great ones, too. But this guy...."

Louison Bobet, the 1956 winner, had watched the race on television and commented the next day, "I have lived through an extraordinary afternoon. All night long, I dreamt of Paris-Roubaix. Eddy Merckx has done something unbelievable. His skill and efficiency astonish me."

Not even a cold caught during the Tour of Belgium could knock out the Belgian champion. In the plains of Picardy, bordering on the north, Merckx was plagued by this respiratory ailment. He slipped back into the depths of the field, all the way back to the automobile carrying his directeur sportif. "I wasn't feeling well enough to place," he later explained. "I wanted to give up." "Give up?" scoffed Guillaume Driessens, rejecting any such thought. "We'll see about that. Meanwhile, take off that jacket and breathe hard. You'll get better."

Merckx even had his share of bad luck. His derailleur jammed before Valenciennes and he blew out a tire before the trench at Arenberg, which he had to cross in a downpour. Luckily, Georges Vandenberghe was there to pass him a wheel. In all, he overcame four changes of either bike or wheel.

Fifty-six kilometers from the finish line, another blowout slowed his pace and threw him behind a second group (which included Godefroot, Sercu, Verbeeck, Rosiers, Sels, Dancelli, Poulidor, and Monséré). Four hundred meters in front of him, in an effort to thwart his comeback, Schotte's men assumed the team time-trial formation.

## Hell eclipsed at a record pace!

Merckx caught the second group, then pushed ahead of them and never looked back. His next pursuit lasted 16 kilometers and reached a ferocious pace over roads the color of soot, pitted with flooded ruts. Just when he seemed on the verge of committing athletic suicide, he entered the town of Flandria still waging his incredible comeback, with only Éric Leman ahead of him. Exalted by the prospect of having to beat just one remaining opponent, the Cannibal caught up with his compatriot and blew by him. After the last cobblestone section, at Hem, he hit the tarmac going 50 kilometers an hour, driven to new heights by the prospect of his imminent triumph.

"This was perhaps the best race of my career," he allowed after his arrival. What an outlandish performance! He had crossed the hell of hells going at the speed of an hour record. Thanks to Merckx, an epic achievement had come to sports.

"Is Merckx the best racer history has ever produced?" wondered Pierre Chany, polling the readers of *L'Équipe*. "Now that we've witnessed this legend's latest feat, is there any reason to doubt it?"

Merckx's last Paris-Roubaix victory in 1973 was probably his most staggering performance of the three. But gone was the angelic face that had characterized the first two happy victories. Instead, his expression was blank, his eyes were sunken, and his face belied the formidable toll of combat. There was almost melancholy in that look.

Was Merckx already thinking ahead and deducing that it would be extremely difficult to win Paris-Roubaix for a fourth time? Poulidor thought so. Merckx, he tells us, was always "fussing about the future," even though on this particular Sunday of lavish mud baths and slick pavement constituting a giant skating rink, he had once again left behind the opposition at a more than respectable distance. Walter Godefroot and Roger Rossiers finished 2 minutes, 20 seconds behind. The fourth finisher, Walter Planckaert, trailed by over 7 minutes.

"This Paris-Roubaix was harder than those I won in 1968 and 1970, and maybe the hardest of all the ones I have participated in," Merckx reflected. "When I took off with De Vlaeminck, at 56 kilometers from the finish, I had to assume all the work. Roger refused to cooperate with me. He complained about an arm being hurt [an injury suffered a few days before at Ghent-Wevelgem]. I left him without accelerating, with 47 kilometers still to go. Godefroot and Rossiers were only 200 meters behind me. It was not an easy task to beat them out."

Indeed it wasn't, especially if one considers what followed for Merckx: yet another fall (after his bike got entangled with a motorcycle), a change of bicycle, and a lingering fear of injury. Yes, fear. Even this world-class athlete had to dig deep within himself at times to find the moral strength to carry on. "I was very afraid after that accident," he recounted. "It was heavy going out there, and I took it easy on the turns. One more fall and I could have been splattered all over the place."

It was the stuff of legend: Merckx riding off alone on his apocalyptic mission. Merckx having to extract himself from a maelstrom. Merckx hobbled but still victorious. "Merckx

outdoes Merckx," ran *L'Équipe*'s headline the day after this savage escapade.

In 1977, one year before ending his prodigious career, he bade farewell to Paris-Roubaix with an 11th-place finish. In all, he had entered the race twelve times without ever abandoning it—no surprise, really, since he always finished his races.

At the start of each Paris-Roubaix, Merckx always donned new clothes so that, as he put it, "I could feel like I was starting from scratch." Whatever he had done in previous editions had no bearing. He aimed each time to give it his all. After all, why dwell on past successes that were already in the bag? He detached himself from those. They existed only in the minds of his fans, whereas he continued to carry on his shoulders the nobility of cycling.   J.-L. G.

1973. Merckx has just dropped De Vlaeminck (who'll finish eight minutes behind) and he's now on a solo run over the final 44km, chased by two more Belgians, Walter Godefroot and Roger Rosiers. The press motorcycles are so close that one of them will cause Merckx to tumble with 36km still to ride. His heart pumping after changing to a new bike, Merckx goes on to win, but this is his hardest Paris-Roubaix.

# Roger De Vlaeminck

## The fanatic

**(1972, 1974, 1975, 1977)**

**1975. This shoulder-to-shoulder confrontation between Roger De Vlaeminck (at left) and André Dierickx recalls a similar one, if in different circumstances, between Jacques Anquetil and Raymond Poulidor on the Puy de Dôme at the 1964 Tour de France.**

He was nicknamed the Gypsy, though Roger De Vlaeminck didn't much care for that label. According to legend, his family came from very modest social origins. His father was reportedly forced by necessity to temporarily house his wife and children in a van, from which he sold soap bars and towels door-to-door. At least that was the legend.

If the name stuck, it was no doubt because De Vlaeminck was driven by a sharp instinct and constant opportunism. He had a propensity to stay alert and make his move at just the right time. He made snap decisions about when to attack or to sprint. He showed a rare agility in Paris-Roubaix.

What's more, this young man who paraded from one podium to another was as handsome as the devil; his face was

tan from a life spent outdoors and subjected to winds blowing from the North Sea and across the capricious skies of Flanders. Rather than being called the Gypsy from Eeklo—his hometown, between Bruges and Ghent—Roger De Vlaeminck much preferred the nickname Mr. Paris-Roubaix, which he earned in 1977 after his record fourth victory. This unique achievement legitimized his enthronement. No one before him and no one since has succeeded in claiming that many editions on the cobblestones of the North.

Nor has anyone shown greater longevity or consistency in the event. De Vlaeminck's participation covered three distinct decades (1969 to 1982) and included four second-place finishes. In thirteen of his fourteen races he finished among the top seven; only once, in 1980, did he abandon the race. "The way Roger could leave the cobblestones unscathed remains a mystery to me," allowed Brik Schotte, known as the last of the racers from Flanders, a few years before his death. "Besides his training in cyclocross, I attribute his success to the perfect way he mastered the race. He was always well positioned at the strategic points. He seemed to glide over the rocks. But to prove oneself that adept in this kind of race you not only have to be talented but also very intelligent."

## "At 27 years old, I'm too young to die"

"He had an amazing feel for this race, rolling over stones as if he were on asphalt," recalled Franco Cribiori, the Italian directeur sportif with whom De Vlaeminck collaborated during most of his career. "The evening of Paris-Roubaix, we threw out all the wheels except those belonging to Roger, which were still serviceable. In fact, they were like new."

This virtuoso on cobblestones, this fanatic of Paris-Roubaix, also possessed an iron will and immeasurable pride. As an amateur, he refused to sign with Merckx's team, spurning his compatriot's generous offer. As De Vlaeminck explained, he preferred to keep his distance from Merckx and fight the great champion head-on.

Indeed, De Vlaeminck provided the most solid opposition to the Merckx regime in the domain of the classics. Paris-Roubaix in particular proved an extremely fertile ground upon which their rivalry grew. In contrast to Merckx, who dreamed of absolute conquest across the board, De Vlaeminck sought out select victories within his grasp. The former summarily executed his foes in silence; the latter drew his motivation from his sense of pride and fed it with worked-up controversies.

Whereas the suave Merckx commanded adoring crowds, De Vlaeminck was widely viewed as unruly and even rebellious. Thus, when the two of them sprinted toward the finish line at the conclusion of Paris-Roubaix 1975, Luc Varenne, the popular commentator, blurted, "Oh shit, it's De Vlaeminck!"

This discrepancy in treatment spurred the Gypsy whenever he entered the dangerous roads leading to Roubaix. "It's

1973. Even training as much as 400km a day in preparation for his favorite classic, Roger De Vlaeminck isn't always at his best. This year, he still had thirty stitches in an injured left arm from an earlier fall, yet he still seems to slice effortlessly though the Arenberg trench.

the most beautiful race, the hardest to win, and it's mine," he declared with passion. And his unparalleled results in this super-classic bear him out.

The 1972 edition: "Success of the rocket De Vlaeminck," read *L'Équipe*'s first-page headline. The wind was bothersome that day. Then a glacial rainfall appeared. At the town of Bachy, 23 kilometers from the finish, De Vlaeminck surged ahead of his surrounding foes, including Merckx. He then caught up with Willy Van Malderghem, who was alone in the lead. At Cysoing, De Vlaeminck's objective was clear: win the race. Nor was he lacking in preparation, having recently completed 1,000 kilometers in just four days! He flew toward his first success at Roubaix.

"In my hurry beforehand, I had forgotten to eat something and a collapse was not far off," he later revealed. "Luckily, I was saved by a few small chunks of sugar at the bottom of my pockets."

1974: "De Vlaeminck leaves Merckx in hell," screamed *L'Équipe*'s headline this time around. Always on the lookout for opportunities, the winner-to-be started out trailing Merckx, who was trying desperately to catch up with the young Italian Francesco Moser. At 33 kilometers from the end, De Vlaeminck launched a blistering attack. As was frequently the case, Merckx could not count on any cooperation to mount a pursuit. It took 20 kilometers for De Vlaeminck to reach Moser, whom he forced into making a faulty turn 7 kilometers from the finish line. The victorious Belgian had given it his all. The following day he discovered that his efforts had triggered tendinitis in his Achilles' heel.

1975: "De Vlaeminck thwarts Merckx," ran *L'Équipe*'s headline. This was his most beautiful Paris-Roubaix. During the sprint he collected his third victory, beating Merckx, who was clad in the rainbow jersey. The deplorable state of the cobblestones, covered by a coat of viscous earth, made the race

1974. On cobblestones covered with a thin layer of clay, De Vlaeminck chases solo leader Francesco Moser for 20km. After being caught by the Belgian, Moser crashes in a turn with 7km to go, and De Vlaeminck goes on to score his second Roubaix victory.

1972. Once he has caught solo breakaway Willy Van Malderghem, De Vlaeminck rides like a rocket to eventually drop his fellow Belgian and win his first Paris-Roubaix by two minutes. De Vlaeminck almost runs out of energy, but he luckily gets some sugar lumps just in time.

mystery have racked their brains without obtaining the slightest satisfaction."

## A workaholic for training

No doubt De Vlaeminck's introverted character had something to do with his up-and-down existence. Success had somehow failed to appease this tormented soul, who had become a cycling champion in order to escape a lifetime at the textile mill he had entered at the age of 15. The man was completely overwhelmed by the loss of his best friend, Jean-Pierre Monséré, killed in a race while wearing the rainbow jersey. He was also deeply disturbed by the sufferings of his oldest brother, Éric, a seven-time world cyclocross champion who fell prey to drug addiction (which he eventually overcame). He was ruined by a divorce, and devastated by the tragic death of his nephew Geert in a bike race. Given all this, is it any wonder why De Vlaeminck was enigmatic, distant, ferocious, and boorish in public? That said, he could be a rather amusing sort in private and a perpetual prankster. One day when he visited Merckx's home, he entered the living room on his bike, exited by the kitchen, and descended the exterior staircase—all without leaving his saddle.

But in the peloton, no one was more fickle than he. "He would sometimes enter the showers singing, and leave cursing," recounts his former teammate Johan De Muynck.

Sometimes, his outlandish behavior in public hid a natural inner anxiety. Resting on the eve of one Paris-Roubaix, he sud-

even more savage and its image even more archaic. Despite his great skill at balancing, De Vlaeminck fell twice. "I am the champion of the world at cyclocross [as of two months earlier], but if someone proposed a race of that sort over a course like this, I would refuse to participate. At 27, I'm too young to die." To win Paris-Roubaix, however, the leader of the Brooklyn squad would stop at nothing.

1977: "It's Mr. Paris-Roubaix," blared *L'Équipe*. The results were predictable. De Vlaeminck finished alone, with more than a minute-and-a-half lead over Merckx, Freddy Maertens, Moser, Jan Raas, Walter Godefroot, Marc Demeyer, Hennie Kuiper, and yet again the valiant but washed-up Raymond Poulidor. De Vlaeminck now resembled the dominant Rik Van Looy of fifteen years earlier.

De Vlaeminck had once again enriched his prestigious collection of spring triumphs. By now, Maertens, though at the twilight of his career, had replaced Merckx as De Vlaeminck's enemy number one. A few days earlier Maertens had goaded De Vlaeminck, "Your legs look a little thin to me. Can they really get you as far as Roubaix?" Retorted De Vlaeminck, "Don't worry about those. They are still solid and they're going to make you suffer come Sunday." And he kept that promise.

On the eve of the Gypsy's fourth and final victory at the northern velodrome, Pierre Chany, *L'Équipe*'s special correspondent, dwelt on the winner's perplexing personality. "All those who have tried to analyze his psychology and pierce his

**1977.** This sector of pavé is difficult, but De Vlaeminck is the strongest. Riding between the cobblestones, badly filled potholes, and a stony roadside, he breaks clear of the peloton and no one can follow him. He'll be christened Mr. Paris-Roubaix after he finishes more than 90 seconds ahead of the runner-up to take victory number four.

denly called for his domestique, Ronan Demeyer. De Vlaeminck had become such a nervous wreck that he figured only the presence of this teammate could put his mind at ease.

In a race, De Vlaeminck was a greyhound. While training over the years, he became a workaholic. He made sure he worked harder than anyone else to gain a psychological edge, especially before the northern classic. "I would leave for practice at five in the morning," he recalled, "and by the time I met Walter Godefroot at his place I had already done 120 kilometers. But I led him to believe that I had just arisen from bed. It was important for me to know that I was doing more than the others. I also wanted people to say, 'De Vlaeminck is so classy, he wins without much training at all.'" In truth, he had plenty of class but he trained a lot.

Before Paris-Roubaix, he would ride up to 430 kilometers in one day.

In 1986, his cycling career over and his finances drained, De Vlaeminck mounted a comeback in cyclocross, thanks to the extended hand of a patron who knew him better than most anyone else. This same man is depicted in a painting belonging to Mr. Paris-Roubaix, showing the two of them going elbow to elbow over the cobblestones of Hell. He was none other than Eddy Merckx.   J.-L. G.

# Francesco Moser

### (1978, 1979, 1980)

## Uno, due, tre!

**In 1986, six years after his third and final win, Francesco Moser is still fighting like a lion. But the cobblestones won't return the love that he has shown them.**

Lapize, Octave Lapize. In 1980, Italian cycling fans discovered the name of this French cyclist from the distant past, the man who had won three straight Paris-Roubaix from 1909 to 1911. His record and intimate connection to the great French classic made news across the Alps because of a similar exploit achieved sixty-nine years later by that champion from Trento, Francesco Moser.

This racer with a very modern approach to his profession rose to the level of Lapize's astonishing achievement when he himself won Paris-Roubaix three straight times from 1978 to 1980. Moreover, the final scenarios, impossible to arrange in advance, played out in much the same decisive manner: each time, Moser reached the northern track in glorious solitude.

The Belgian Roger De Vlaeminck, a great lover of the Queen of the Classics, won it four times before bowing to Moser's domination, which he fought to his last drop of sweat. Before the Second World War, another Belgian, Gaston Rebry, won it three times, a feat duplicated in the 1960s by yet another compatriot, Rik Van Looy. Finally, of course, Eddy Merckx left his mark in the legendary mud fest by likewise compiling three victories. But none of them had matched the consistency of performance registered by Lapize at the start of the century.

Francesco Moser, for his part, found the formula for total success, applying all his cycling know-how in a race that does not, as everyone knows, lend itself to exact science.

## His mother's regrets

Moser's power and suppleness made for an ideal combination to overcome the cobblestones. The athlete (1.84 meters and 80 kilograms) attacked the course in an almost floating style that made it appear as if he rolled along the cobblestones on some sort of air cushion, immune to the terrible vibrations that hampered other cyclists. His approach was consistent, as he explained. "In Paris-Roubaix, my only tactic is to provoke the maximum number of mechanical failures among the competition so that I can break away," he said. Rather than launching outright attacks, Moser imposed a sustained rhythm at a break-neck pace on those who tried to stay on his tail—like Dietrich Thurau in 1980. Moser had three commandments for victory: be strong, ride in front, and get lucky. His springtime campaign invariably began with Milan-San Remo and ended with Paris-Roubaix. In order to ensure that he would be in top form, this highly disciplined Italian led a monastic existence. He applied himself with grace and commitment, because he was devoted to his sport above all.

Francesco Moser belonged to a clan that included five brothers. Aldo, the oldest, was the first champion. Enzo strove to imitate him, but it was Diego who wore the pink jersey in the Giro d'Italia. Francesco was 18 when he escaped his native Trento. Before then, in his adolescence, he would often spend up to ten hours a day in the field, stooped over and toiling beside his mother and father.

In 1974, Moser's mother watched her son's extremely encouraging start in Paris-Roubaix, which he achieved while assisting De Vlaeminck.

"You know he could become a great champion," offered *L'Équipe*'s Christian Montaignac after Moser's surprisingly strong showing. "Yes, maybe," sighed Moser's mother, "but he was already a great cultivator."

Perhaps it was that love of the land that enabled Francesco, the most gifted of the five brothers, to become such a master of rural roads. Some were so ripped apart, in fact, that even the local peasants hesitated to drive their tractors over them. Finishing second in the Paris-Roubaix of 1974, after discovering Hell, he concluded, "Difficult, yes, but not as bad as the mountains." Moser, who again finished second in 1976, finally achieved consummation in 1978, a confirmation in 1979, and an affirmation of superiority in 1980. And in two of those editions (1978 and 1979) he had to beat out his protégé, Mr. Paris-Roubaix himself, Roger De Vlaeminck.

The Belgian master, who had already battled Merckx and Godefroot, finally found a roadblock in the Italian upstart. In 1978, the two rivals both rode for the Sanson team, and both were unaccustomed to sharing glory. But the Belgian reluctantly agreed to play the role of the good teammate. Their non-aggression pact enabled Moser to streak toward victory over an abominable course. De Vlaeminck was nonetheless tempted to break the deal. "Moser was a natural, a great champion, but extremely selfish," opined the Gypsy. "Besides, we didn't talk to each other. He took off right when I was planning an attack, on the cobblestones of Bachy, 20 kilometers from Roubaix."

Much later, the Belgian confided to Philippe Brunel of *L'Équipe*, "I had to respect the team dynamics, so I offered a fair amount of money to Jan Raas [who rode for a rival team] so that he would lead me back to Moser. He tried everything to get me there, but once Moser had taken off, there wasn't much anyone could do to catch him."

## "I knew I would win it one day"

The Italian's mud-splattered rainbow jersey became an instant icon after he triumphed in the epic edition of 1978. Pierre Chany's report the next day was entitled "A Triumph at the Limits of the Possible." And it began as follows: "This demented course over carpets of mud that give rise to great legends, this savage and suspenseful dash, has taught us at least two lessons we should never forget. First, Francesco Moser, an associate of our own outstanding Gypsy, is a virtuoso in his own right over this impossible terrain, and he must now be counted among the most prestigious winners of the world's most difficult cycling race. Second, we have witnessed, this April 16, 1978, the extreme limit of human endurance in the makeup of this course."

"At last!" were the first words from the winner whose eyes were reddened by the superhuman effort, and whose face was streaked with mud and tears. "I knew it! I knew I would win it one day. It's my kind of race. I discovered that in 1974, when I first competed in Paris-Roubaix. To win here is a dream, and one that will never be repeated," he predicted. Prematurely, as it turned out.

When he won his second Paris-Roubaix in 1979, on dry earth this time, Moser did not forget to remind everyone that he "owed nothing to anyone." And certainly not to De Vlaeminck, who had become, once again, a direct competitor.

But even if the Italian had no personal debts this time around, he was beholden to the elements and to his own good

"Be strong, ride in front, and have a little luck." These are the three commandments that bring Moser three consecutive wins at Roubaix. Here, in 1979, he's on his way to the second victory. "I don't owe anything to anyone," he says, directing his comment to those who intimated that his 1978 win was made possible by his teammate De Vlaeminck.

1980. With 15km to go, the champion of Italy drops his last breakaway companion, Didi Thurau of Germany, and heads to his third win in a row. Octave Lapize was the only previous rider to achieve this special hat trick back in 1911.

luck—or rather, to the bad luck of Marc Demeyer, Hennie Kuiper, and De Vlaeminck. They all got flats in the interminable tunnel of Wannehain, 14 kilometers from the finish line. Four kilometers farther on, the Italian himself endured a similar misadventure, but without suffering grave consequences.

As he had the previous year, Moser was able to penetrate the velodrome of Roubaix in perfect solitude. He thus became the first Italian to collect two victories in this mythical place, a feat he deemed "excellent for our national prestige."

## "I went looking for luck"

In the 1980 edition, Moser faced two great protagonists: Jan Raas, a favorite, and the irrepressible De Vlaeminck, still in the hunt. But how could they possibly outmaneuver a Moser at the height of his powers? His very image was that of an implacable horseman, as *L'Équipe* aptly called him the day after his fantastic final gallop. "I was never so confident," Moser said. "It was pointless to hide my intentions. I wanted to arrive alone in Roubaix, just as I had in 1978 and 1979." The performance started early, 90 kilometers from the finish line, when Didi Thurau, Gilbert Duclos-Lassalle, and De Vlaeminck were still in the thick of things.

But after flatting for the second time in two years, the Belgian, who had until then generally evaded fatal pitfalls, finally had to face the music: his luck had run out. Moser prof-

ited from the windfall. His attack confounded the brave Duclos-Lassalle, who ultimately finished second despite three falls down the stretch. Only Thurau remained in serious contention. The German chained himself to the Italian champion like a condemned prisoner, until 15 kilometers from the finish. After that, he was compelled to watch as Moser's rear wheel faded into the distance. Entering the track, Moser wiped his hand on his face and stroked his hair. Then he raised his hands high into the sky, well before and well after the finish line, as if to register that moment for all eternity.

"I started my attacks as soon as it was possible; if anyone says I got lucky, I would say I went looking for luck, that's all."

And so Moser would cap his historic run. But while he would manage, at the twilight of his career in 1984, to set a new hour record, his tally of victories at Roubaix would evolve no further, despite more entries on his part. In the 1990s, a younger generation of Italians, led by Franco Ballerini and Andrea Tafi, sought new glory on the cobblestones. And they readily conceded that they would pursue their dreams by feeding off the legend of their great predecessor.     J.-L. G.

# Bernard Hinault

**(1981)**

## Driven by hatred

1981. On the velodrome, Bernard Hinault has delivered a phenomenal effort to take the final sprint. He absolutely needed to overcome the challenge of the cobblestones, to prove he could win a race he called rubbish. To add such a classic to your palmarès makes a great rider even greater. Hinault has just done so.

Bernard Hinault was poised to win Paris-Roubaix in 1981. He was wearing the world champion jersey on his back, had victories in two Tours and one Giro under his belt, and was ready to defy any bad luck that might come his way. Still, he hated this race, with its cobblestones and cursed dust that irritated his eyes. "I believe I've already shown that I am the strongest rider," he groused, "and now I have to prove that I'm also the best on those wretched cobblestones."

Indeed, he had reached a kind of athletic apogee that spring. The proof? He had always found it a struggle to get into top shape before the dog days of summer, and yet he had already registered a clean sweep at the Critérium International, winning the road race, the hill climb, and the time trial.

Better still, he had stolen the Amstel Gold Race, which had pitted itself against the classics that year. He had outsprinted such fearful rivals as Roger De Vlaeminck, Jan Raas, Sean Kelly, and Pierino Gavazzi.

This success on Dutch turf showed that the Breton had become almost invincible, even in his rivals' favorite stomping grounds. But that did not prevent him from expressing his

misgivings about Paris-Roubaix. His impressive performances in the cobblestone stages of the latest Tours (1979 and 1980) did not alter his negative sentiments toward this northern peculiarity, nor did they diminish his apprehension. "This is like pigs at play," he scoffed to the journalist Jean-Marie Leblanc, after he dominated the fearsome Hennie Kuiper during a northern Tour stage through Lille under abominable weather conditions. Nevertheless, Hinault felt immense pressure to win the Queen of the Classics. He knew well that public opinion demanded no less. For in the early 1980s, champions were still judged not just by the depth of their palmarès but also by their diversity.

"Those who demand that I win Paris-Roubaix at any cost are not those who pedal themselves. After all, I don't go around to people's offices to tell them how they should be doing their jobs." But a Hinault who simmers is a Hinault who stews. He may not have liked the Classic of Classics—that's an understatement—but he relished challenges. In fact, that was his modus operandi. "You want me to win Paris-Roubaix? Well then, stand back and let's see what I can do!"

1981. Before finishing off the job in the velodrome, the French world champion was prominent in the morass he so detested. Here he's riding so strongly that stars like Moser, De Vlaeminck, and Demeyer have a hard time staying on his wheel.

## A royal sprint between stars

When the leading pack entered the velodrome at the conclusion of the 1981 edition, the clamor became deafening. They were six in all, a galaxy of stars. But the frenzied crowd chanted one name alone: "Hinault, Hinault!"

To get that far, the Badger had already overcome numerous twists of luck. At the crossing at Neuvilly, where he first saw cobblestones, rivals passed him left and right. He was in the third subgroup at the hill of Saint-Python, and he needed a providential realignment just to get back into the race by Valenciennes. Then there were flat tires, and a fall when the Belgian Gerrie Verlinden crossed his path. For this Paris-Roubaix was being contested in the mud, as if the elements had ganged up against Hinault. To avoid a pileup of racers, he went around a curtain of fans for the length of a ditch, his bicycle on his shoulder. Finally, on the fat cobblestones 12 kilometers from the end, he sent a pesky little black poodle airborne with his foot. Well, it had long been said that Hinault would stop at nothing to achieve his goals.

The six contenders who presented themselves at the gates of the velodrome were all great names. Hinault was by no means the favorite when up against Roger De Vlaeminck, the record winner of this event, or Francesco Moser, who had registered his third straight win the year before. Another former winner in the crowd was the great Marc Demeyer, as well as the tough Hennie Kuiper, who would win the event two years later. Only the speedy Guido Van Calster had yet to figure in the palmarès of this race.

Hinault didn't fool around—that wasn't his style. As soon as he entered the track, he burst into the lead, setting a faster and faster pace by using his big gear. Louison Bobet, who had been invited to follow this edition marking the 25th anniversary of his personal triumph, was overwhelmed by this crazy spurt. "What a beast!" he gasped. Hinault first repelled an attack by Marc Demeyer, then Roger De Vlaeminck, who tried unsuccessfully to pass on the outside. Hinault was the strongest, that's all there was to it.

On the podium, he bristled with smug satisfaction. "Take it, here's your cobblestone," he snapped, handing his trophy to Maurice Champion, one of Cyrille Guimard's assistants on the Renault team. "It will wind up in my cellar," he promised, feigning a complete lack of interest. But the fact is, *all* of Hinault's trophies wound up in his basement. And, as it turned out, that cobblestone was not consigned to such a bad place after all.

"I'm not going to tell you that I like this sort of race now that I've won one," Hinault declared. "It has too many pitfalls, too many motorcycles, and too much dust." Deep down, though, he was elated—not so much because he had beaten the absolute best in De Vlaeminck and Moser, but because he had silenced the critics who had demanded he prove his caliber.

Another small detail: when Hinault went to the anti-doping control station, someone pointed out a small white spot on his front tire. It was punctured. Hinault seized the wheel and worked out a section of the inner tube with his thumbs. He then gave the tube a mighty squeeze with his fingers, producing a loud bang. "There," he laughed, "now it's dead." That was one less tire that could go on him in the middle of a sprint. Clearly, it was in the cards that Hinault would win a Paris-Roubaix at all costs.  P. B.

# Sean Kelly
**(1984, 1986)**

## Power wins twice

1992. Eight years after he first won Paris-Roubaix, Sean Kelly is still in the thick of things. After all, the mud, as befits his rugby-playing countrymen, is as Irish as his pedigree.

It wasn't really Sean Kelly's style to put on a show. He wasn't known for great solo flights but rather for his extraordinary efficiency. He rarely took the initiative, but he excelled in the art of counterattacking. At any rate, the Irishman with the rustic look reigned over the classics in the mid-1980s. He imposed his rule on every race, no matter its style. It was thus entirely natural that he asserted himself in Paris-Roubaix as well, while still at the peak of his powers.

His two successes, in 1984 and 1986, fell squarely within his best years. At the time, he was practically invincible in March and April. To fully appreciate the extent of his domination, one must recall how both his triumphs in the Queen of

the Classics fell in the middle of impressive runs. In 1984, for example, he had already won Paris-Nice, as usual (he was in the midst of a seven-year streak), followed by a victory in the Critérium International. He almost won the Tour of Flanders too, but was robbed by the surprising Johan Lammerts. Kelly prevailed again in the Tour de Pays Basque and, capping off this exceptional campaign, in Liège-Bastogne-Liège as well. It was thus no surprise to see him enter the velodrome of Roubaix in the lead, accompanied only by Rudy Rogiers, a promising young Belgian. Winning the sprint was a mere formality for Kelly.

Kelly's second win in 1986 was preceded by another dominant spring campaign. Once again he won Paris-Nice, followed by a victory in Milan-San Remo. To be sure, the Tour of Flanders still eluded him (as it would his entire career), when the Dutchman Adrie Van der Poel caught Kelly by surprise and erupted in a victorious sprint. But Kelly did not dwell on this disappointment. That same evening, he headed off for the Tour du Pays Basque where, a week before Paris-Roubaix, he would again flaunt his winning ways. Though he knew how to pace himself in stage races, he was never content to dog it and simply rack up kilometers. He won one stage after another. In fact, the insatiable Irishman seemed intent on winning every stage no matter how bad the weather got. And that year, it snowed heavily the first two days and flooded the rest of the week. "He could make that kind of effort because for ten years he had been living the life of a monk, just like Bobet in his prime," explained his proud directeur sportif, the late Jean de Gribaldy.

## No effort spared, just 36 hours before Paris-Roubaix

During the week of the Tour du Pays Basque, the classics of the North seemed far from the Irishman's mind. He alluded to them only once, on Wednesday evening, when he casually inquired, "Who won Ghent-Wevelgem?" Told that the Italian Guido Bontempi had prevailed in a sprint, Kelly showed little reaction and asked no further questions.

Moreover, as the last stage of Pays Basque approached, Kelly appeared on the verge of losing this especially tough edition despite his spirited performance. The modest Italian, Maurizio Rossi, the author of an escape during the long first stage, held a 3-minute, 40-second lead over the implacable Irishman. The gap seemed hopelessly wide, considering the 18-kilometer time trial still ahead. But the unexpected transpired. Unsparing in his efforts just 36 hours before Paris-Roubaix, Kelly reversed the standings. At 6:00 on Friday evening, he mounted the podium facing the Plaza Mayor in the village of Andoain. Nearly an hour later, he was still up there, collecting all the jerseys and cups corresponding to various categories of distinction. Finally he drove off to catch a flight to Paris. Upon his arrival in the French capital, Marcel

Tinazzi whisked him off to his hotel in Compiègne, the starting point of Paris-Roubaix. That Sunday, picking up where he had left off, the Irishman easily nailed his second victory in the event.

## Tough preparation

Sean Kelly never balked at tough preparation. And the rigorous regimen he followed often allowed him to inflict a similar punishment on others. Once in the shower reflecting on the race, he was often surprised by how passive his foes had been. They had made the fatal error of shaping their strategy around whoever had been favored to win. When Kelly forced the pace, the peloton accelerated. When he slowed down, so did the others. Finally, he found himself that year on the streets of Roubaix in the company of a determined Rudy Dhaenens, a courageous Ferdi Van den Haute, and a thorny Adrie Van der Poel, his

nemesis in the Tour of Flanders. This time, Kelly firmly invited the Dutchman to start a relay, and Van der Poel accepted. In this 1986 edition, the finish line faced the headquarters of La Redoute, the sponsor of the race. The ambience of the velodrome was sorely lacking, but the result was the same. Kelly broke away and easily disposed of his companions.

The tireless Kelly registered so many successes in the mid-1980s that it's easy to overlook just how numerous and impressive they really were. He had an entirely personal perception of fatigue. "It's a mind game," he said. "You only get tired when you're holed up in some hotel room and have time to think about it." How Kelly loved the outdoors, whatever the weather.   J.-L. G.

1986. Like a true athlete of the bicycle, Kelly puts all of his energy into pulling his machine out of the mud and steering it onto a less cloying surface. By taking the race in hand like this, he goes on to take his second Roubaix victory.

# Marc Madiot

**(1985, 1991)**

## The classic in his blood

Marc Madiot brandishes the winner's cobblestone he so much wanted. This is his second Roubaix trophy, six years after the first.

In 1991, no one tipped him to win. At 32, he's returning from the depths of a long career, but he works so hard that he's able to create a huge surprise. And this time he does it in dry weather.

In big races, Marc Madiot had a habit of sticking out his tongue whenever he felt stressed. So he did on April 14, 1985, for it was a big day indeed. He had just claimed his first major professional victory, Paris-Roubaix, a race he had also won six years earlier as an amateur. In 1983, he again showed a predisposition for this race when he finished fifth. In fact Paris-Roubaix resembled his own character, in the sense that Madiot was one of the last true romantics, who stoically tolerated all that shaking for the love of the sport.

In the far right lane where he had crossed the finish line, he shook hands with Cyrille Guimard, whom he had known for some eight years, since his junior days. Madiot reflected on Merckx and De Vlaeminck, the icons of his youth. And in his happiness, he let his emotions override his pain. "Before I got to the velodrome, I slipped into my 12-tooth gear and I gave it all I had, just for the thrill of it," he said.

His first success in Paris-Roubaix was the fruit of much patience. He was already 26, in his fifth professional season. Up to that point, his achievements had fallen far below expectations, considering his ample skills. But he had shown class, to be sure. And above all, he worked hard. Finally, beneath it all, he had an abiding love for the bicycle. "For me it's not just a job," he explained. "It's my life." It took an old-style race for this modern champion to finally blossom. He had to be caked

in mud to show his true face as a young winner. Yes, it took Madiot a while to get to his goal. But one conviction drove him. "I refused to be rushed," he said, "because I knew my time would inevitably come."

## Like a lifestyle

Madiot sensed the hour was at hand when he reached the sticky cobblestones at the crossroads of l'Arbre. Francesco Moser, competing in his final Paris-Roubaix, committed a marvelous sin of pride by attacking 80 kilometers from the finish line, defying a headwind. The Italian's subsequent capitulation led to Éric Vanderaerden's euphoria. The latter was already on a roll, having registered a memorable exploit the previous Sunday in an apocalyptic Tour of Flanders, followed shortly thereafter by a another victory in Ghent-Wevelgem. But the young prodigy, drenched in sweat and wearing his Belgium champion's jersey, was also withering from the intense wind sweeping the gray and desolate plain.

Madiot, for his part, knew how to bide his time before making his move. He felt in exceptionally good shape. He calmly pedaled along as if riding on velvet. "Yes it's true, I'm going to win this thing!" he told himself 14 kilometers from the velodrome, when he suddenly let loose, never to be seen again from behind. When he finished, he expressed his feelings with a touch of exaggeration. "A victory, for me, whether in the Tour de Vendée or in Paris-Roubaix, is essentially the same thing," he declared.

What he really wanted to say was that riding well in the sport he adored gave him great pleasure. "What I love above all is the thrill of the race—it matters little which one," he explained. "I'm intoxicated by the experience. I need to see the bicycles and their whirling wheels, even if it's just an amateur race near my home. That's real cycling. You thrash the pedals,

1985. On this day of mud and headwinds, two careers cross. That of the veteran Francesco Moser, a three-time winner, who's still racing at the top, but hits some trouble, and that of the young Marc Madiot, who wins with the wisdom of an old dog. So what if he gets a bit worked up after the finish?

smell the fries, and when you're done, you relive the race fifteen times over. In the final analysis, it's a lifestyle."

One of Madiot's great talents was that he knew how to bite off full mouthfuls of that life. But it is no coincidence either that his most notable accolades include choice morsels. There's Paris-Roubaix, of course, but also the Championship of France (1987). Indeed, he coveted those races that evoked within him a lifelong passion.

## Same time, same place

Six years separated Madiot's success in the amateur Paris-Roubaix from that of his first pro victory. Six more years would elapse before his return to the podium. He was nearly 32 when he won the Queen of the Classics for a second time. That was in 1991, when no one really expected him to win it. Madiot thus completed his crossing of the desert. His last previous vic-

tory, a stage of the Critérium International, was more than two years prior. A broken pelvis, a falling-out with his old friend Cyrille Guimard, and a shaky transition to the Toshiba team conspired, according to his Toshiba teammate Jean-François Bernard, to make Madiot a virtual has-been. Many others had come to a similar conclusion, though Madiot still kept his enthusiasm for the sport.

He began the 1991 season wearing the RMO jersey, and he sensed the start of a comeback when he finished sixth in the Tour of Flanders. This surprising result not only confirmed that he still had abilities but also showed his profound motivation.

And then, at last, he put together the perfect race in Paris-Roubaix. He felt not a wisp of air during the first few hours, thanks to the shelter provided by his brother Yvon. Nor was he worried about the morning breakaway, which gained a lead of seven minutes. "When I'm in a race," he allowed, "I focus on no one else. I live my own life." He bet his success on his superior

1985. Six years after he won the amateur riders' version of Paris-Roubaix, Madiot confirms his inherent talent against the inner circle of the sport. At 26, he forces the pace in the mud until the top men are stuffed and then makes his decisive attack at the Carrefour de l'Arbre.

serenity and experience. The impetuous winner of 1985 had given way to a calm messenger with a total inner fullness. He won his first in a blizzard. This time a luminous sky witnessed his resurrection in the race that had made him a star. He was in the company of the Italian Franco Ballerini and the Belgian Hendrik Redant when he launched his attack, at the crossroads of l'Arbre, just as he had six years earlier. "I took off at exactly the same spot," he recounted. "I said to myself that Ballerini would certainly take care of us in a sprint. So I did something of a bluff. Not a real break. I just spun hard for a kilometer and a half and that did the trick."

## A femur fractured on cobblestones

In 1985 he had been in a hurry to finish, but this time around he wanted to savor the moment. "I knew where I was going. I knew that I had won it," he said.

Seventy years after Henri Pélissier (1919, 1921), Madiot became the first Frenchman to win two Paris-Roubaix. His destiny was now complete. He would return to the Hell of the North again and again, until the twilight of his career, but without attaining strong results. By 1994, he was clinging to

the last branch of the very modest Catavana team. But his faith in himself and love for the sport were undiminished. One day, he accomplished a monumental training stint of nine hours, all alone. "That really wracks the body," he conceded. "Come the evening of April 10 I don't want to have any regrets, to tell myself I should have done this or that."

Madiot knew the end was near, that he must soon walk away from this sport that had made his heart beat. "This wine is so good that I want to drink it until I am no longer thirsty," he reflected days before the contest began. "And I feel there are still a few drops left." His adventure ended at a turn in the road, on the cobblestones of Famars. His femur fractured, Madiot would soon be a racer no longer. But he would leave the sport with no regrets. He could not have chosen a better way to exit than to fall on that battlefield of honor known as Paris-Roubaix. P. B.

# Gilbert Duclos-Lassalle

## Cobblestones with béarnaise sauce

**(1992, 1993)**

After finishing second to Moser in 1980, Duclos-Lassalle knows he can win this race. A year later, alone in the lead for 20km, he looks as though he'll achieve his dream, but he will flat on the Wanneheim section of pavé, and then crash. He'll finish 22nd.

Twenty-eighth in 1978, 25th in 1979, 2nd in 1980, 22nd in 1981, 20th in 1982, 2nd in 1983, did not finish (dnfs) in 1985, 34th in 1986, 17th in 1987, did not finish in 1988, 4th in 1989, 6th in 1990, 12th in 1991, 1st in 1992, 1st in 1993, 7th in 1994, 19th in 1995...

This barrage of statistics sums up the saga of Gilbert Duclos-Lassalle in Paris-Roubaix. It conveys his longevity, his patience, and his long frustration, followed at last by his deliverance. It reflects a life spent on a bicycle, a nineteen-year career with seventeen entries in this classic, including his great success on his 14th try and his euphoric repeat on his 15th.

He had already discovered the cobblestones when he was 23. Yet he did not execute his masterpiece until the age of 37 years and 8 months, and he was nearly 39 when he claimed his second win. In that lengthy interim he had registered only two dnfs, one in 1985 and the other in 1988, and only one non-entry, in 1984, owing to a hunting accident that nearly cost him his left hand. This litany of results, which stretches through three distinct decades, allows us to see something of the personality of Duclos-Lassalle.

Yet his full sporting history cannot be boiled down to statistics alone, for it also includes the vivid memories of challenges and sufferings. And in those two domains, this good man was abundantly experienced well before he realized his dream of victory.

As early as 1978, just before his first Paris-Roubaix, the Flemish press had already singled out Duclos-Lassalle as a potential star. He was 23 at the time, and an apprentice with the Peugeot team. Earlier that year, he had been the only Frenchman to finish Ghent-Wevelgem (in 18th place), battling a snowstorm. He defied the prevailing perception that only Belgians can endure such harsh climatic conditions. In fact, this young man came from the foothills of the Pyrénées, in the province of Béarn after which the famous sauce is named. In his debut at Roubaix, he proved once again that he was made of rare metal, finishing a surprisingly strong 28th.

In 1980, Duclos-Lassalle got off to his best start ever. He won in succession the Tour of Corsica, Paris-Nice, and the Tour of Tarn. He lined up for the start of Paris-Roubaix in excellent shape as attested by his recent seventh- and eighth-place finishes in the Tour of Flanders and the Amstel Gold Race, respectively. Naturally, he was among the favorites to win, despite the supremacy of Francesco Moser the preceding two years.

## The surgeon worked miracles

Endowed with a fiery temperament but a solid head, Duclos-Lassalle refused to sell his services to the Italian champion, despite the latter's healthy offer. Still, the Frenchman's resolve didn't change the outcome of the affair: Moser won again and Duclos-Lassalle finished second, nearly two minutes behind. "Moser attacked twice, and twice I responded. Had it not been for all my problems, he would not have been able to drop me so easily," insisted Duclos-Lassalle. Problems? They included two blowouts and, in the final stretch, two falls.

Despite the Frenchman's disappointment, he began to believe that he would one day prevail. But he also knew that if he was to attain greater success in this warrior's race, he would need the patience of a monk. "Now the difficulties will begin for me. I will be a marked man; everything will get harder," he predicted. Still, Maurice De Muer, his coach, insisted that his racer's spirit and outlook remained positive. "In just one move, he went ten steps forward," said De Muer. "But he remains humble."

The following year, 1981, Duclos-Lassalle undoubtedly commanded greater public attention in Paris-Roubaix. But Bernard Hinault and his rainbow jersey stole the show. The distinguished Breton had grudgingly made up his mind to win this race, even though it repulsed him as much as it attracted him.

Duclos-Lassalle's hour of glory would come, no doubt, but when? Two years on, 1983 was not quite the year either, though he finished a strong second behind Hennie Kuiper. The Dutchman had finally prevailed on his 11th try, setting a good example for the Frenchman, who by this time had a relatively modest six attempts under his belt, with two second-place finishes to show for his efforts. His obsession with Paris-Roubaix grew, though his surprising win in Bordeaux-Paris a few weeks later temporarily distracted him.

Between the Queen of Classics and the "Marathon of the Road," Duclos-Lassalle had already proved that he was a racer of distinction. In the winter, when he carefully stored his bicycle, he indulged in his second passion, hunting—a dangerous pastime indeed. In the fall of 1983, a bullet went through his left hand, leaving, in his words, "a gaping hole the size of a 5-franc coin." The surgeon had to work miracles so that Duclos-Lassalle's rehabilitated hand was sufficiently firm to grasp his handlebars, even over cobblestones. But his comeback proved agonizingly slow. Duclos-Lassalle returned to Paris-Roubaix in 1985 only to abandon it. He was not again a factor in the race until 1989, when he finished in fourth place. Still, it was a great performance considering that he had fractured his kneecap that February and had been laid up for a month.

"I came because I love Paris-Roubaix above all and I love to shine in it. For as long as this race exists, I will participate in it," he promised. But his opportunity for glory seemed to be slipping away. His son Hervé, born three months before Duclos-Lassalle first ascended the podium in 1980, was already in boarding school and aspiring to become a professional racer just like his dad.

On Sunday, April 12, 1992, his father lined up for the start of Paris-Roubaix for the 14th time. The recent success of the 36-year-old Sean Kelly, winner of Milan-San Remo, gave Duclos-Lassalle renewed hope. Moreover, in the recent Tour du Pays Basque, which over the years had become his training ground for Paris-Roubaix, he had shown himself among the best climbers.

## "I could quit racing now, but I won't"

Duclos-Lassalle quickly imposed his pace. He pulled himself out of the trench at Arenberg with Jean-Paul Van Poppel and Rik Van Slycke on his wheel. He still had another 115 kilometers and fifteen cobblestone sections to go. Twenty-five kilometers ahead of him, four racers were in the lead. Three of them had left the forest together; the other, Thomas Wegmüller, was the only one of the morning breakaways who had rebounded back in front. Behind Duclos-Lassalle, controlling the peloton, were his teammates Greg LeMond, Jean-Claude Colotti, and Philippe Casado. A win seemed within Duclos-Lassalle's grasp. He hit his stride 45 minutes from the finish line, near Ennevelin, where he decided to tempt fate. "I had no choice," he said. "Van Poppel was no longer earnestly collaborating with me, and he was the faster sprinter. I thought of Merckx and Moser, who had also taken off far from the end. I gave it my all."

He gradually built a lead of 1 minute, 30 seconds before his reservoir of energy began to dissipate. His pace became erratic. The extreme length of this Sunday and his solitude weighed heavily on his mind. Yet, had he not dreamt all these years that he would one day find himself leading this race all alone?

Now that he was approaching the summit of his athletic life, there was no way he was about to back off. But the threat of Olaf Ludwig loomed large. The overpowering German arrived at the crossroads of l'Arbre having cut the Frenchman's lead to just half a minute. "When he approached, I had to figure out his speed so that I could maintain the same rhythm as he," Duclos-Lassalle disclosed. "I took note of the time differences as related by the time-check motorcycle and other allies. To get away with this, you have to be an 'old' racer. You need at least two friends among the motorcyclists, the Republican Guard, or the photographers who are willing to inform you. That goes along with senior privileges."

His resistance was both heroic and touching. A delirious crowd, totally taken by his noble cause, hailed his entry into the velodrome. Duclos-Lassalle himself was overcome with emotion. "With all that encouragement, I think I could have done three or four more laps around the track without my legs acting up. I could quit racing now, but I won't. This victory makes me want to win one more."

## Ballerini bluffed

The following year, 1993, when he transformed his wish into reality, he was pleased to have shown the full array of his skills. "I attained my first success with flair. In the second, people finally discovered another side to Duclos-Lassalle: my knowledge of the race, my strategizing, my tactics, and my experience. I had to outmaneuver a man who was stronger than I. Upon arriving at the crossroads of l'Arbre, Patrick Lefévère, Ballerini's coach, screamed to him to drop me. I was suffering, but I went all-out for the next 200 meters to stay on his wheel. I looked right at Ballerini and cracked a smile. I was bluffing, hiding my pain, so that he would stop attacking. I'm not sure that a younger racer would have been able to stay on him as I did. Then I took advantage of the smooth sections to catch my breath and relax a bit. I no longer forced the pace. Ballerini kept saying to me, 'Pass, pass.' But I replied, 'No, no. You're the faster one.' That's when he came unwound."

The Italian was clearly superior to the Frenchman. But the latter trusted in his lucky star. He knew his adversary well, although they had never hung out together. For Ballerini

1992. A dozen years after his second place, Duclos chooses the cobbles at Ennevelin, with 45km to go, to make a long-distance solo attack, just as Merckx and Moser did in years past. Chased by the German Olaf Ludwig, Duclos uses his experience to match his pace to that of his pursuer to preserve his winning margin.

reminded him of himself back in the 1980s, when he was something of a mad dog. The young and impetuous Duclos-Lassalle had repeatedly allowed success to slip though his hands by always trying to stay in the lead, without thinking about how to conserve energy for the long haul.

For the lap and a half he still had to do at the velodrome, Duclos-Lassalle marshaled all the strength he had left, and deftly exploited his knowledge of track racing gleaned from his winter participation in Six-Day races. He took advantage of the track's banking to launch his sprint from far out, for he knew that he was inferior in pure speed. The two men threw their bikes to the line. Ballerini raised his arms toward the sky in victory. At last! He had joined his countryman Francesco Moser in the record books—or so he thought.

Duclos-Lassalle, for his part, calmly awaited the verdict of the photo-finish. The development and analysis of the document took several minutes, a seeming eternity. He dared not even hope until it was delivered. "Duclos-Lassalle is the winner!" bellowed the announcer, Daniel Mangeas. The long mur-

mur that had persisted during the interlude erupted into an extraordinary outburst of joy, shared by that of the champion. The emotion reached a pitched fervor.

"With this second win, I enter into the legend of Paris-Roubaix," crowed the veteran (38 years and 8 months), now the oldest winner ever, having edged out the Belgian Pino Cerami (38 years and 1 month, in 1960) for this symbolic honor.

Ballerini was crushed. His dream had fallen only 8 centimeters short. What a nightmare! "I'll never return to Paris-Roubaix," he vowed. When a journalist asked him if he had committed any errors, the crushed Italian let his immense distress get the better of him: "Yes, I made the mistake of becoming a bicycle racer."

## "In this race, I was as fussy as a fawn"

Gilbert Duclos-Lassalle was past 40 when he finally bade goodbye to the classic of his heart. That was in 1995, the year of

**1993. In an explosion of joy, Duclos celebrates his second consecutive victory after finessing with his breakaway companion, Franco Ballerini of Italy. At the velodrome, the French veteran makes out he's spent and then jumps from behind with a half lap of the track to go, and Ballerini's late charge comes just too late. At 38 years and 8 months, the classic's oldest winner has a right to roar.**

Ballerini's revenge. Later on, the organizers honored him by naming a bridge in Wallers "Gibus," his nickname as a racer, meaning "fancy hat." It seems to date from a stage tour when he nonchalantly donned a hat, and perhaps stuck on account of his high-profile image as a hunter.

His longevity did not stem from any secret but rather from his natural good health and his assiduous daily care. "I was fortunate to receive an excellent constitution from my parents," he gratefully acknowledged. "That allowed me to get through the cold, the rain, and the sun. To that I added the discipline of a strict life, from which I did not deviate. I took care of my body. After every long training ride, I made sure I got a massage. In winter, I went for long walks with my dog. At times I walked 50 kilometers with only an apple in my pocket."

"Whenever a big race approached," recounted Maïté, his wife, "I warned the children to behave because he was on edge. My daughter had the annoying habit of spilling water on the table, and he got furious every time she did that, as if she had opened floodgates! Even when he was at the Tour du Pays Basque, you could feel the tension permeate the house." The

morning of his second Paris-Roubaix victory in 1993, recalled Hervé, who would become a professional racer in his own right, "we waited for him in the hotel lobby. I cried 'Bonjour papa!' But he was so deep in thought that he didn't reply or even look at me. Here I was—anonymous to my own father! That's tough on a 13-year-old." Smiled Duclos-Lassalle, "The day after Paris-Roubaix my entire family was as emotionally spent as I was. It seems that, in this race, I was as fussy as a fawn." J.-L. G.

# Johan Museeuw

**(1996, 2000, 2002)**

## The Lion revived

In 1996, the Mapei team brings anticlimax to the race's centennial edition when three of its stars break clear and ride in a slow-motion parade around the velodrome to hand the victory to team leader Museeuw. Even so, the race isn't without its emotion, as here, when an angry Museeuw threatens a motorcyclist who, blinded by the dust, almost causes the Belgian to crash.

During the 1990s, Johan Museeuw was the racer who best personified a lion, the symbol of Flanders. In northern cycling races, black icons of that animal often appear on banners with a yellow background, proudly hoisted by Flemish fans. Just as Basque flags flourish in the foothills of the Pyrénées whenever a Tour stage passes by, so, too, does the lion of Flanders abound along the routes of the Ronde van Vlaanderen (Tour of Flanders in the local dialect) and Paris-Roubaix.

The Flanders lion left large and deep footprints on both sides of the Franco-Belgian border, especially along the cobblestone roads of northern France. These tracks lead directly to the radiant persona of the highly disciplined Museeuw. Perhaps the images that stand out most in retrospect are the three times he stood in the center of the velodrome of Roubaix to collect his trophies (1996, 2000, 2002). But just as vivid, if deeply disturbing, is the agonizing look on his face when he gravely injured a leg in the trench of Arenberg in 1998.

Museeuw's intimate affair with Paris-Roubaix began in 1994, when he barely lost out in the pursuit of Andreï Tchmil over a swampy course. Two years later, he had joined a powerful Italian-Belgian coalition, the Mapei team, which reigned grandly over all the northern French and Flemish classics.

In principle, having an abundance of strengths is no handicap on the booby-trapped route of Paris-Roubaix, where it is best to have a few cards to play to overcome the hazards. And yet. . . .

In the 1996 edition, three racers led the pack 86 kilometers from the finish line, all members of the Mapei team. They were Johan Museeuw, Gianluca Bortolami, and Andrea Tafi. They had long fought for a common cause. But as the end of the race loomed, a bitter internal conflict arose. Who would win this race? Or, perhaps more to the point, who should win it?

"That would be I," asserted Museeuw to the two Italians, basing his claim on the unspoken rules that govern the hierarchical world of professional cycling.

Why the Belgian? Because, of the three, he was the best-known racer. But the two Italians merely scowled, prompting Museeuw to confront each one individually: "Who is the leader of this team—you or I?"

The Italians acceded to Museeuw's wishes, and they even took care to wait for him after he flatted 8 kilometers from the velodrome. But the squabble continued, turning now to the thorny issue of who would get second place. By default, that would fall to Bortolami, thanks to his victory in the World Cup of 1994. Tafi nonetheless pleaded that he would be a father for the third time within hours, and that a second-place finish could have a positive impact on his nursery.

"To put an end to all these discussions, I put my foot down," recounted Patrick Lefévère, the directeur sportif and mentor to the Flemish star. "I imposed a sequence in line with their respective rankings: first, Museeuw; second, Bortolami; and third, Tafi." Lefévère even consulted by telephone with Giorgio Squinzi, the CEO of Mapei, a multinational corporation specializing in chemical products and based in Milan. The latter eventually went along with the plan, but not before exploring all the possibilities. "Couldn't they all cross the finish line at the same time and share the victory?" Squinzi asked innocently. Replied Lefévère, "No, that's impossible. There must be a first, second, and third finisher." Squinzi thought for

a moment. "Very well, then. Let all three of my racers arrive at the velodrome at the same time. Then you can decide the order of finish."

Lefévère's decision nonetheless proved highly controversial. "The three Mapei racers displayed a lack of decency and self-control before millions of television viewers," thundered Jean-Marie Leblanc, the director of the race, who had the distinct impression that the public dickering had brought discredit to his event. "Their machinations have led fans to conclude that this race lacks the proper sporting spirit."

The headlines in the Italian press seethed with anger on a different score. "Scandal at Roubaix" (*Corriere dello Sport*); "A Betrayal for Its 100th Edition" (*Tutto Sport*); "An Italian Sponsor Against Italians" (*Corriere della Sera*); "The Italians Give Away Paris-Roubaix" (*Gazzetta dello Sport*).

This harsh reaction, along with other vitriolic commentaries, deeply disturbed Squinzi. "I am very disappointed with the Italian press and its chauvinist reaction," he said. "Enzo Ferrari was right not to want an Italian leader for his fleet of F1s, fearing that sooner or later that arrangement would lead

Third in 1995, winner in 1996, third again in 1997, Museeuw has big hopes for 1998. Unhappily, he crashes on the mud-slick cobbles of the Arenberg forest and breaks his left knee. The grim-faced race doctor, Gérard Porte (at right), helps the Belgian to an ambulance, unaware that the mud-infected wound will turn gangrenous.

Museeuw wins his second Paris-Roubaix in 2000. Two years after almost losing his leg to gangrene, his comeback is called a miracle, one that he shares with the crowd by pointing to his left knee as he reaches the finish line.

to major problems. Next year, I will either get out of cycling altogether or I will build a team without Italians."

As it turned out, he did not make good on either of those threats.

## In 2000, a battered leg displayed in victory

Museeuw deserved far more than a tainted victory in Paris-Roubaix. To get something better than that, he had to wait four long years. For in 1998, halfway through his legitimate quest, the accident occurred. He fell heavily in the muddy trenches at Arenberg, shattering a kneecap into numerous pieces. A serious infection followed. Museeuw was tormented by the threat of an amputation, which he barely escaped.

Two years later, happily recovered, he donned his battle gear one more time and returned to the scene of the crime. He wore no helmet but rather, in the fashion set by the "pirate" Marco Pantani, he wore a bandana. Naturally, it featured the Lion of Flanders, which was roaring once again.

Crossing the finish line, the usually discreet Museeuw, who had always been careful to hide his sentiments, liberated his battered left leg and lifted it high in the air. At the same time, he pointed to his painstakingly reconstructed kneecap. His was a solitary victory and a stunning comeback after the ordeal of 1998. He richly deserved his monstrous ovation.

This day of great happiness did not, however, fully erase the nightmare of one terrible Sunday—or, for that matter, the large scars still showing on his leg. But at least his mental scars were soothed. "It's a dream, a hugely emotional moment, for it was two years ago almost to the day that I nearly lost my leg," allowed an emotional Museeuw, on the verge of tears. "Many doctors told me to forget about cycling. I worked extremely hard to get back to this level. So naturally, after all that I've been through, there's nothing more beautiful to me than victory in Paris-Roubaix."

The last hurrah for the hero now widely known as the Lion of all Flanders was reserved for spring 2002, in his 37th year. The old warrior had one last score to settle with destiny. A fall in the summer of 2000, this time from a motorcycle, had caused multiple fractures. To enter into the legacy of Paris-Roubaix without having to knock at its door, Museeuw penetrated the velodrome alone one more time, three minutes ahead of his nearest pursuers. He was covered with a thick layer of mud, like a statue of duty accomplished.   J.-L. G.

# Tom Boonen

**(2005)**

## Born on the cobblestones

2005. Tom Boonen is all in but still has the strength to lift the winner's cobblestone. He's from a new generation of winners that eats up the pavé and can smile about it later.

In the spring of 2002, the old lion Johan Museeuw roared victoriously for the last time. On the cobblestones he crossed his successor, a cub who had already developed sharp claws and who had placed himself directly in line for the throne.

The newcomer was Tom Boonen, a name that sounds like a cartoon hero. He's a good-looking young man and a magnificent athlete (1.9 meters and 80 kilos). He is gifted, supple, solid, elegant, intelligent, and even charismatic. In sum, he has everything it takes to succeed.

What's more, he fears no one and nothing (he is seemingly immune to the intense pressure of big events). His Herculean strength is activated by powerful levers and enhanced by a hunched posture calculated to lower his center of gravity.

Boonen has mastered northern routes with such ease that he appears to have been born on the cobblestones. When he was just 21 and a member of the U.S. Postal team, he even rode at a faster clip than his team leader at the time, the American George Hincapie, despite the latter's greater experience.

The strong bond between the cub from Antwerp and the Lion of Flanders was made crystal clear on Easter Sunday 2002, when the neo-professional and the venerable Museeuw fought it out for 235 kilometers over muddy terrain and in cold weather. Without the formidable resistance of the apprentice champion, the older one and his powerful cobblestone-crushing machine would have utterly dominated the race.

"I'm not trying to imitate Museeuw; I just want to be Boonen, that's all," he replied testily as he descended from the third plank of the podium. This declaration should not be interpreted as an idle display of vanity. The prodigy does indeed prefer to distance himself from the living legend of Belgian cycling out of respect for the man and his achievements.

But this respect did not prevent Boonen from publicly denouncing the reception he received from fans stationed along the edges of the road. "In the final stretch, the Flemish spectators whistled at me because I trailed Museeuw. I will never forget that, and I will remind them of that when I become great," he warned with a self-assurance that stunned his listeners. Of those three promises he made—to never forget, to avenge himself, and to become great—he will keep only one. But that is by far the most important one and the only one that really matters: he will in fact become great. He added wisely, "For now, I am only Tom Boonen. It will be a long time before I can equal Johan's career."

## A sprint by the old soldier

The day he bade farewell, in 2004, at the Grand Prix de l'Escaut, Museeuw moved Boonen with a symbolic gesture: he offered the young man the rosary beads he had worn under his jersey. The moment the champion went into retirement, Boonen inherited his role as the leader of Quick Step. The booing of 2002 aside, the spontaneous gift from the Lion of Flanders ensured a deep public affection for his successor.

2005. When two former winners, Jean-Marie Wampers and Johan Museeuw, talk during the race, Wampers says, "Boonen pedals so easily, without any expression on his face, it's obvious he's going to win."

Boonen's victory in the Tour of Flanders on April 3, 2005, brought the Belgian's career to a boiling point. A week later, in Paris-Roubaix, came the formal proof that Belgian cycling had produced its greatest genius and its most precocious cobblestone champion since Roger De Vlaeminck some thirty years before. At the tender age of 24, Boonen would register a double victory in the Tour of Flanders and Paris-Roubaix. This golden boy of the new generation is only the ninth racer in the history of cycling ever to achieve as much. During the French classic, he was especially impressive, eschewing any mistakes. He had patiently awaited his hour to strike without falling into a funk.

Boonen's team showed its confidence in the new leader by initiating a sprint 80 kilometers from the finish line. Nor was Boonen bothered by the fact that his teammates had disappeared before the final stretch. As an amateur, he frequently found himself having to fend for himself, and he knew exactly what to do.

At the velodrome in Roubaix, two other candidates presented themselves: his old leader, George Hincapie, and Juan Antonio Flecha. The American and the Spaniard were fairly fast and experienced riders. And neither nationality has ever won at Roubaix. But it was still not to be their day. Once on the track, the Belgian performed like a wily soldier. Sure of his strength, he waited for the last turn to erupt, and surged ahead at the finish line.

After the race, when Boonen exited the car driven by Jean-Marie Wampers, winner in 1989, Museeuw looked on with bated breath. The former commented to the press, "Boonen pedaled easily, without making a face. It was evident that he would win. At that point I turned to Museeuw and said, 'You see, Johan, the racer before you will certainly win over eleven categories in the world cup [the total number of Museeuw's career victories in that event].' He did not answer me."

On the eve of the Queen of the Classics, Museeuw had speculated about Boonen's prospective victory. "What if Tom wins Paris-Roubaix just a week after he prevailed in the Tour of Flanders?" Museeuw said. "Will he have anything left to shoot for the rest of the season?" A few months later, Boonen gave a resounding answer in Madrid, where he was crowned world champion.    J.-L. G.

2005. Boonen is concentrated, sticking out his tongue, just like Marc Madiot did, on his way to his first Roubaix victory at age 24. There's sure to be more wins down the road.

# CHAPTER XI

# THE ANGELS OF HELL

Paris-Roubaix is a miracle—a living, vibrant monument and a true love affair. It's a unique challenge, dreamt up by capricious organizers, animated by revered racers, praised by clever journalists, followed by loyal fans, and preserved by exceptional friends.

**Fever pitch**
**1939**

Émile Masson has barely finished the race before his father (center), a former champion himself, along with journalists, race followers, and spectators, come to congratulate him, question him, and tap him on the shoulder. It's a certain excitement that Masson, the oldest living Roubaix winner, now in his nineties, will never forget.

**A living fresco
1986–1989**

To transform the cobblestones
into a work of art, or Paris-Roubaix
into a giant, living masterpiece
that features the racers and the
spectators, was maybe not a
dream of the Flemish masters, but
Algerian artist Mohamed Ben
Bella did it in 1986. His colorful
treasure survived for four years.

# The guardians of the temple

Milan-San Remo and the Tour of Lombardy proceed from the land of the commedia dell'arte; Liège-Bastogne-Liège and the Tour of Flanders arose from ancient Flemish mysteries. Bordeaux-Paris and Paris-Brest-Paris represent formats that have largely disappeared due to their excessive lengths and overly demanding formats. Then there's Paris-Roubaix. It remains a distinct and exemplary race—the only one, in fact, to have largely preserved, since its creation in 1896, the same drama, the same environs, a similar route, and even, in some sense, a similar fan base. It is the unchangeable and obligatory challenge, cycling's own living museum.

Here, when dust does not give the racers a face of flour, it's because rain has fixed upon them a mask of mud instead. Here, the battle between legend and reality is authentic. The racers fall, moan, curse, flat, restart, and bleed.

Paris-Roubaix thrives on drama and mystique. The race still harkens back to the song-and-dance shows characteristic of the region's carnivals and Mardi Gras celebrations of long ago. It has long been held on Easter Sunday. And that's no coincidence.

Jean Bobet once wrote that his famous brother, Louison, celebrated Easter Sunday. But Jean did not mean that his brother attended a church service or indulged in the traditional seasonal cakes from Provence. Rather, Jean meant that his brother partook in the bicycle race that in some quarters has become practically synonymous with the holiday itself (it is even known in France as La Pascale, or the Easter event). For Roubaix, after all, is in the north of France, where pointed cabbage heads and round beet plants abound. Where the hills are so eroded that even if you placed one on top of the other, you still wouldn't have an ascent comparable to that of the mighty Mont Ventoux. And when you speak of shells around here, chances are you don't mean the almond-filled desserts of Carpentras, but rather the ubiquitous cobblestones of sandstone or granite that the locals tolerate much as they do codfish oil—by holding their nose before swallowing.

## A tapestry of motion

Or course, the actors and spectators have changed since 1896. But they become like figures in a fresco—preserved for eternity in a kind of "tapestry of motion," as the journalist Antoine Blondin put it one windy day. Yes, the Queen of the Classics, with its 40 or 50 kilometers of cobblestone, now belongs to the golden legend of cycling. To win at Roubaix is to touch the Holy Grail. Whether they devour or finesse the cobblestones, all those who finish Paris-Roubaix, all those who savor the rejuvenating showers at the velodrome, have acquired an aura with which nothing else compares, not even finishing the Tour. As much here as there, one becomes a giant of the road.

The spectators are not mistaken about the beauty of this race. If you take a good look at them, you'll see that they are no ordinary fans. They not only line the route, they help to create and preserve its character. At one point, they plant a "Giant of the North," one of the obligatory carnival characters seen at festivals throughout the Pas-de-Calais province. In another, they have revived a long-abandoned windmill just to enhance the local scenery. Elsewhere, they applaud wildly, many with hands full of calluses as a result of having volunteered before the race to reset stray cobblestones. Over there, in the trench of Wallers-Arenberg, you might find the movie director Claude Berri. In 1992 when he came to shoot outtakes for his film *Germinal*, he could not resist alluding to certain figures germane to this race.

The first and most important of these, even if he is not much in evidence today, was no doubt Philippe Auguste. This Capetian king reigned from 1180 to 1223. It was he who ordered that his kingdom be paved with cobblestones, and it was he who crushed Otto IV, the emperor of Germany, and his ally the count of Flanders, at Bouvines, near the race's crossroads at l'Arbre. And with a godfather like Philippe Auguste, how could this race have become anything but a fierce, hand-to-hand struggle?

## Jules Verne too

The second major benefactor of this race was a certain Victor Breyer, a journalist with *Le Vélo*, the newspaper that initiated this competition. After the inaugural run, widespread complaints about its difficulty and bad weather nearly forced Breyer to abandon a second running. He himself was a former cycling champion who had covered only a portion of the route by bicycle; the rest he had traversed in one of the first automobiles.

**René Deruyk (with Jacques Anquetil)**
**1983**

An excellent journalist at *La Voix du Nord*, René Deruyk didn't miss reporting a single edition of Paris-Roubaix from 1955 to 1989. Besides getting several scoops on stars like Fred De Bruyne, Noël Foré, and Felice Gimondi, Deruyk wrote a memorable book about the race titled *Les Dessous du Pavé* (The Hidden Side of the Cobblestones).

Passing through Amiens, Breyer made the acquaintance of the third major figure in this saga, a certain Jules Verne, author of *Journey to the Center of the Earth*, *Twenty Thousand Leagues Under the Sea*, and other noted works. But in this race, you don't go underground or underwater. You just have to stay balanced on the frequently slippery and treacherous cobblestones, which, in Verne's time, also meant holding tight to the handlebars of a bicycle with no brake and a fixed gear. Not an easy assignment by any means.

This grand outdoor adventure proved even more amusing to the writer in that Amiens, his city, was at the midpoint of the race and the place where the difficulties started. Rumor has it that Verne furnished the first-place prize money in 1896, generally attributed to the Welshman Arthur Linton. Be that as it may, Verne was indeed fascinated by the pneumatic clincher tires made by Dunlop and how they could solve the problem of shock absorption. The clouds of dust raised by the pioneers also made him recall the Siberian treks on horseback undertaken by Michael Strogoff, the intrepid imperial messenger in his novel of the same name.

If we can suppose that Verne closely followed the exploits of his neighbor, the diminutive Italian racer Maurice Garin, we can be equally certain that he would have noticed Victor Bagré, a renowned professional walker. The latter got a chance to teach the kings of the pedal a lesson, the first editions of Paris-Roubaix being wide open. Alas! He discovered that cycling competition, even if halting at times, was indeed an acquired art. The neophyte finished 24th, 8 hours behind the winner. Nevertheless, the audacious Bagré earned his place in the race's hall of fame, next to Théodore Vienne and Victor Pérez, the two industrialists from Roubaix who teamed up with *Le Vélo* to organize the contest and have it end in their velodrome.

## A race with many twists

In 1895, these weaving specialists built a velodrome in the middle of Barbieux Park. This patch of green in the heart of the city was originally intended to give the city's numerous textile works a clean break from the dozens of grimy chemical plants where they worked hunched over, ten hours a day, six days a week. But while the residents of the wool capital of France were inclined to applaud bicycle racers, they were also drawn in

their meager spare time to the 2,400 local cafés. Vienne and Pérez, creative entrepreneurs, shrewdly recognized that having a road race end on their premises would help attract a whole new clientele.

Before long, they also realized that they could expand the format to bring in even larger crowds. They thus created a similar race for motorcycles and light automobiles. They failed, however, to adopt new security measures and, inevitably, tragedies followed. In April 1900, a motorcycle veered into a crowd assembled at the forest of Saint-Germain and crushed the leg of a female spectator, whose husband happened to be Charles Bos, a local deputy. In 1898 the race was also opened to pedestrians. The organizers had to slow down the walker Ramogé, who went so fast he threatened to arrive at the velodrome before the crowd. Uninhibited by notions of fair sportsmanship, Mr. Pérez intercepted the fleet champion at Seclin, and forced him to shave, take a bath, and eat lunch before he could resume. Even with the forced delays, Ramogé managed to arrive in Roubaix four hours ahead of the pack. "At least the format was saved," wryly commented the journalist Robert Coquelle, a farsighted witness to those heroic times.

Jules Verne died in 1905. Curiously, that year also marks the emergence of Mr. Accou and Mr. Dussart, two figures from Roubaix who likewise demonstrated a flair for futuristic technology. To be sure, unlike Verne, they were not concerned with submarines or blimps but with something far more mundane. They introduced the "ideal elastic fork" for bicycles. A former pacer in Paris-Roubaix, Mr. Accou designed his spring fork so that it could be installed on all machines in a matter of minutes, to absorb road shock and reduce shaking. We cannot say for sure if Louis Trousselier, Henri Cornet, or Georges Passerieu employed this novelty in their triumphs at this time. But that seems unlikely, considering that Mr. Accou apparently failed to make a fortune.

## Roger Labric, journalist, writer, racer

A happier figure connected to this race is Roger Labric. He was perhaps the only journalist-writer, along with Émile Masson and Jean-Marie Leblanc, to have entered it as a competitor. In 1921, he finished 21st in a memorable contest rendered epic by extreme wind and cold and dominated by the Pélissier brothers. His firsthand impressions are little known (see the anthology at the end of this book), yet he rubbed shoulders with a stars like Costante Girardengo, the first Campionissimo, and also with unknown Flemish racers. He overcame potholes and punctures before reaching the velodrome "following a series of small, complicated roads lined by two rows of stoic spectators who never stopped encouraging us, all the while indicating the route."

A participant in the 1920 Tour, a renowned automobile pilot and a great aviator, Labric was a daredevil who, in the same period, roller-skated on the edge of the Saint-Michel bridge in Paris.

In 1925, another journalist, André Reuze, infiltrated the race's portrait gallery to aggrandize his own reputation. Unlike Labric, however, he was never actually a contestant, nor was he connected to the organizers. Yet he opined in *Le Miroir des Sports*, "As for the famous cobblestones of the North, they are only a factor in automobile races. The cyclists simply roll along the sidewalks in single file. But it's customary to talk about how vexing they are—it makes for greater drama."

In fact, the journalist exaggerated a bit, as is often the case. To convince oneself of this, one need only look at photos of the 1929 Paris-Roubaix,

**Jean-Claude Vallaeys and Alain Bernard**
**2000**

If Paris-Roubaix has survived after overcoming several crises, it's largely due to these two men from the Association des Amis de Paris-Roubaix. They have jealously guarded the heritage of the pavé while putting on exhibitions and receptions with former winners to publicize their cause.

**The passionate Henriette Herbin**
**2005**

Flanked here by technical director Jean-François Pescheux (at left) and race director Jean-Marie Leblanc, Henriette Herbin is an inseparable part of the event. She's another of the Friends of Paris-Roubaix who has worked hard to preserve the cobblestones along the race route.

which produced a new heroic figure, the champion Charles Meunier. Already third in 1928, he won the following year, despite the dust and the cobblestones. And there were quite a few obstacles along the way, especially within cities like Arras. He also had to carefully negotiate his way over the dirt track at the Amédée-Prouvost stadium, like a skilled miner, lest he fall. In fact, Meunier was a real miner, who must have cast a curious glance at the slag heaps and mining villages that the course passed for kilometers on end. Having worn his boots in such environs for years, he knew that riding a bike over cinders was just as dangerous as riding over loose sand. Consequently, when he got to the track, he did not start a sprint—unlike Georges Ronsse, his companion in their breakaway, who promptly fell and had to cross the line with his bicycle draped over his shoulder. The miner smiled softly under a mask of black dust with two blank spots surrounding his eyes, left behind by the large glasses he had just removed.

## Two young faces full of marvel

An uncooperative knee forced the Belgian champion to abandon the race in 1932. He thus had to retreat to the depths of the mine at Hainaut and endure its inglorious dust until he reached the age of 55 years. Truly the stuff of an Émile Zola novel.

Still, this 1932 edition was truly magical. Along with the unfortunate figures of Joseph Curtel and Jean Maréchal, it produced two young faces full of marvel: Henriette Herbine and Jean Devys, who were there observing the racers of Paris-Roubaix for the first time. These two authentic children of the local countryside are still with us today, and their unfailing good nature endures as well.

Jean remembers how his father despaired one day in 1936 when Romain Maës was disqualified from the race, a disappointment that lasted until the Belgian Émile Masson at last erased the bitter memory with his triumph in the 1939 edition. "He finished on the avenue Gustave-Delory," recalls Jean, adding, "In 1943 they arrived at the new velodrome for the first time. I know. I was there."

Each year, Henriette, like Jean, joins the crowd awaiting the racers at the Roubaix velodrome. She nonetheless waxes nostalgic about the assemblies of old. "The giant electronic screens of today, often poorly situated, are no substitute for those old-style rallies, complete with march-

ing bands and majorettes. They used to be such a bonus that three or four hours would go by and I wouldn't even notice."

When it comes to bicycles, they both know what they're talking about. Henriette, an accountant with a local cookie maker, has practiced not only cycling but also swimming and rifle shooting. Jean, for his part, is a master at Ping-Pong and an accomplished cyclist, with numerous traces of Paris-Roubaix under his belt.

Since 1950, they haven't missed a single edition. He has long planted himself at the crossroads of l'Arbre "near the battlefield of the Bouvines and its church with twenty-one stained glass windows 6 meters high." She follows the route and the racers with her car, over the cobblestones dubbed "blue cows" in the Pévèle region. Then she sprints back to the velodrome to see the racers arrive. Today, given the traffic congestion, she is usually a nervous wreck by the time she gets there.

These two cases underscore the fervor, love, and attachment many locals feel in relation to the race, the countryside, and the racers. To tap and encourage this sentiment, Jean-Claude Vallaeys, a local hairdresser, founded in 1981 the highly influential association called the Friends of Paris-Roubaix.

But while Jean Devys knows the entire history of his region bearing on the race, right down to his fingertips, Henriette's passion is simply overwhelming. She can expertly weigh the chances of all the participants, and recount from the bottom of her heart all the delusions and triumphs of the past fifty years. She has experienced them intimately by encouraging, advising, and consoling the racers, at times even waiting it out with their families. Among the stars she has known personally: Duclos-Lassalle, Jalabert, Marie, Durand, Moncassin, Agnolutto, Demeyer, Cerami, and Godefroot.

And since the day she happened to chat with Jean-Marie Leblanc, Henriette has enjoyed excellent relations with the former director of the Tour and of Paris-Roubaix, who is still active in the Amaury Sports Organization (ASO). Leblanc knows that a fan of this caliber is priceless, that she proceeds directly from the soul of this race. Invited to ride in his VIP car during the 2005 edition, Henriette even managed to watch the race from the sky, aboard a helicopter. She's familiar with everything cycle-related, but her passion for Paris-Roubaix knows no bounds. She has acquired all the related cassettes and books—even samples of cobblestones. She has transformed her apartment in Roubaix into a veritable Paris-Roubaix museum.

Jean-Claude Vallaeys is but a humble choirboy next to such a phenomenon. He, too, discovered the race during his childhood. He was born just 300 meters from the track and the café Chez Petrieux, which faces the velodrome, which belonged to his godfather. He was 9 years old in 1949 when he saw his first edition, and what a memorable one that was. Serse Coppi and André Mahé were declared cowinners in a virtual dead heat, several months after the scandal-plagued race ended. At the time, Vallaeys was a bit disoriented by the misdirected Mahé, who failed to enter the stadium at the appropriate point, and by the sprint that favored Fausto Coppi's little brother. Vallaeys was a bit older in 1955, when he strained his ears to overhear a shouting match between the Campionissimo and Louison Bobet in the showers. "The two champions told each other off in no uncertain terms for their failure to pursue Jean Forestier, who consequently enjoyed an easy victory by default."

## Daddy De Bruyne spends a night in his car

An unexpected and precious witness, Vallaeys was back monitoring the race in 1957, hanging out in the family café, into which Belgian fans started flowing on the eve of the race. At the Petrieux café, they discussed the chances of their countrymen while freely enjoying glasses of Picon, a cocktail banned at that time in their homeland. That particular year, the father of Fred De Bruyne had a few too many, and he spent the night dozing in his car. He was still there the next afternoon, his tickets to the velodrome in hand, when his son crossed the finish line as the surprise winner.

But Vallaeys's greatest memory dates from 1984, when his student, Alain Bondue, crossed the finish line in third place. He could have, and should have, won. Still, third place was splendid indeed. Bondue was himself living out a love affair with this race that he had frequented since childhood. At the edge of the route, with his parents, he had seen Eddy Merckx pass by. "That must have been in 1967," he recalls. "It was cold. Merckx had flatted. My ears were glued to my transistor radio. I was 8; I still remember the motorcycle escort."

Bondue remembers every little detail of his own race, every paved sector nearly to the meter. It's staggering. And he recounts like no one else how he entered certain sections trailing, only to gain ground by the exit. Which leads him to say, "Here, bad luck does not make you lose and good luck does not make you win. The race is never lost as long as no one has crossed the finish line." Today, this ex–directeur sportif and consultant follows the race on television. His knowledge of the route is so perfect that, when the commentators misreport the position of the racers, he immediately calls them to set them straight. He is so enamored with Paris-Roubaix, he dreams of the day when one of his racers will win it. At that point he will surely explode with emotion. No other reaction is conceivable.

## René Deruyk's scoops

Bondue's third-place finish in 1984 was a sacred victory, not only for one who grew up on the spot, but also for the entire region so proud of its champion, and for a handful of personal friends like Vallaeys. "It was Jean-Claude who created the Vélo Club in 1966 to enliven the track," recalls his friend Devys. "He was also the only one who believed in Paris-

Roubaix when it was threatened, the only one who wanted to save it even if he had to move heaven and earth. Few would have thought this modest barber on de Lannoye street was up to the task."

Before he enjoyed his retirement at Anduze, Vallaeys found a worthy successor in Alain Bernard. But that transition did not prevent Vallaeys from crossing France, helter-skelter, whenever the Friends of Paris-Roubaix held an important meeting or received an exceptional guest, like Émile Masson, winner of the 1939 edition, who recently visited Roubaix at the age of 90. Jean Devys and Henriette Herbin in particular were deeply moved to see the old champion whom they had applauded roadside as children.

René Deruyk represents a modern version of Labric or Reuze, with one small difference: he is actually from the area, being a journalist with *La Voix du Nord*. Perceptive, clever, jovial, and talented, Deruyk has covered the contest thirty-five times, from 1955 to 1989, with such insight that he has become without a doubt a major figure of this epic.

With him, you are smack in the middle of the classic. Examples of his acuity are to be found by the dozens in his reference book *Les Dessous du Pavé* (The Hidden Side of the Cobblestones). For example, Belgian journalists have maintained that their compatriot Fred De Bruyne had to brake in the 1956 edition, to let his teammate Louison Bobet pass him. But Deruyk extracted from the Belgian racer a firm and droll denial: "No, I didn't brake—I just stopped pedaling." In 1959, Deruyk knew before anyone else that Nöel Foré would win Paris-Roubaix. Eight days earlier, when the racer had finished the Tour of Flanders in last place, he had confided in the journalist, "No, there's nothing wrong with me. I'm just preparing for Paris-Roubaix, which I will win."

He was still there in 1966 when Felice Gimondi's team, along with its team director, Luciano Pezzi, conducted a secret reconnaissance mission to scout out the route. He knew then and there that they were serious about winning the race, which they did. Gimondi would even enhance his already stellar image by performing a remarkable 40-kilometer solo breakaway.

Once he gets the heroes to make their confessions, he is in the enviable position of being able to hustle over to the newspaper office—a mere fifteen-minute car ride away—and get right down to work. Some things, however, he chooses not to reveal. For example, that Guillaume Driessens, the celebrated directeur sportif, had been a bad sport once again—deliberately opening his car door to impede those in pursuit of his racers.

## Françoise, the mother hen of Paris-Roubaix

Two more inescapable figures are Françoise, the owner of the café of the same name, at the entrance of the first paved sector at Troisvilles, and Yorann Vandriessche, the owner of the celebrated Taverne de l'Arbre, at the crossroads near Roubaix where the race is often decided.

At Chez Françoise, customers savor the famous runny Omelet Maroille all year long, but especially in the period starting fifteen days before and one month after Paris-Roubaix. For over ten years the race regulars have lined up here. They are part of the family and, if the bar is full, they sit down in the adjacent dining room. Here you meet people from all over France and Italy, organizers, journalists, high school students, and even ex-champions like Raymond Piotte and Jean Stablinski.

**Madame André Farine**
**2004**

It's thanks to this widow of a passionate race supporter and editor of the *Nord Éclair* newspaper that all the sails on the windmill at Vertain—site of one of the rough sections of cobblestones—now greet the racers every year.

They have come to show that, even if they have lost their pedal stroke, they are still pretty deft with their forks. And when Françoise places her 3-meter-tall giant statue in front of the café, known as the "small Françoise," it signifies that judgment day is not far off.

At Yorann's tavern, the ambiance is unique. A stone's throw from the battlefield of Bouvines, the place is conveniently located and the décor exceptional. It boasts five fresco murals by Christian Guillaume, alias Teel, the superb cartoon artist, cycling fan, and illuminator of the race that has gotten under his skin. Roubaix, as all the winners know, is just 15 kilometers away. It is here where the racers hit the wall and come unstitched. There is ample dust and mud. Some, like Johann Museeuw, wore helmets and glasses. Others, like Eddy Merckx, Roger De Vlaeminck, Francesco Moser, and Rik Van Looy, did not. The establishment is open all year long—except the day of the race.

## Ben Bella, the cobblestone painter

When the racers pass by the hill of Templeuve, they can admire the fully functional windmill at Vertain, which salutes them with all its wings in motion. It is operational now in large part thanks to Mrs. André Farine, the widow of the former editor-in-chief of *Nord Éclair*. Her husband was a long and fervent fan of Paris-Roubaix who appreciated its broad appeal to cycling fans and the general public. In her own magical way, his spouse has managed to extend their shared passion.

It's a passion that allows certain dreams to come true. The painter Mohamed Ben Bella, for example, aspires to bring art—so often an elitist pursuit—directly to the people. So it was that he conceived of a work that would forgo the canvas and transform an ordinary object of everyday life into an expression of art: a road. That's right, he wanted to paint a road. After he was refused permission to alter the main arteries at Lille and Tourcoing, he, a sports fan and a former soccer standout, set his sights on the small, declassified roads of Paris-Roubaix. Those used but once a year and made of cobblestone, naturally.

The idea appealed to Jean-Claude Vallaeys and the race organizers, notably Jacques Goddet. Even the local council and the roads department were open to the idea, provided that the artist not make the road any more slippery. Ben Bella was energized at the prospect of having a canvas 12 kilometers long and 3 meters wide. He was thrilled at the idea of

"creating a work of art on which peasants, champions, riverside residents, and tourists alike can circulate and live." It was to be something truly unprecedented. The multicolored serpent took form near Gruson, and wound up at Hem with a finishing flourish. It was no easy task, as it would take eighteen tons of red, blue, and white paint, which then had to be injected with sand to make it nonslippery. He had to import the red from Berlin and the blue from London. And he had to paint.

The result of this epic undertaking surprised the participants and followers of the 1986 edition. "Moser was afraid he would fall down," Ben Bella confides, "but he quit before he got there. As for Sean Kelly, the Irish winner, he told me it cheered him up." The racers in three subsequent editions would profit again from the coloring of Hell, before the combined effects of rain, snow, ice, and pedestrian use returned the cobblestones to their original gray. "Jacques Goddet wanted to renew the operation, but for me it was a onetime proposition," explains Ben Bella, adding, "It took the jubilee of Duclos-Lassalle to induce me to paint all those cobblestones one by one." The artist still gets goose bumps whenever he sees the champions mount their bikes. But, at this point, he shows his appreciation by offering them monster blocks to display proudly above their fireplace. A painted cobblestone makes for a sacred trophy indeed. Vallaeys may have had the original idea of awarding the winner a cobblestone trophy, but Ben Bella has added a unique artistic dimension.

This initiative that embellished the legend appealed to Jean Stablinski, who is perhaps the most sympathetic figure in this portrait gallery. An authentic miner of the deep, he returned to ground level to become an immense champion. He was the one who, in 1968, told organizers about an obscure cobblestone section of road near Arenberg, in the woods at Wallers where he used to gather edible boletus when he was not hunting there. He knew it would make the race even more difficult, and thus enhance its declining image. During that 1968 edition, when Stablinski entered the trench and struggled to keep his balance, he thought movingly about his old companions who had continued to extract coal 300 or 400 hundred meters below. As the visionary Antoine Blondin wrote in 1955, "Hell is worthy of this place."

SERGE LAGET

**The sidewalks
1925**

According to writer André Reuze, in the 1920s, the competitors shouldn't be condemned for riding on the sidewalks instead of the cobblestones. At the time, there are so many cobbled sections that the organizer doesn't bother to count them. Things have changed over the years.

### Jean Stablinski
### 2004

It's not by chance that Jean Stablinski is wearing a red jacket. He's one of the devils of the Hell of the North, who in 1968, when still a racer, tipped off the organizers about this now infamous section of pavé in the Wallers-Arenberg forest. Before that, he was a miner who worked underground no more than 300m away from this place where the racers suffer. Quite a destiny.

### The inspection
### 2004

Is the trench still practicable? Amaury Sport Organization competitions director Jean-François Pescheux (at right) and Jean-Claude Vallaeys from the Friends of Paris-Roubaix (center) have come to see for themselves. A few changes are needed, mainly from the standpoint of crowd and rider safety, before the race finds its Alpe d'Huez.

**The Carrefour de l'Arbre
2002**

It was closed down once,
but the tavern at the famous
Carrefour de l'Arbre's pavé
section is in business again,
perhaps ladling out riders'
"grimace" soup, much to the
pleasure of the fans who
watch the key breakaways
form here.

**Homage
2005**

At the Arbre, they really
applaud, as if to thank the
riders who've already
survived for 250km and
have enough respect for the
race to carry on to the finish.
There's always new history
in the making.

**Chez Françoise**
**2004**

At Troisvilles, just before the
first section of pavé, the Chez
Françoise café has become a
favorite rendezvous for race
followers, journalists, and
organizers. Here, over a
runny omelet made by the
welcoming Françoise, the
race goes into orbit yet again.

# LETTERS
# OF NOBILITY

The author René Fallet (at left) and his friend Georges Brassens, the famed singer/poet, follow the race in 1971. Raymond Poulidor comes to meet them before the start. The French racer knows Fallet very well, but Brassens only by reputation. Proud to be there, Brassens is struck by the serenade of the cars' klaxons, the length of the race, and the finish on the velodrome.

A handful of French celebrities have managed to watch Paris-Roubaix as official race followers. They range from volcano expert Haroun Tazieff to singer Georges Brassens, and include filmmaker Louis Malle, artist Jacques Faizant, former prime ministers Edouard Balladur and Pierre Mauroy, comedian Raymond Devos, and the stuntman Rémy Julienne. All were struck by the rigors of the race and the heroism shown by the racers. Among these rare witnesses are a few writers. We rediscovered in the columns of *L'Équipe* the accounts of their experiences in the Hell of the North. Some, like the frequent observers of pro cycling Antoine Blondin, René Fallet, and Louis Nucéra, are hardly unexpected guests at this rendezvous on the cobblestones. But there are also complete surprises, including screenwriters Alphonse Boudard and Guy Lagorce, novelists Georges Conchon and Yves Gibeau, authors Guy Croussy and Jean-Edern Hallier, film director and novelist Sébastien Japrisot, and journalist Françoise Xénakis. The first great witness, who recounts a race in which he actually participated, was Roger Labric, in 1920. . . .

## 1920
# The misfortunes of a Paris-Roubaix
BY ROGER LABRIC (1893–1962)

*A writer, journalist, aviator and car racer, this phenomenon was also a bicycle racer. Roger Labric, whose brother was the mayor of the free community of Montmartre, participated in both the Tour de France and Paris-Roubaix in 1920. Here's the proof.*

Before I wrote about this race, I wanted to experience firsthand the effort and the suffering of a racer launching himself, on a bicycle that was still far too heavy, over the horrible roads of the postwar era.

We started out as 140 "toughies," for it was cold that morning, down in the Suresnes neighborhood of Paris, just in front of the Belle Gabrielle café. And by the climb up to Pecq, before reaching the Saint-Germain forest, the peloton had already splintered into several groups riding in jerseys already covered in mud. It had rained all night long. Just before Lens, tragic in its ruins, we took to a rugged and punishing route alongside the old battlefield with its poorly filled potholes that really tested our rims and forks.

My first puncture, just after Meru, threw me to the ground, right where another racer was changing a tire. He wore a tri-colored jersey, covered by an oily sleeveless vest that passed as a rain jacket. It was Costante Girardengo, the reigning Tour of Italy champion. A malfunctioning pump compounded his troubles. I passed him mine and then we took off together toward our destination, chasing a peloton that was in echelons, racing into an icy wind. Not having, as I soon realized, the same cadence as the Italian campionissimo, I had to drop off his wheel and regretfully let him rejoin the lead group alone, just before the feed zone at Amiens.

As the kilometers passed and the low sky remained menacing with gusting snow, riders dropped out one after the other, even the champions. With no higher ambition than to finish, I resolved to soldier on. After Arras, I rolled along for some time drafting a sort of blond giant, who raved on in an incomprehensible dialect. He was, it appears, a Flemish racer whose name I never did discover.

He dropped me too, and I was all alone when I arrived at the Stadium of Roubaix, after following a series of small, complicated roads between two lines of stoic fans who never stopped encouraging us, and all the while showing us the way.

I didn't have to complete the obligatory lap around the cinder track where Paul Deman had triumphed earlier. He, too, had been well behind the estimated time schedule. An official handed me a pen to sign the finishing sheet.

Alas, a thousand times alas! I was so cold that my numb fingers couldn't hold the pen properly. My scribbling was worse than illegible.

The race was judged truly hard, very hard, as much by the bad weather as by the deplorable state of the roads, which had become as slick as billiard tables.

In spite of four punctures, I had completed one of the most punishing editions of Paris-Roubaix the sport of cycling had ever known.

In the name of the fraternity of journalists, I could not have asked for more.

(This appeared in *L'Équipe* in 1950.)

## 1954
# The spire over a pointed arch
BY GABRIEL AROUT (1909–1982)

*This playwright and screenwriter (including* The Cracks, *directed by Alex Joffé), a friend of Jacques Goddet, was also inspired by Paris-Roubaix.*

Among the many peculiarities of our time is one based on a misguided notion: the passion for originality.

It's never easy for an author to write about simple, commonplace ideas or themes already addressed by great writers before him. But there was a time long ago when contemporary painters and authors made it a point of honor to apply their talents to the same subject. And they were right to do so, as true originality does not consist of inventing the "never before seen," but rather showing some character, not necessarily unique, in everyday situations. That is what truly distinguishes an original author.

If five authors were to write five plays this year about the story of Jesus and Judas, critics might complain that this was four plays too many. But I would happily see all five, and I am sure that each one would interest and enrich me.

So what have these philosophical musings to do with Paris-Roubaix? you might ask.

Well, if it is true, as Jean Giraudoux claimed, that his *Amphitryon* was the 38th production of the nineteenth-century play, then yesterday we witnessed the creation of the 52nd Paris-Roubaix. And this living work of art, vivid, diabolically loud, resonant, panoramic, and rich in color, like the most modern movie, is timely confirmation of my thesis. Because this production, different every year, is nothing more than a retelling of the same subject.

The facts are simple. Some two hundred guys on bicycles cover a ribbon of roads always over a similar distance, terrain, and surface, driven by a common desire to finish their tiring trip in the front. Even so, each one of the preceding fifty-one races from Paris to Roubaix had its own special character.

And what similarities there may have been were due to the similar atmospheric conditions and the temperament of the men who played a preponderant role in the outcome. It's a fact that the heat, the rain, and the head or tail winds play the role of a tragic, comic, humorous, or melodramatic inspiration in the structure of a race, as they do in the path followed by an architectural project.

Nevertheless, within these similarities, there's always a singular and mysterious element that justifies the curiosity, the infatuation of the crowds . . . and the individuals.

A bicycle race is a collective production, a work of art that's built like a cathedral: a solid, compact, and almost squared-off mass at the base, which then stretches upward, thinning out and sharpening itself like a bell tower, to leave at its extremity a single man, his arms raised in victory, crossing the symbolic line that marks the end of the work.

And also like a cathedral, it is the work of countless anonymous workers, who build and decorate it, enrich and perfect it, to the best of their abilities, leaving us in the end with but one name from among the many, as if to underscore the fact that from the beginning each one had an equal right to sign off on the project.

Incidentally, this point applied well to yesterday's race. The 52nd Paris-Roubaix, slowed by an unfavorable wind, kept the solid form of its base for a long time, before it soared above the pointed arch defined by the twelve early breakaways so that a group of great and small masters—Petrucci, Hassenforder, Fornara, Koblet, Papazian, Bobet, Kübler, Rémy, Scodeller, Surbatis, and Blusson—finally put their stamp on in a flamboyant proliferation of points and embellishments, until its final spire emerged in the chubby figure of a valiant and potent little Belgian named Impanis.

## 1955
## Black faces

BY YVES GIBEAU (1916–1994)

*A journalist and writer, the author of* La Ligne Droite *and* Allons z'enfants, *this lover of sports was also a regular contributor to* L'Équipe *in the 1950s.*

The followers of bicycle races are like innocent disciples of the Marquis de Sade. At the start of Paris-Roubaix, all of them bundled up, they go and sound out the mood of the riders, look with a jovial air at their frozen thighs dotted with goose bumps, and say with a compassion masking their feigned despair, "It's not so warm, is it guys? What a weird spring! You're going to have to move around, right?"

And in getting back into their cars, the followers plead with all their heart, barring terrible heat that can also be infernal, for rain, wind, sleet, or snow, the other imponderables of our legendary cycling classics, along with renewed bravery and surprises, imagining what the famously slippery stretch between Moncheaux and Mons-en-Pévèle will be like if God or the devil cares to intervene on this Sunday devoted to the joys and indulgences of Easter.

Right on schedule, a fine, cold rain came down. After the jolting climb at Doullens, the peloton was splintered into several groups of dripping-wet, frozen racers, their faces the color of their team jerseys like red or violet, yellow or white, shrouds.

Fausto Coppi, his racing cap crumpled, his locks of black hair stuck to his forehead, is nothing less than an emperor, and this *commedia dell'arte*, an impromptu Italian play, was suddenly enriched by a walk-on actor of quality battling the wind and cold and also, no doubt, a crazy temptation to renounce everything—job, pride, paycheck—to return home on different roads and eat eggs with his family. The once dapper and dashing riders, greeted with cheers of admiration by the inebriated crowd, were already assuming the somber masks, like characters in Dante's *Inferno*, before descending into hell.

The villages and towns, far from being cordial, offered a prison's blackened brick walls, the streets devastated where gutters, gullies, and ruts were just so many traps, and where the old mine shafts bristled with disparate scrap metal eerily resembling a line of gallows. As if no one dared be alone to confront the dreaded road of the cross awaiting them after Moncheaux, the grave-looking racers passed through the village elbow to elbow, knowing full well that within a few hundred meters they would split up despite themselves and their collective will and that solidarity would no longer be appropriate.

The race followers were getting what they wanted, beyond their wildest dreams. The road had become a quagmire where the machines skidded with every push on the pedals. Roadside bike paths, which the uninitiated had counted on to reduce their torture, resembled rutted dirt paths pitted with open sewers where ghosts of men, their fingers numb, their thighs frozen, collapsed and could not go on.

In the land of coal miners, other black-faced workers had come as a source of Sunday entertainment with the strength of their legs, their breath, and their stubbornness. Their team jerseys had no more symbolic power. The names Mercier, Gitane, La Perle, Bianchi, had all disappeared. There was total anonymity beneath the coating of mud, mixed with dirty water, sweat, and maybe even some tears. We could barely distinguish, among the contorted faces, the pinkish wounds of their mouths, which were edged with a trace of foam.

Every time a lone rider brushed against the fans, on tearing his bicycle away from the coal-like deposit, they would yell at him from the pit of their stomachs: "It's almost over, buddy! It's over—go!"

Even the strongest of them, those who were presumably prepared for all the pitfalls, for all the martyrdom—and I'm thinking in particular of Antonin Rolland—shake their heads like condemned prisoners who we vainly encourage before the big sleep, ready to swear, if they could have unglued their lips, that they would never do this again.

At least not till next year.

## 1956
## Cobblestones at the base of the "big throat"

BY ANDRÉ DUQUESNE (1911–1979)

*A prolific Belgian author of whodunits under the pseudonym Peter Rand (some three hundred novels, including* Une Poupée dans le Tour, *in collaboration with Ange Bastiani), Duquesne, born in Marcinelle in Flanders, also brought his magnifying glass to cycling's Hell. He inevitably encountered plenty of victims and an executioner.*

They told me it was Hell; you bet it was! In the beginning, in spring sunshine as bawdy as a dirty old man with three chicks, we're about to have a good laugh because our chauffeur Pugneite has accidentally smashed his liter of wine instead of drinking it. At least the red is in play.

We scramble away, just ahead of the peloton. And then we wait for them to catch up. No, forget that! At Chantilly eleven guys have already broken away and it's our job to follow them. I'm having a chuckle, too, as their Hell, right now, is more pastoral than anything else. It's fun, as pleasant as you can imagine, full of pretty girls on the sidewalks. . . . For sure, there are some motorcyclists . . . and, yes, they whistle nonstop, but no one cares a whit about them. . . . To amuse ourselves, we start a betting pool. A small one, mind you, not what you might think, just one to predict the winners. I pick Van Steenbergen, Ockers, and Impanis. The others are all born losers, so I laugh to myself. Good. The race hasn't changed: still eleven guys relaying each other well, but they have no chance. Just cycling claptrap. In this sport, you have what we call the "big guns," that is, the guys who have huge calves and something extra in their noodles—smart enough not to show themselves until the final 50 kilometers. Those eleven, they're big too, but I won't say big whats. . . .

At Hénin-Liétard, the shadow of the great Gaston Rebry is cast over the race. He's one big gun! They call him "The Executioner." "And what about Hell?" I ask, with a smile that's half-facetious, half-serious.

And then we were there. Oh, my God! It was a certain Garnault, a race official, who revealed it, and Paris-Roubaix had again found an executioner. He showed us the way. All of a sudden, there was a turn . . . not even a right angle. And the Garnault in question, his face coal-black above his red vest, seemed like he was pitching us in with his satanic gesticulations. As Hell, it was no doubt nothing awful, but as a road, it evoked mass murder or a Chicago slaughterhouse. A true monster. A road . . . no, let's just say a dirty thingamajig that doesn't even resemble a road. It is a stingy two meters wide. Down the middle, the cobblestones are humped like a donkey's back—a pig-headed donkey at that. And then there are the shoulders of flint, cinders, and the like—nothing but holes with a little edging around them.

Into that Hell, a fantasia of cars, motorcycles, and bicycle racers launch themselves like lemmings. God recognizes his own here. The countryside has a cloud of dust over it, as if it's hiding its face, and it screams, squeals, creaks, and cries out in agony. In the distance looms the eerie silhouette of a monstrous slag heap. Below a sky they no longer see, their tires moaning and brakes squealing, the racers suddenly appear as if possessed. And just as quickly there's nothing. It's like the serenity one finds in the mountains following an avalanche . . . a total calm. The road appears to be solid, and even has true edges. They look at it, dumbfounded.

A trifling cop motions us forward. He thinks that we still have somewhere to go when in fact we have just left something huge, breathless and disoriented.

We have lost the peloton in there but we know whoever emerges in front won't be just anyone. Then there's the velodrome, the finish line, and the thundering crowd that's wisely penned in and obediently unruly. The finish is no more than a formality to settle our bets. My friend Radice has bet on the top three. That's so cunning. He's a pervert; by playing the top three, he knew he couldn't lose.

They told me it'd be Hell.

## 1959
## The black ballet

BY ANTOINE BLONDIN (1922–1991)

*Writer, novelist, winner of the 1959 Interallié Prize for* Un Singe en Hiver, *Blondin was also one of* L'Équipe's *most brilliant columnists. His best-selling novel* La Semaine Buisonnière, *along with his carefully crafted columns from twenty-seven Tours de France and the Olympic Games in Rome, Grenoble, and Tokyo, filled several generations of readers with wonder. We wouldn't want to miss his expert eye on the Hell of the North.*

When they requested the honor of participating in this cycling event, each one of the riders apparently owned a distinct personality. One could distinguish between the pretentious and the unpretentious, the plodder on wheels and the dandy of the highways, the rich and the poor, the city rat and the field mouse. Their respective behavior suggested a great diversity in lifestyles, even among their wives, to whom they still seem attached by a certain bond, confirming with their differing views and choice of clothing that a true hierarchy exists between them. It extends as far as their baggage, piled up every which way in the trucks, which doesn't respect the fraternal divide that separates the pigskin from the canvas suitcases. Yet, in truth, the supreme nuance that to our eyes divided them into distinct systems was that the young and the old could coexist in a stormy atmosphere on the same planet. Still, the heart judges whether they're to be cherished or feared, and the spirit aims to choose among them, while the memory consults their palmarès and identification papers to set them apart. They say that the younger, precocious racers have set their sights high this year.

Whatever, an excellent writer once wrote something along these lines: A generation is not made up of individuals of the same age, but by men who make the journey together.

The riders of the 57th Paris-Roubaix illustrated this suggestion beyond all expectations. Hell, just as we are promised in the Last Judgment (whatever the verdict of the finish-line judge), puts everyone on an equal footing—all dead perhaps, but destroyed by the mud, melted in the communal clay lining of a symbolically sumptuous fireplace, beaten down by Satan's boots. From the grand Fausto Coppi down to the modest André Retrain, they all belong, for one day at least, to the same class, where the rain and the wind, the pavé beneath a pool, a pool beneath the pavé, all help create a solidarity of anonymity that is the peloton's *raison d'être*.

On this Sunday, the bitter duel that everyone expected between Jacques Anquetil and Roger Rivière rapidly gave way to a brawl between trash men, suitably unrecognizable, rolling out their garbage cans. The first victim was Jean Robic, a returning warrior, who suffered a nasty blowout. His red jersey, on which one almost expected to see his bicycle manufacturer, "Fatalitas," go up in flames, squirmed at the roadside while his too-old face expressed the hopelessness of a detained child. His small silhouette took its place for a moment in a countryside covered in gray, and then seemed to pop back into the box of lead soldiers from which it never should have left. That bad twist of rubber, truth be told, wiped out poor Robic.

This red light at the tail end of the caravan, this flash in the pan, only highlighted the extraordinary black ballet that was now freely unfolding, without even mentioning the broom wagon where characters hooded in dust buried themselves to gather their courage for another day. As custom dictates, the holiday was at the same time as this race, both forward and back. In the back, Fausto Coppi counted himself fortunate to reach the finish; in the middle, Brik Schotte brandished his 39 years over the stones, before he served himself and uncorked a libation of a similar name at the end of the race; and up front, Noël Foré, who had flatted last year while in the winning break, took full revenge and proved that even a puncture victim has the right to believe in Santa Claus. It's no longer necessary, at this emotional point, to establish a distinction between the young ones and the old ones. All of them, on arriving at the velodrome, seemed to say, "I made it; we've all made it." Then they headed toward the Roubaix boys' school, where a hive of showers sheltered five groups of riders. They were nude for a moment, convenient for those who wanted to come to life again, who wanted a facelift. Then they reclaimed their suitcases and, with them, their sense of etiquette, and we saw them reappear, the small and the big, the ugly and the handsome, the tight-fisted and the astounding, the elegant and the diffident. Then we noticed that the racers who finished were not necessarily the ones we had expected. At last, they rejoined their wives, and asked them, understandably, what they'd been up to all day long.

## 1961

## Every man for himself

BY GUY LAGORCE (BORN IN 1937)

*This brilliant journalist and writer, awarded the Goncourt Prize for his novel* Héroïques *(1980), was also a distinguished international athlete. His strong athletic sensibility comes through in this report.*

At kilometer 56, shortly after Clermont, in a long and beautiful straightaway, we suddenly catch a whiff of our childhoods. The road winds around the side of a small hill. Two children, 10 and 12, pedaling old bicycles with all their might, try to reach the course on a little side road before the racers pass by.

These two awestruck kids: that was us, they are us, all the race followers, several years before the circumstances of life threw us willy-nilly into this incredible world that doesn't disappoint those who believe in it. For "incredible" is not too strong a word. Paris-Roubaix starts like a party and ends like a bad dream. Until Doullens, the follow cars salute one another with jolly blasts of the horn, the different crews exchanging friendly waves, while the riders themselves quietly chat; they say that, after all, this race is like many other races.

Then suddenly, there's Doullens: a long and clear-cut climb that dissects two rows of trees standing to attention. The moment they come off that hill, something has changed; the riders' faces have become serious, their eyes more tired; their mouths become thin lines as they tear along at 55 kilometers an hour.

In the wind, the peloton deploys into wide echelons. Many of the racers, their heads in their handlebars, their hips rocking, lose one, two, five meters, then catch back on, their eyes staring ahead. Once more, they get dropped, then catch back on. It's a very physical race, merciless, of frightening clarity; it's an unbearable hour.

Already at Bailleul, the first slag heaps appear on the horizon, the old mining towns and villages flashing past, as we head through them between two lines of yelling faces at the ends of craning necks.

The fever rises. We rumble faster and faster; the race crushes all. Suddenly, just after Moncheaux, at kilometer 220, a turn like any other plunges the race into Hell. Within 200 meters, everything has changed. The 25 kilometers that follow are virtually indescribable.

It's a narrow maze of wretched roads where one car takes up all the room, wretched roads paved with ruts and humps.

You either persevere or puncture. Those who flat, and they are numerous, will not come back. To the left and to the right, they fall heavily. On their dazed faces, blood blends with the dust. The others pass by without even looking. It's every man for himself.

Behind, amid the lively honking we heard before, follows an infernal racket. Cars, motorcycles, and bikes brush past one another in a prolonged and miraculous balancing act. The race knots and unknots its dramas in an unimaginable scrum. It cries, it shifts, it

yells; it's a terrible din. In one monstrous velo-cacophony, the legend of Paris-Roubaix springs to life.

The brilliant and airborne butterflies of the first 200 kilometers have turned into blackened bugs. In faces of stone, their eyes shine through. The entire race has caught the fever. From a group of nine, whose Hell is pure purgatory, Rik Van Looy bolts clear. Feline and ferocious, he escapes, bursts out. His hips, back, and head remain motionless as his legs pump like pistons on his pedals. Superb! Noël Foré, like a demon, tortures his machine, but he can only watch helplessly as Van Looy's red jersey becomes smaller and smaller. It's over. Every man for himself, and Van Looy is the man who has done it.

Behind, the unhappy and heroic Rolf Wolfshohl pursues his Calvary of falls and flats. He was the one who launched the race into Hell, and it's he that Hell has treated the worst. Christian Raymond, the former amateur champion of France, finishes twenty minutes behind Van Looy. In the shower he repeats, "I don't care. I proved to myself that I was a man, because I suffered, but I still finished." He repeats, "I finished."

Overcome by suffering, he had begun to believe that his ordeal would never end. He, too, had won his own race.

## 1979

## Nasty spring

BY RENÉ FALLET (1927–1983)

*A journalist, writer, and winner of the 1964 Interallié Prize for his* Paris in the Month of August, *and also the author of* Triporteur, Beaujolais Nouveau Est Arrivé, *and* Soupe aux Choux, *this screenwriter was mad about bicycles and a friend of Georges Brassens, with whom he followed the race in 1971, before returning eight years later.*

Nasty spring. It makes you wait weeks. You freeze in the streets and under the umbrellas, the rivers overflow, and—bang—the day of Paris-Roubaix hits me right on time. I don't know if you're like me, but I can only conceive of Paris-Roubaix in the rain. I won't go as far as snow, mind you, because they'll call me sadistic for my preference for precipitation. It's a matter of applying poetry to sport. In the rain, the plains are clearly more desolate than in full sunshine, and a wet cobblestone is more aesthetic than a dry one, in the manner of an empty font in a deconsecrated church. Marcel Carné, in his films of poetic realism, tolerated only cobblestones that were slick and shiny under the streetlights. In short, on this day, I long to see spectators trampling through the dripping forests, and riders shivering in their toe-clips, as rain trickles from their cotton caps. Yesterday it neither bucketed down nor rained cats and dogs—so much for the picturesque. I had to take my Paris-Roubaix just as it came, dusty like the noble old-timer that it is. I thought a lot, while going along, of the race's technical director, Albert Bouvet, because he has taken it upon himself to weave together all the cobblestone sections from one end to the other into the infernal itinerary we demand. It's a wonderful little job that would have thrilled the nineteenth-century humorist Alphonse Allais, the job of uncovering the cobblestones. Bouvet still manages to make ends meet by creating new sections, but for how much longer? Until the course itself is declared a national monument, the most rugged bike race in the world—and in my view the most beautiful—Paris-Roubaix will be hanging by a thread, like the one that connects the whaler to the whale, threatening the latter with extinction. As for the lucky climbers, no one will ever steal their mountains. Pity the poor cobblestones specialist, whose profession is threatened with extinction. The De Vlaeminck brothers are just as endangered as baby seals. Leaving aside this bleak future, let's get back to the present, which is called the spring, because it was springtime yesterday. It was even an Italian one, like last year. For some time now, Francesco Moser has had the knack of displacing the Riviera to his liking. It's constantly drilled into us that Paris-Roubaix is a lottery for cyclocross riders, et cetera. But they're pulling the wool over our eyes. If it's a lottery, then the zero rarely wins the pound of sugar. Yesterday morning, the experts were citing the names of Moser, Roger De Vlaeminck, Jan Raas, and Marc Demeyer. And, sure enough, like clockwork, they were all there at the finish, plus a couple of others named Hennie Kuiper and Joop Zoetemelk. The lovers of the lottery will have to try again. At this exact moment of truth, that can even be discouraging. Bernard Hinault was there too, thank goodness, as the first Frenchman to cross the line, a role that fell so often to Raymond Poulidor. But cycling enthusiasts like to see Tour winners go on to win Paris-Roubaix, just like Fausto Coppi, Louison Bobet, and Eddy Merckx. Hinault didn't stay away from the more beautiful of the two yesterday. And I hope that one day, perhaps in 1980, he places a beautiful cobblestone of the North on the fireplace mantle of his Yffiniac home. That's the most understated and most magnificent of *objets d'art*.

## 1980
## To everyone his El Dorado

BY LOUIS NUCÉRA (1928–2000)

*A writer, journalist, and columnist, he loved cycling so much that he died a victim of his passion, cut down by a crazy motorist. He won the 1981 Interallié Prize for* Chemin de la Lanterne, *and the grand prize for sports literature in 1987, for* Mes Rayons de Soleil. *He cultivated friendship like no one else. The proof,* Le Roi René, *is a vibrant tribute to the cycling champion René Vietto, the idol of his youth.*

"Things are always less beautiful than the dreams we have of them." So said French author Marcel Proust. That stopped being true yesterday, on the road that leads from Compiègne to Roubaix. The one who dreamed about watching "the Easter race" since he was in short trousers, and who had never been able to fulfill that dream until this Sunday, saw everything that he had imagined exceeded by the actual experience. He's now in worlds that don't claim to have the virtues we should have renounced.

Everything conspired to create the triumph: a sky that had put on summer finery, racers who never insulted the legend of this event, and the redemption of the French who hadn't had such success since French resident Tino Sabbadini placed second twenty years ago.

It was an opera of catastrophe, an opera of sand, with all its acts, successively mixed together, being offered to the race followers.

An opera of catastrophe, because bad luck is dealt out to the riders: multiple flats for the cherubic René Bittinger, a broken frame for the cavalier Marcel Tinazzi, crashes for Jan Raas and Gilbert Duclos-Lassalle, serious injuries to Roger De Vlaeminck and Michel Pollentier. The bloody face of the latter, bludgeoned by fate, will not be forgotten soon, especially by those who took care of him.

An opera of sand because, with stupefied looks, we catch sight of the racers on the cobblestone sections as if they were crossing a desert. The directors of this tragedy, who are the bike race organizers, had managed to bring together the wind at the same time as the blue skies. As a result, dust joined the mix. And everyone fought for his own El Dorado according to his heart.

In the end, it was a superb opera, for high speeds left their mark on the race. It was merciless and turned into a battle of attrition.

So, while Demeyer and Hinault refused to give in to fatalism, while De Vlaeminck was left twisting in pain on the road, and while Didi Thurau and Duclos-Lassalle outdid each other with their courage, Moser the magnificent, with the heavy baggage of hope, flew like a hawk on the hunt. The velodrome at Roubaix was approaching. The opera was about to play its final chords. And no lack of taste could now bring them into disrepute.

It's been a long time since the one who scribbled these lines had dreamed of Paris-Roubaix. He dreamed above his means. It was the era when Gaston Rebry was the boss, when René Vietto, a climber, aimed his rims onto hostile roads. The years passed. And finally the project has come to pass. It would have been inopportune for the kid who had grown up to refuse his pleasure. The nostalgia for something you hadn't really experienced was often intense. But when a race attains the quality of yesterday's, any attempt to destroy the memories is useless. Those secret odysseys have now been transformed into reality.

## 1982
## The saints go to hell

BY YVES BERGER (1931–2004)

*A writer and editor, this southerner who loved American Indians won the 1962 Fémina Prize for* Le Sud *and the 1994 Médicis Prize for* Immobile dans le Courant du Fleuve. *A cycling fan, he was an attentive follower of Paris-Roubaix.*

I was sure of this, from my career as a writer and editor: words do not lie. And now I can confirm that they do indeed apply to Paris-Roubaix, for I have just lived them. Don't hunt around for other expressions; for the eighty years this race has existed, its chroniclers have used these words and these alone. By necessity. What words, you ask? Beauty, sadness, pain, courage, injustice. Paris-Roubaix resembles no other race precisely because it elicits those nouns. For me, witnessing my first Paris-Roubaix on April 18, 1982, I would start with the word beauty. I saw it at the base of the hills, and after I returned to my car, at the summit where motorcycle lights flicker. I saw it in the immense sheeplike backs of the racers who are glued together, and in their fantastically efficient organization, proving that beauty does indeed spring from order. And, finally, I saw beauty in the racers themselves, as they lined up on their machines and pedaled without swaying, elbows tucked into their bodies. Serge Demierre, a Swiss rider, left me with the same unforgettable image of perfection that I got from his countryman Hugo Koblet, when the latter passed Avignon in a stage of the Tour back in 1951.

Sadness comes from following—or preceding—your favorite racers, only to learn from the car radio that they are losing their advantage as the peloton closes in. What can you do about it? I had been tracking Patrick Bonnet and Gotz Heine (his name alone destines this German for glory) for several hundred kilometers. Okay, but what about injustice? Duclos-Lassalle, Kuiper, Contini, Moser, and Willems were all victims and repeat victims, whereas Raas, Hinault, and De Vlaeminck got off scot-free.

I will never forget number 92: Frank Hoste, winner of Ghent-Wevelgem. We were behind him, and he was among the best. We saw him plunge into a hole and we heard, in our hermetically sealed car, his frame crack. Parodying Malraux, we affirmed without blinking that Paris-Roubaix is the intrusion of eternal fatality into individual destiny.

I saw Fons De Wolf, who was not fully a man; indeed he was almost an adolescent carrying all the baggage of this overly brief state built on the tender remains of childhood. He flatted a second time, while he too was riding along in the large breakaway group of thirty. Right then and there he lost his chance at the great year my colleagues and I at *L'Équipe* had forecast for him. Hell indeed. In fact, I now realize that I had forgotten to include that principal descriptive at the start of this article, when I ticked off the words describing this race like a litany. Though hackneyed, it is strong, and it forces itself upon me like a black vision, before delivering me to my night of sleep.

Hell, these innumerable straight, laborious, tortured, and gutted roads and paths spiked with glistening and slashing cobblestones, where one is astonished to see bicycles hurtling along, and where one doubts that even a single racer will get through unscathed. On top of that, in this infernal landscape, are the insufferable cars that rock and rub one another. Miraculously, thanks to the dexterity of the drivers, they manage to avoid stray racers and onlookers. Then the motorcycles. And the stream of horns and sirens. At ground level, the holes, ruts, stones, sandstone, and the miserable aging tar only add to the hellish racket.

Even the geography is something of a Hell. That evening, this Paris-Roubaix seemed like all the others I had read about the day after. Similar and yet unique, because this time I had seen and lived it myself. I could now relate to all the familiar names of places, towns, villages, and hamlets such as Neuvilly, Marchiennes, Orchies, Lesquin, and Cysoing. As sleep began to descend upon me, I took one last look through the dust rising from the paths at the mud-splattered and tortured faces of the racers. I realized that for eighty years now, once a year, the saints go to Hell.

## 1983
## The fatality of destiny

BY GUY CROUSSY (BORN IN 1937)

*Guy Croussy, a university professor, is the author of numerous novels selected for consideration for the Goncourt Prize, including* Les Bleuets, Le Loupcervier, *and* La Tondue. *He is also a northerner who is passionate about sports, cycling in particular. In Paris-Roubaix, he rediscovered the places where most of his books take place.*

The North produces rain, prime ministers, and wet cobblestones. There, near the North Pole, they still live in the Stone Age. Every year, at the same time, racers take over the small country roads whose origins have been lost in the night of time. There's nothing more terrible than a cobblestone road. You'd think it was a chunk of some distant star. A cobblestone is slightly rounded, a bit rough, and it provokes the earthly shakings so appreciated by the spectators. For their own pleasure, the fans have created mud, umbrellas, and wet cobblestones. The first Sunday after Easter, over these ensnaring roads, accidents can happen. It's hardly surprising. After all, their occurrence is scientifically planned.

At Neuvilly, the first staggering breakaways have lodged themselves into the throat of the monster. Pascal Simon sinks into a rut. All of a sudden, everyone gets a rude awakening. Here, they can appreciate how fragile hope becomes in the face of such stark reality. They reassure themselves that the quirks of fate would never dare tangle with a legend so widely anticipated as Paris-Roubaix, where courage must surely be rewarded. Alas, that's not the case! Fons De Wolf had already fallen. Yet, on the asphalt, he knows how to do extraordinary things. Like an angel, he can fly over the pavement. There, like others in this race, he is no longer composed of anything but his head, torso, and thighs. Looking at his head, you might conclude that he's thinking about the beautiful women of Limbourg. But if one can believe the latest polls, the women of that Belgian city prefer angels over the demons who fall into ditches. It seems they do not like the disgrace of bad fortune. The fans tell themselves that De Wolf cannot possibly disappoint those women of Limbourg. But he does. Suddenly, their idol is nothing but a dethroned angel thrown to the ground.

What adds interest to the spectacle is that after Neuvilly, all of a sudden, the racers have embers in their eyes. Some appear possessed, jumping alarmingly from one edge of the road to the other. A very important nuance, however, distinguishes their pure hallucination from that of the spectators. In the latter case, it is often a pretext for the intoxicated souls who gather where the racers are expected to fall, to watch them break into pieces. In the racer's case, hallucination can be sudden and fatal. It gives birth to a great faith in universal order. The racers dutifully fall where the fans have assembled. One can never emphasize enough how perceptive the fans are, and how much they love the fatality of destiny. But don't believe for a moment that they know only the good side of life, or that they pass their existence listening to the rainfall along the muddy roads. The fan is also an office head, a judge, a psychologist, a lover of balanced budgets, a worker in a factory about to disappear, a retired executive, a connoisseur of Louis XVI commodes or shopping carts.

The fans are reenergized. They tell themselves that, come what may, Bernard Hinault is not about to launch himself into a fit of somber glares and bitter denunciations, that he can't possibly throw in the towel before the decisive part of the race, that he will grab fate by the scruff of its neck. Alas, no. He has abandoned smack in the middle of the race and there are indeed plenty of somber glares.

From the village of Aulnoy-lez-Valenciennes, the fans begin dreaming of a victory by Alain Bondue, who has already gained the stature of a Francesco Moser and whose future seems bright. The time has passed when our racers resembled farmhands, mute Belgians with clumsy hands. They have become elegant young men. After this they will no doubt become part of the jet set. One tells oneself all the same that it's not possible that such a determined soul could fall victim to the foibles of fate, that Bondue has promise, that he is in good company with Gilbert Duclos-Lassalle and Francesco Moser, that he won't be struck by bad luck. And yet he is. Between Orchies and Mons-en-Pévèle, he falls, gets up, and falls again. His front wheel gives out, his victory gives out, and the crowd gives out. One time, two times, a hundred times. At Martinsart, he falls again. Barely arisen, he falls yet again. No one can know the hearts of certain men. No one. Not even those who brought them into this world. Today, Bondue possesses the class of Moser, the courage of Duclos-Lassalle, and the elegance of De Wolf. Tomorrow or the day after tomorrow, Bondue will cross the cobblestones without trouble and win Paris-Roubaix. It's written in the sky and in his sheer will.

Suddenly, the mud and cobblestones are behind us. There's asphalt once again. Moser, Duclos-Lassalle, and Marc Madiot take off like meteors. Trees are flourishing in sunny prairies. Around here, the sky is more beautiful and vast than elsewhere. In the distance, in the plain, a train makes its way toward Paris. Only a short while ago, a spectator could have run to catch up with the racers. "The surroundings of Paris are the most beautiful in the world," said the humorist Alphonse Allais. And so, too, are the surroundings of Mons-en-Pévèle. Here the legend ends. Here one loses a sense of history; the epic is denied and destiny thwarted. Here takes place the inversion of all inversions, and the race defies all predictions. Jan Raas is beaten. Wilfried Peeters is beaten. Hinault is beaten. Duclos-Lassalle senses happiness, and his head starts to spin. He accelerates at full speed. Suddenly, you have to tell yourself that the race can't possibly revert to madness. Surely a Dutchman won't win this thing one more time. But he does. Yes, Hennie Kuiper comes back from the edge of hope and sails on alone toward victory.

## 1984
## The cross of the heroes

BY ALPHONSE BOUDARD (1925–2000)

*A sensitive novelist who cultivated slang, Boudard authored masterpieces like* La Métamorphose des Cloportes *and* Les Combattants du Petit Matin*, for which he won the Renaudot Prize in 1977. Here he writes about other combatants with a zany talent.*

To wait for my 58th year to follow my first Paris-Roubaix, that's a heap of time! Better late than never, et cetera. So here I am at long last, in a follow car to see for myself if the papers had bluffed me a bit all those years since I first developed a passion for the sport of cycling. I knew all the buzzwords: Hell, the cobblestones of the North, the mud, this race from another era.... And I knew the palmarès . . . nothing but the upper crust, prestigious names like Coppi, Van Looy, Bobet, De Vlaeminck, Hinault, not to mention Merckx and Moser.

The 1984 vintage has been announced with several casualties . . . deserters who won't face the trench at Arenberg. Scrub Hinault, Moser, and Raas from the list of starters, along with a few lesser names. We would just have to do without them, and once the race begins they'll be of no more importance than the champions of old.

The race takes off in the misty morning, with a nip in the air that penetrates your shoes, jacket, and pants. Before that, though, here you are in front of the palace of Compiègne for the starting cer-

emonies. I recognize Laurent Fignon passing by, with his adolescent mug. I also see Joop Zoetemelk, the bravest of the brave, who has traversed every imaginable terrain and fought the bloodiest of battles. I shake hands with Jean-René Bernaudeau, who must have thought I was the deputy mayor.

The participants, including some heroes, and the journalists are all there. The public is scrunched up behind the barriers, while big policemen try to contain their enthusiasm. What strikes me the most is the pervasive camaraderie; no one takes himself too seriously here, not even the winner or the unlucky loser.

And then we're off. We go ahead of the race. A few brave ones break away, taking one or two minutes, but they're of no consequence. I have time to savor, if that's the right word, the scenery. The countryside and townships through which we pass don't encourage me to frolic in the grass. The small villages barely reveal a joy for life. The gray sky is low. Farther off there's nothing, just gloomy plains. A few furtive touring cyclists stand in small groups next to red brick houses. We spot a few grandfathers who saw Henri Pélissier pass by, maybe even François Faber. I don't know for sure; I'm making my own memories.

In any case, I wait for the famous cobblestones, the legendary assassins of tires—those nasty things that make the pens of journalists shake. And there they are! I admit I too have a hard time hanging on to my felt hat. They haven't been deluding me, after all. After Neuvilly, it's a quagmire, with potholes everywhere. You can barely see the cobblestones, so submerged are they in crap. There are holes and ponds galore. And the stench makes me squirm in my car seat. We await the poor cyclists. A mass of people thirst for live entertainment, as if they're in a Roman arena. They want to rejoice over the racers' crashes, blowouts, and abandons. They want to see those athletes suffer. There's no other way to explain why all these people came from who knows where to watch this carnage.

In the more humane sections of the route, the fans of Alain Bondue, a local boy, have come to wave banners of encouragement . . . and to wish him a happy birthday. He turns 25 today. And if Alain can stick out this Paris-Roubaix, that would send a shockwave through the thatched cottages of the North. He escapes with his teammate Gregor Braun in the famous forest of Arenberg. In a setting from the 1914–1918 war, only the echoes of artillery fire are missing. A light drizzle falls, but that doesn't stop Bondue from becoming part of the race's legend. He's going to hang on almost to the very end . . . until the invincible Sean Kelly, escorted by Rudy Rogiers, comes and joins him. But still he fights, inspired by his 25 years and his many friends who cheer him on. And then, rotten luck, the angel falls. He gets up, but Kelly is already headed to another victory.

At Roubaix, Bondue will finish only third but he has won the hearts, and a hero's medal, in what has turned out to be the most fabulous race of the year.

The sun at last pierces through the haze over the velodrome. The racers arrive in small groups, encrusted up to their eyes, before breaking into a sprint to improve their final placing. I linger for a while on the infield to await the survivors. After all, it's not every day that I get to see a Paris-Roubaix. They announce the arrival on the track of the veteran Zoetemelk. He has again withstood the battering, traversed the cobblestones of bad intentions in the Hell of the North, braved the fickle weather and the tons of crappy mud. He is without a doubt the old man of the competition, yet he never gives up. For a man who has won the Tour de France and many other races, to finish 36th in this Paris-Roubaix doesn't seem at all dishonorable. On the contrary. I told you he was the bravest of the brave.

## 1985
## A classic tragedy

BY JEAN-EDERN HALLIER (1936–1997)

*Writer, journalist, and inveterate polemicist Jean-Edern Hallier was a Six-Day racer before founding a leftist newspaper,* L'Idiot International, *and authoring rich works ranging from* La Cause des Peuples *to* Le Premier qui Dort Réveille l'Autre, *along with reporting for* Paris-Match, Le Matin, *and* L'Équipe.

That was the least of it, that a Breton should win, for my first Paris-Roubaix. An elementary courtesy from the organizers, maybe! Or a thoughtful gesture on the part of the racers! The Belgians had so well understood this need that they had immediately punctured, abandoned, or exhausted themselves racing into the wind, like Éric Vanderaerden. The result was played out in advance between two Bretons, me and Marc Madiot. My head and his legs!

What's more, it was the first weekend that I prayed for bad weather. God answered. He served up rain, cold, and wind. Inevitably, it can't be a true Paris-Roubaix without sadomasochist conditions. The true sadists were the spectators, who deliberately plant themselves in front of the biggest puddles, the sharpest cobblestones, and the corners that promise the most crashes. They resemble the people of the Middle Ages who turned out to watch victims in the stocks. Blood, voluptuous pleasure, death. Or rather mud, cold, a free-for-all . . . as it's the racers who are the masochists. Melancholy madmen with wild eyes and ravaged faces! As a sadomasochistic ceremony, I've never seen anything better.

Had Madiot not won, the reader has no idea what sort of article he would have read. I would have had the tone of Louis Pauwels in *Le Figaro* magazine, defending the moral order. I would have written, "Down with bike racing!" I would have denounced Sean Kelly, Gilbert Duclos-Lassalle, and Francesco Moser with Christian indignation. Do you realize what this means? The racers would not go so fast if there were no houses of ill repute in Roubaix. I saw them myself. They are the velodrome's communal showers where the racers exhibit themselves naked and muddy in front of television cameras—whose operators will no doubt resell their photos to gay magazines. Paris-Roubaix is the glorification of vice! Even the masses, happily under the influence of far-right nationalist leader Jean-Marie Le Pen, have turned away from it. At the roadside, there were only drugged countesses, marquises with big guts from guzzling the beer of the North, all the aristocrats who make up the peeping Toms' guard of honor in the Bois de Boulogne. It's scandalous!

But since Madiot won, I prefer not to go down that road—which is, like that of our heroes, paved like the Appian Way. Besides, I really believed for a moment that we were headed for Rome. As everyone knows, all roads lead there. Especially as the weather almost improved midway through. I said, "Shit, the sun!" Happily, it didn't last. There were big icy showers, hailstones on the lanky legs of the Belgians. The closer one got to the end, the farther away Roubaix became. It was a bit like a scene from *The Castle* by Kafka! To the extent that they finish it on a section of cobblestones, you get a second helping. Not a second of boredom, of relaxation, and yet, it was interminable! It could have gone on for a lifetime, at this level of cycling perfection, this last modern tragedy—and this bicycle race that is the only domain where ancient values, like courage, still apply. It was so slow, and so dazzling at the same time, that I saw Vanderaerden and Moser, the two favorites, fall in the hallucinating passage to Kafka's Castle: they were still 60 kilometers from the finish, but they believed they were already in Roubaix, making the same errors as a beginner. Moser was done in by a premature breakaway, falling like an honorable old soldier, while Vanderaerden executed a beautiful attack, but it was savagely useless in the fierce head wind.

What's more, with their muddy trappings they couldn't see anything anymore. Happily a few, like Greg LeMond, were on cruise control, as the team Radar–La Vie Claire requires. Had he not relied on radar, LeMond, whose eyes you couldn't even see at the end, would never have finished fourth. Of course, I would also have liked to see Hennie Kuiper win. Or a youngster like Bruno Wojtinek or Dominique Lecrocq. Except that there was Madiot, a child of Brittany. On this day, he was Merlin the magician who knew how to make a difference, physical of course, but also metaphysical. He knew how to step up to a superior pace; he had a spiritual shift in gears that left his foes behind. Whether he ever wins a race again has no importance. He won Paris-Roubaix, the most beautiful, the most moving, of all the classics, in the full sense of the term—with pure class.

When he entered the track, I saw his radiant and heartbreaking smile. He was like a child entering a magic circle, on his shiny finishing path of cement. It was almost supernatural. When the race is so beautiful, you become not only a onetime winner but also a champion forever. Madiot is one of those.

## 1986
## I wanted to see

BY GEORGES CONCHON (1925–1990)

*A journalist and author, winner of the Goncourt Prize in 1964 for his book* L'État Sauvage, *Conchon was also a brilliant and prolific screenwriter:* Judith Therpauve, La Banquière, Sept Morts sur Ordonnance, La Sucre, *and* La Victoire en Chantant. *An amateur cyclist, this writer from the Auvergne had a special affection for the cobbled classics.*

I wanted to see Steve Bauer and I saw Steve Bauer. I had already seen the Canadian come within a hair's breadth of winning the Tour of Flanders, and I firmly hoped to see him give a repeat performance, to race assertively if not victoriously, in Paris-Roubaix. I saw him, fleetingly, several kilometers from the finish line. Sean Kelly (and company) had just dropped him. To be sure, Greg LeMond was with him, after suffering a flat, it's true. At the next turn, floating in the hands of fans (or perhaps cameramen sent by CBS), was the star-spangled banner. Clearly, the United States had suffered a blow. True, it was no Pearl Harbor, but LeMond was nonetheless stopped in his tracks, like a plow striking a rock.

Speaking of plows, I saw more than one field where wheat was piercing through the soil. And this germination alone should have consoled me for what the great experts of Paris-Roubaix agreed was not producing a particularly good crop. But it was my first and I had much to feast my eyes on.

I wanted to see young talent rise up, and mature as well. I had long believed in Dominique Lecrocq; he was a prospect. But Christophe Lavainne also pleased me. He moves like a rower with an air of detachment. I saw him get dropped not too far from Roubaix, his face scrunched up with the calm acceptance of one who knows he has given it his all. He had a certain elegance about him that not all racers have; they usually get annoyed.

I wanted to see Gilbert Duclos-Lassalle, but I learned that he had broken his handlebars. I was intrigued by such a detail; it shows not only a strong man, but also that impetuous temperament that many of us admire in Duclos.

Above all, I wanted to see suffering. Everything seemed to lend itself to that; it was snowing at the start in Compiègne. I ran into the commentator Robert Chapatte, who seemed to be a bit ahead of the other race followers to get to the lunch stop; he didn't mince words: "Around midnight, we'll have to go looking for the racers on the farms." I knew he was exaggerating, but I suspected he was taking me for the greenhorn that I was. For it was almost turning nice. We were barely in the trench at Arenberg when the worst forecast came: moments of sunshine.

I had heard talk of mud that would repulse even sewer workers, but I hadn't seen much of that. Except toward the end, thanks to a welcome little drizzle, but that mud was erased by the paintings of Mr. Ben Bella. The Algerian artist had chosen to create a rather cheerful exit to the gates of Hell by painting the cobblestones, though that was a little too much.

I was assured that even worse than the mud was the dust. But I didn't see it at all, even when the cobblestones were still dry—just a thin layer of compact mud, almost imperceptible.

In sum, it was too nice for once, miraculously, in this shitty spring.

I especially did not want to see Kelly—that is, to see him win. Enough is enough. Already as a small child, I had a big grudge against Gaston Rebry, the unflappable winner at Roubaix in 1931, then 1934 and again in 1935, until the blessed day in 1936 when Georges Speicher finally won. Many years later, on this April 13, 1986 (God, how time flies!), I had pinned my hopes on Pascal Jules. For a long time, as far as Mons-en-Pévèle, I told myself this gem: Jules is the sort of guy who can win what we used to call *la Grand Pascale*, the Great Easter Event.

You know what a mistake that was!

I was left with Adrie Van der Poel. The Irishman Kelly, or the Flemish guy—neither really appealed. But I will always take a Flemish racer over an overly glorious Irishman, especially since the former had already thumbed his nose at the latter in the Tour of Flanders. To see them together at Cysoing and again at Camphin, and still at Chéreng and finally at Hem, struck me as a fairly well-concocted drama in the absence of anything better (a French racer, that is). Though Sundays rarely resemble one another in cycling, could this one not produce the same sort of miracle as the previous week? I wanted that all the more since *L'Équipe* sportswriter Pierre Chany had upset me when right here the previous Monday he went on about "Van der Poel with his golden eyes." What a pleasure that would have been, if Ferdi Van den

Haute had not launched his sprint prematurely, to make myself appreciated, in the same vein, by talking about a "Van der Poel deluxe"! But it was not meant to be. I believe in omens: of the four poodles I observed with their mothers at the edge of the cobblestones, three were rigged out in cardigans of a green that was obviously, outrageously Irish.

## 1987
## The dynasty of forsythias

BY SÉBASTIEN JAPRISOT (1931–2003)

*This writer of books and screenplays, author of* Compartiments Tueurs, La Course du Lièvre à Travers les Champs, *and* Un Long Dimanche de Fiançailles, *thoroughly enjoyed the suspense of Paris-Roubaix.*

The Paris-Roubaix of my childhood, those of Coppi and Van Steenbergen, were gray, rainy, cold, anguished affairs. The Hell of the North was paved with bad intentions. And this morning, as I stood in the square by the Palais de Compiègne, to witness the start of my first race but the 85th overall, it was likewise cold and gray. Anxiety also prevailed—in the eyes of Francesco Moser, in the tight jaws of Luc Vandenbroucke, in the big-veined calves of Joop Zoetemelk. Only Sean Kelly, perhaps, and Bernard Hinault seemed relaxed. The Irishman's expression was rugged and impenetrable. In contrast, the beloved Badger displayed a glowing smile and so much affability that everyone hoped he would add to his palmarès a second victory in this great classic.

"There they are!" We would hear this cry all day long, starting from the first turn of a wheel, all along a nondescript hedge of redbrick homes with gardens bursting with forsythias. Paris-Roubaix, for as long as it has tar under its rims, causes the curious locals to appear at their doorsteps in bathrobes or with curlers in their hair. It even attracts children who have just left Mass with their hands full of palm branches. In their eyes you can see their happiness that this long-awaited event is finally under way. Watching Paris-Roubaix, especially when the rain holds off, is like receiving an old friend who drops by every year at the same time.

There they are! When the same cry resounded about a half-hour after the start, it was to salute the first breakaway, led by Charley Mottet and followed by sixteen other audacious racers. No one thought much of them. Someone explained to me that the group simply hoped to reach the first cobblestones before their doomed cohorts, but after that they wouldn't get far. Wouldn't get far? The breakaway would last five hours and 200 kilometers! They were sixteen at the start, and after a strenuous effort, one was still alive and about to sail home. His name was Theo De Rooy. Then he fell too. Who didn't take a spill in this Paris-Roubaix? That low sky evidently is there for a reason.

There they are! I saw them after their arrival in Roubaix, in the showers. I saw bloody fingers, bruised arms, scratched legs, and ripped jerseys covered by mud. All those baggy eyes with blank expressions were no doubt still seeing the trench at Arenberg, and the crowd gathered along the embankments on either side of a meter-wide band of tough guys that stretched endlessly into the distance in a tunnel of skinny trees.

I would be told—later on, not that evening—that this wasn't a great Paris-Roubaix. That it wasn't like those of my childhood that had aroused my enthusiasm. That it wasn't like the one Hinault had won, who seems so serene today now that he has pocketed a victory. I recalled Vandenbroucke's enraged bursts to rejoin the leaders, after a flat had ruined all his hopes. I recalled Kelly's fall and Éric Vanderaerden's immediate attack. I recalled how, a few kilometers from the end, the blond Éric had relentlessly overtaken Patrick Versluys and Rudy Dhaenens before beating them out in the sprint. The victor spread out his arms like the Christ-figures on all the crucifixes that stake out the road to Hell. It was raining. The rain, wind, and dust rebounded to the very end. This race had everything. I can now savor, with a light heart, its harsh character. I will even watch the race again on television. King Kelly, this evening, must have one of those famous cobblestones weighing on his heart. Had he not fallen, would he have kept pace with the supercharged Vanderaerden? Would there have been a fairy-tale ending, a thrilling final sprint that everyone had anticipated? The mystery will remain. But mystery is the instigator of legends. A noble defeat in Paris-Roubaix can be worth two victories and install the loser as part of a dynasty, alongside such illustrious figures as Coppi, Van Steenbergen, Bobet, and Merckx. Not to mention Anquetil, the magnificent performer of 1958, who would never win the race. These perennial champions constitute a dynasty much like that of the first yellow flowers of spring. Every year, they accompany the winner and his adversaries through every village along the long northern roads. I say "adversaries," for there are no losers in Paris-Roubaix.

## 1988
## Thirteen, eleven, five, two...

BY FRANÇOISE XENAKIS (BORN IN 1930)

*A journalist, writer, and radio commentator, Xenakis has authored some twenty novels dealing with malice, including* Elle Lui Dirait dans l'Ile; Moi, J'aime Pas la Mer; Zut, On a Encore Oublié Madame Freud; La Vie Exemplaire de Rita Capuchon; *and* Mouche-toi Cléopâtre. *On Paris-Roubaix, she fully appreciated its history and said she was hoping to return to the race, just like the riders.*

Who says dreams never come true? I had a dream: to follow the Tour de France and Paris-Roubaix. For Paris-Roubaix, at least, that has happened; I followed it, thanks to those who invited me. But did I see a real one?

Did I see *the* race, the craziest race, the most inhumane, with some two hundred masochists who willingly sign up every year to be watched by several million sadists who demand, from the comfort of their armchairs, the going in for the kill of the upstart who broke away all alone, the flight of the favorite golden boy who took off only to be cut short by a piece of wax paper in his derailleur, and the crowd that screams with dread—or should I say with pleasure?

Of course, some of the greats have been cut down, not by a knockout punch but simply because the criterium specialists happened to take off first. From the very start, and ignoring the paradox uttered by French poet Jean de la Fontaine and God, that the first shall be last, they stupidly sprinted away from the start hoping to win!

8:30 A.M. Compiègne. "Shit, it's all screwed up, it's going to be a nice day!" This driver, doing his 28th Paris-Roubaix, knows what he's talking about. And it's not just going to be nice, it's clear that it is and it will be a downright gorgeous day, and already, at the start, a veil of discouragement hangs over the race followers. Say goodbye to mud crusted on faces wrinkled by suffering, goodbye to spectacular falls magnified by oceans of mud....

The racers arrive. My, they're handsome. I still had a false memory from childhood, an image of racers looking much older than their age. Laurent Fignon? He's ravishing. As svelte as a dancer. Yes, they're all good-looking, their legs shaven and oiled, wearing strange rocking clogs covered by white socks, and walking like Chinese women with bound feet. "There's Fignon, get his autograph . . . there's Kelly. . . ." And did someone say, "Look, there's Demol"? No, why would you ask me that? Who's Demol? Look, if his mother was there, she might have seen him autograph the sign-in sheet and line up with the others, but she would have been the only one to pay any attention to him.

At kilometer 44. "Breaking apart," I rasped. They've been riding for an hour, and thirteen of those criterium specialists have bolted. Their lead will reach 5:40 over the peloton. "But this can't be true!"

It's me, always me, the neophyte, who says that. It's also me that says that, in this good weather, those unknown guys who have nothing to lose will win the race. But the pros, for I am in a car full of pros, settle me down. Seeing my astonishment at their lack of reaction, the most experienced race follower lets out a calm "Just wait. They'll get caught." And so I waited.

1:30 P.M. The race drones on. The brave criterium racers (the specialists in my car have now conceded, "Sure, they're the good ones") are still in the lead. But a cry, "You'll see, the Arenberg section is coming. That'll get them." And there are so many people in that trench that the heads of those on the left almost touch the heads of those on the right. And the fathers holding kids at the end of their arms lean them even farther out, no doubt in an unconscious effort to protect themselves. Yes, everything changes at this point.

At last! The peloton is starting to get uneasy. It's as if there was one who said to the others, "That's not the end of it, guys! Now, if we get down to it, we can start the second round." And there's Fignon. Fignon wants to put on the pressure. But no one wants to follow him. No one wants to do their bit. No one wants to stick their neck out. There are too many stars, that's clear. And what's more, Fignon's team-mates are on the roadside, their bicycles broken, and their team cars have jumped ahead to follow Fignon; that's the protocol. So he's alone.

Finally, five kilometers from the end, Fignon must have said to himself, sublimely, "Shit, I'm going to attack." For the voice of the commentator became animated: "Fignon has broken away. He's moving clear." And over the microphone, quite indiscreetly, a bitter voice adds, "It's about time."

No, it was too late. A certain guy arrives in the winners' circle. After drafting the entire race on the wheel of Thomas Wegmüller, whose derailleur got jammed by a piece of trash, this guy lifts his arms with a contented air. He has won. Who is he? They say his name is Dirk Demol.

Postscript: I would like to return to see a real Paris-Roubaix, if only because Roubaix is a fine town—blowing another of my pre-conceived notions. That said, bravo, Mr. Demol.

# PALMARÈS

**1896**
1. FISCHER Josef (GER)
2. MEYER Charles (DEN)
3. GARIN Maurice (ITA) **(1)**

**1897**
1. GARIN Maurice (ITA)
2. CORDANG Mathieu (HOL)
3. FREDERICK Michel (SWI)

**1898**
1. GARIN Maurice (ITA)
2. STEPHANE Auguste (FRA)
3. WATTELIER Edouard (FRA)

**1899**
1. CHAMPION Albert (FRA)
2. BOR Paul (FRA)
3. GARIN Ambroise (FRA)

**1900**
1. BOUHOURS Emile (FRA)
2. FISCHER Josef (GER)
3. GARIN Maurice (ITA)

**1901**
1. LESNA Lucien (FRA)
2. GARIN Ambroise (FRA)
3. ITSWEIRE Lucien (FRA)

**1902**
1. LESNA Lucien (FRA)
2. WATTELIER Edouard (FRA)
3. GARIN Ambroise (FRA)

**1903**
1. AUCOUTURIER Hyppolite (FRA)
2. CHAPPERON Claude (FRA)
3. TROUSSELIER Louis (FRA)

**1904**
1. AUCOUTURIER Hyppolite (FRA)
2. GARIN César (FRA)
3. POTHIER Lucien (FRA)

**1905**
1. TROUSSELIER Louis (FRA)
2. POTTIER René (FRA)
3. CORNET Henri (FRA)

**1906**
1. CORNET Henri (FRA)
2. CADOLLE Marcel (FRA)
3. POTTIER René (FRA)

**1907**
1. PASSERIEU Georges (FRA)
2. VAN HAUWAERT Cyrille (BEL)
3. TROUSSELIER Louis (FRA)

**1908**
1. VAN HAUWAERT Cyrille (BEL)
2. LORGEOU Georges (FRA)
3. FABER François (LUX)

**1909**
1. LAPIZE Octave (FRA)
2. TROUSSELIER Louis (FRA)
3. MASSELIS Jules (BEL)

**1910**
1. LAPIZE Octave (FRA)
2. VAN HAUWAERT Cyrille (BEL)
3. CHRISTOPHE Eugène (FRA)

**1911**
1. LAPIZE Octave (FRA)
2. CHARPIOT André (FRA)
3. VAN HAUWAERT Cyrille (BEL)

**1912**
1. CRUPELANDT Charles (FRA)
2. GARRIGOU Gustave (FRA)
3. LETURGIE Maurice (FRA)

**1913**
1. FABER François (LUX)
2. DERUYTER Charles (BEL)
3. CRUPELANDT Charles (FRA)

**1914**
1. CRUPELANDT Charles (FRA)
2. LUGUET Louis (FRA)
3. MOTTIAT Louis (BEL)

**1919**
1. PÉLISSIER Henri (FRA)
2. THYS Philippe (BEL)
3. BARTHELEMY Honoré (FRA)

**1920**
1. DEMAN Paul (BEL)
2. CHRISTOPHE Eugène (FRA)
3. BUYSSE Lucien (BEL)

**1921**
1. PÉLISSIER Henri (FRA)
2. PÉLISSIER Francis (FRA)
3. SCIEUR Léon (BEL)

**1922**
1. DEJONGHE Albert (BEL)
2. ROSSIUS Jean (FRA)
3. MASSON Émile (BEL)

**1923**
1. SUTER Henri (SWI)
2. VERMANDEL René (BEL)
3. SELLIER Félix (BEL)

**1924**
1. VAN HEVEL Jules (BEL)
2. VILLE Maurice (FRA)
3. SELLIER Félix (BEL)

**1925**
1. SELLIER Félix (BEL)
2. BESTETTI Piero (ITA)
3. VAN HEVEL Jules (BEL)

**1926**
1. DELBECQUE Julien (BEL)
2. VAN SLEMBROECK Gustave (BEL)
3. REBRY Gaston (BEL)

**1927**
1. RONSSE Georges (BEL)
2. CURTEL Joseph (FRA)
3. PÉLISSIER Charles (FRA)

**1928**
1. LEDUCQ André (FRA)
2. RONSSE Georges (BEL)
3. MEUNIER Charles (BEL)

**1929**
1. MEUNIER Charles (BEL)
2. RONSSE Georges (BEL)
3. DÉOLET Aimé (BEL)

**1930**
1. VERVAECKE Julien (BEL) **(2)**
2. MARÉCHAL Jean (FRA)
3. MAGNE Antonin (FRA)

**1931**
1. REBRY Gaston (BEL)
2. PÉLISSIER Charles (FRA)
3. DECROIX Émile (BEL)

**1932**
1. GIJSSELS Romain (BEL)
2. RONSSE Georges (BEL)
3. SIERONSKI Herbert (GER)

**1933**
1. MAËS Sylvère (BEL)
2. VERVAECKE Julien (BEL)
3. LE CALVEZ Léon (FRA)

**1934**
1. REBRY Gaston (BEL) **(3)**
2. WAUTERS Jean (BEL)
3. BONDUEL Frans (BEL)

**1935**
1. REBRY Gaston (BEL)
2. LEDUCQ André (FRA)
3. AERTS Jean (BEL)

**1936**
1. SPEICHER Georges (FRA) **(4)**
2. MAËS Romain (BEL)
3. REBRY Gaston (BEL)

**1937**
1. ROSSI Jules (ITA)
2. HENDRICKX Albert (BEL)
3. DECLERCQ Noël (BEL)

**1938**
1. STORME Lucien (BEL)
2. HARDIQUEST Louis (BEL)
3. VAN HOUTTE Marcel (BEL)

**1939**
1. MASSON Émile (BEL)
2. KINT Marcel (BEL)
3. LAPÉBIE Roger (FRA)

**1943**
1. KINT Marcel (BEL)
2. LOWIE Jules (BEL)
3. THIÉTARD Louis (FRA)

**1944**
1. DE SIMPELAERE Maurice (BEL)
2. ROSSI Jules (ITA)
3. THIÉTARD Louis (FRA)

**1945**
1. MAYE Paul (FRA)
2. TEISSEIRE Lucien (FRA)
3. PIOT Kléber (FRA)

**1946**
1. CLAES Georges (BEL)
2. GAUTHIER Louis (FRA)
3. VLAEMINCK Lucien (BEL)

**1947**
1. CLAES Georges (BEL)
2. VERSCHUREN Adolf (BEL)
3. THIÉTARD Louis (FRA)

**1948**
1. VAN STEENBERGEN Rik (BEL)
2. IDÉE Émile (FRA)
3. CLAES Georges (BEL)

**1949**
1. MAHÉ André (FRA) **(5)**
1. COPPI Serse (ITA)
3. LEENEN Frans (BEL)
3. MARTIN Georges (FRA)
3. MOUJICA Jésus-Jacques (FRA)

**1950**
1. COPPI Fausto (ITA)
2. DIOT Maurice (FRA)
3. MAGNI Fiorenzo (ITA)

**1951**
1. BEVILACQUA Antonio (ITA)
2. BOBET Louison (FRA)
3. VAN STEENBERGEN Rik (BEL)

**1952**
1. VAN STEENBERGEN Rik (BEL)
2. COPPI Fausto (ITA)
3. MAHÉ André (FRA)

**1953**
1. DERIJCKE Germain (BEL)
2. PIAZZA Donato (ITA)
3. WAGTMANS Wout (HOL)

**1954**
1. IMPANIS Raymond (BEL)

2. OCKERS Stan (BEL)
3. RIJCKAERT Marcel (BEL)

**1955**
1. **FORESTIER Jean** (FRA)
2. COPPI Fausto (ITA)
3. BOBET Louison (FRA)

**1956**
1. **BOBET Louison** (FRA)
2. DE BRUYNE Alfred (BEL)
3. FORESTIER Jean (FRA)

**1957**
1. **DE BRUYNE Alfred** (BEL)
2. VAN STEENBERGEN Rik (BEL)
3. VAN DAELE Léon (BEL)

**1958**
1. **VAN DAELE Léon** (BEL)
2. POBLET Miguel (SPA)
3. VAN LOOY Rik (BEL)

**1959**
1. **FORÉ Noël** (BEL)
2. DESMET Gilbert (I) (BEL)
3. JANSSENS Marcel (BEL)

**1960**
1. **CERAMI Pino** (BEL)
2. SABBADINI Tino (FRA)
3. POBLET Miguel (SPA)

**1961**
1. **VAN LOOY Rik** (BEL)
2. JANSSENS Marcel (BEL)
3. VANDERVECKEN René (BEL)

**1962**
1. **VAN LOOY Rik** (BEL)
2. DAEMS Émile (BEL)
3. SCHOUBBEN Frans (BEL)

**1963**
1. **DAEMS Émile** (BEL)
2. VAN LOOY Rik (BEL)
3. JANSSEN Jan (HOL)

**1964**
1. **POST Peter** (HOL)
2. BEHEYT Benoni (BEL)
3. MOLENAERS Yvo (BEL)

**1965**
1. **VAN LOOY Rik** (BEL)
2. SELS Edward (BEL)
3. VANNITSEN Willy (BEL)

**1966**
1. **GIMONDI Felice** (ITA)
2. JANSSEN Jan (HOL)
3. DESMET Gustaaf (BEL)

**1967**
1. **JANSSEN Jan** (HOL)
2. VAN LOOY Rik (BEL)
3. ALTIG Rudi (GER)

**1968**
1. **MERCKX Eddy** (BEL)
2. VAN SPRINGEL Herman (BEL)
3. GODEFROOT Walter (BEL)

**1969**
1. **GODEFROOT Walter** (BEL)
2. MERCKX Eddy (BEL)
3. VEKEMANS Willy (BEL)

**1970**
1. **MERCKX Eddy** (BEL)
2. DE VLAEMINCK Roger (BEL)
3. LEMAN Éric (BEL)

**1971**
1. **ROSIERS Roger** (BEL)
2. VAN SPRINGEL Herman (BEL)
3. BASSO Marino (ITA)

**1972**
1. **DE VLAEMINCK Roger** (BEL)
2. DIERICKX André (BEL)
3. HOBAN Barry (GBR)

**1973**
1. **MERCKX Eddy** (BEL)
2. GODEFROOT Walter (BEL)
3. ROSIERS Roger (BEL)

**1974**
1. **DE VLAEMINCK Roger** (BEL)
2. MOSER Francesco (ITA)
3. DEMEYER Marc (BEL)

**1975**
1. **DE VLAEMINCK Roger** (BEL)
2. MERCKX Eddy (BEL)
3. DIERICKX André (BEL)

**1976**
1. **DEMEYER Marc** (BEL)
2. MOSER Francesco (ITA)
3. DE VLAEMINCK Roger (BEL)

**1977**
1. **DE VLAEMINCK Roger** (BEL)
2. TEIRLINCK Willy (BEL)
3. MAERTENS Freddy (BEL)

**1978**
1. **MOSER Francesco** (ITA)
2. DE VLAEMINCK Roger (BEL)
3. RAAS Jan (HOL)

**1979**
1. **MOSER Francesco** (ITA)
2. DE VLAEMINCK Roger (BEL)
3. KUIPER Hennie (HOL)

**1980**
1. **MOSER Francesco** (ITA)
2. DUCLOS-LASSALLE Gilbert (FRA)
3. THURAU Dietrich (GER)

**1981**
1. **HINAULT Bernard** (FRA)
2. DE VLAEMINCK Roger (BEL)
3. MOSER Francesco (ITA)

**1982**
1. **RAAS Jan** (HOL)
2. BERTIN Yvon (FRA)
3. BRAUN Gregor (GER)

**1983**
1. **KUIPER Hennie** (HOL)
2. DUCLOS-LASSALLE Gilbert (FRA)
3. MOSER Francesco (ITA)

**1984**
1. **KELLY Sean** (IRL)
2. ROGIERS Rudy (BEL)
3. BONDUE Alain (FRA)

**1985**
1. **MADIOT Marc** (FRA)
2. WOJTINEK Bruno (FRA)
3. KELLY Sean (IRL)

**1986**
1. **KELLY Sean** (IRL)
2. DHAENENS Rudy (BEL)
3. VAN DER POEL Adrie (HOL)

**1987**
1. **VANDERAERDEN Éric** (BEL)
2. VERSLUYS Patrick (BEL)
3. DHAENENS Rudy (BEL)

**1988**
1. **DEMOL Dirk** (BEL)
2. WEGMÜLLER Thomas (SWI)
3. FIGNON Laurent (FRA)

**1989**
1. **WAMPERS Jean-Marie** (BEL)
2. DE WOLF Dirk (BEL)
3. VAN HOOYDONCK Edwig (BEL)

**1990**
1. **PLANCKAERT Eddy** (BEL)
2. BAUER Steve (CAN)
3. VAN HOOYDONCK Edwig (BEL)

**1991**
1. **MADIOT Marc** (FRA)
2. COLOTTI Jean-Claude (FRA)
3. BOMANS Carlo (BEL)

**1992**
1. **DUCLOS-LASSALLE Gilbert** (FRA)
2. LUDWIG Olaf (GER)
3. CAPIOT Johan (BEL)

**1993**
1. **DUCLOS-LASSALLE Gilbert** (FRA)
2. BALLERINI Franco (ITA)
3. LUDWIG Olaf (GER)

**1994**
1. **TCHMIL Andreï** (UKR)
2. BALDATO Fabio (ITA)
3. BALLERINI Franco (ITA)

**1995**
1. **BALLERINI Franco** (ITA)
2. TCHMIL Andreï (UKR)
3. MUSEEUW Johan (BEL)

**1996**
1. **MUSEEUW Johan** (BEL)
2. BORTOLAMI Gianluca (ITA)
3. TAFI Andrea (ITA)

**1997**
1. **GUESDON Frédéric** (FRA)
2. PLANCKAERT Jo (BEL)
3. MUSEEUW Johan (BEL)

**1998**
1. **BALLERINI Franco** (ITA)
2. TAFI Andrea (ITA)
3. PEETERS Wilfried (BEL)

**1999**
1. **TAFI Andrea** (ITA)
2. PEETERS Wilfried (BEL)
3. STEELS Tom (BEL)

**2000**
1. **MUSEEUW Johan** (BEL)
2. VAN PETEGEM Peter (BEL)
3. ZABEL Erik (GER)

**2001**
1. **KNAVEN Servais** (HOL)
2. MUSEEUW Johan (BEL)
3. VAINSTEINS Romans (LAT)

**2002**
1. **MUSEEUW Johan** (BEL)
2. WESEMANN Steffen (GER)
3. BOONEN Tom (BEL)

**2003**
1. **VAN PETEGEM Peter** (BEL)
2. PIERI Dario (ITA)
3. EKIMOV Viatcheslav (RUS)

**2004**
1. **BÄCKSTEDT Magnus** (SWE)
2. HOFFMAN Tristan (HOL)
3. HAMMOND Roger (GBR)

**2005**
1. **BOONEN Tom** (BEL)
2. HINCAPIE George (USA)
3. FLECHA Juan Antonio (SPA)

**2006**
1. **CANCELLARA Fabian** (SWI)
2. BOONEN Tom (BEL) (6)
3. BALLAN Alessandro (ITA)

**2007**
1. **O'GRADY Stuart** (AUS)
2. FLECHA Juan Antonio (SPA)
3. WESEMANN Steffen (GER)

**2008**
1. **BOONEN Tom** (BEL)
2. CANCELLARA Fabian (SWI)
3. BALLAN Alessandro (ITA)

**2009**
1. **BOONEN Tom** (BEL)
2. POZZATO Filippo (ITA)
3. HUSHOVD Thor (NOR)

**2010**
1. **CANCELLARA Fabian** (SWI)
2. HUSHOVD Thor (NOR)
3. FLECHA Juan Antonio (SPA)

**(1)** Maurice Garin gained French citizenship in December 1901.

**(2)** Jean Maréchal (1st) disqualified.

**(3)** Roger Lapébie (1st) disqualified.

**(4)** Romain Maës appeared to finish first.

**(5)** Although he was in the lead, Mahé was misdirected off course by the officials, and finished behind Serse Coppi. Mahé was later awarded a co–first place.

**(6)** Finishing 2nd, 3rd, and 4th, Hoste, Van Petegem, and Gusev were disqualified for ignoring a closed gate at a train crossing.

*general director and publication director*
Christophe Chenut

*assistant general manager of subsidiaries and development*
Xavier Spender

*editorial director for* L'Équipe
Claude Droussent

## Paris-Roubaix: A Journey Through Hell

**BOOK DEPARTMENT**
*Editor-in-chief*
Gérard Éjnès
*Book coordination*
Serge Laget
*with*
Pierre-Marie Descamps, Yann Hildwein, Gérard Schaller
*Art Direction*
Jacques Hennaux
*Assistant*
Matthieu Néel
*Design*
Gilles Montgermont *(Department head)*

**L'ÉQUIPE EVENT PHOTOS**
*Director*
Jacques Deydier
*Department heads*
Pascal Ronceau, François Gilles, Frédéric Mons
*Photographers*
Patrick Boutroux, Alain de Martignac, Michel Deschamps, Bruno Fablet, Jean-Louis Fel, Didier Fèvre, Pierre Lahalle, Pierre Lablatinière, Nicolas Luttiau, Richard Martin, Bernard Papon, Jean-Marc Pochat, Jérôme Prévost.

**DESK PHOTOS**
*Department heads*
Dominique Danne, Ingrid Buzelin, Stéphane Cabaret
*Photo editors*
Grégoire Dubreuil, Philippe Evain, Virginie Hadri, Philippe Le Men, Clara Martin, Christian Naï-Slimane, François Samson, Christian Vail, Anne-Laure Vallet, Alain Vignotte, Cyril Vuilly

**RESEARCH DEPARTMENT**
*Department head*
Danièle Coussot
*with*
Thierry Dangerma (assistant department head), Dominique Bartholomé, Maurice Broquet, Alain Hasse, Rodolphe Meunier

**PHOTO EDITING AND CORRECTION**
*Director*
Bruno Jeanjean

**BOOK MANUFACTURING**
*Director*
Lionel Planquart
*with*
Guy Jouno, Patrick Pastor, Valérie Yanji

*This work was created by the book division of* L'Équipe
*under the direction of*
Vincent Laudet
*with*
Laurence Gauthier (book sales manager)
Isabelle Calais (general manager)
Sandrine Matichard (marketing communication)

*with the help of*
Jean-Marie Scharsch (foreign rights)

*Page layout*
Sandrine Desbordes

*Publisher, French edition*
SNC L'ÉQUIPE
4, rue Rouget-de-Lisle
92793 Issy-Les-Moulineaux

## Special Thanks

*This book would not have happened without the Friends of Paris-Roubaix, official and nonofficial, with special gratitude to:*

Mesdames André Farine,
Françoise (de Troisvilles),
Henriette Herbin,
Mahjoub Ben Bella,
Alain Bernard,
Philippe Conrate,
René Deruyk,
René Devys,

François Doulcier,
Patrick Hollebecque,
Jean-François Pescheux,
Pascal Sergent,
Pic Teel,
Jean-Claude Vallaeys,
and Yorann Vandriessche
(of la Taverne de l'Arbre).

*As for the champions of yesterday and today, they were faithful to their reputation, which is no small thing. We thank them for their patience and their understanding:*

Jean Bobet,
Alain Bondue,
Albert Bouvet,
Albert Dolhats,
Pino Cerami,
André Darrigade,
Roger De Vlaeminck,
Gilbert Duclos-Lassalle,
Laurent Fignon,
Jean Forestier,
Bernard Gauthier,
Walter Godefroot,

Frédéric Guesdon,
Bernard Hinault,
Raymond Hoorelbeke,
Jan Janssen,
Hennie Kuiper,
Marc Madiot,
André Mahé,
Raymond Poulidor,
Roger Rosiers,
Jean Stablinski,
and Rik Van Looy.

Copyright © 2007 by VeloPress, English-language edition
First published in France as *Paris-Roubaix: une journée en Enfer*, copyright © 2006 by L'Équipe

All rights reserved. No part of this book may be reproduced, stored in a retrieval system, or transmitted, in any form or by any means, electronic or photocopy or otherwise, without the prior written permission of the publisher except in the case of brief quotations within critical articles and reviews.

VeloPress
3002 Sterling Circle, Suite 100
Boulder, Colorado 80301-2338 USA
303/440-0601 · Fax 303/444-6788 ·
E-mail velopress@competitorgroup.com

Library of Congress Cataloging-in-Publication Data
  Paris-Roubaix: a journey through hell / Philippe Bouvet ... [et al.] ;
translated by David V. Herlihy.
    p.  cm.
  ISBN-13: 978-1-934030-09-7 (hardcover: alk. paper)
  ISBN-10: 1-934030-09-0 (hardcover: alk. paper)
  1. Paris-Roubaix (Bicycle race)—History.  I. Bouvet, Philippe, 1955–
GV1049.2.P37P37 2007
796.6'20944—dc22

                                                    2007021008

Printed in China

For information on purchasing VeloPress books, please call
800/811-4210 ext. 2138 or visit www.velopress.com.

10 9 8 7

## Photo Credits

**AFP**

*4–5, 20 (left), 20 (right), 21 (left), 21 (right), 22, 27 (top and bottom), 46 (bottom), 72 (left), 90 (left), 94 (bottom), 95, 106, 107 (top, bottom),*

**Les Amis de Paris-Roubaix**

*44, 203 (left), 207 (bottom).*

**BN**

*14, 41, 158.*

**Doerler (Jean-Marie)**

*209.*

**DR**

*202, 203 (right), 205.*

**Ducoulombier (Emmanuel)**

*201.*

***L'ÉQUIPE***

*couverture, 2–3, 4–5, 8, 10, 16–17, 19, 23, 26, 28, 29 (top and bottom), 30 (top and bottom), 31, 32, 33, 34 (top and bottom), 35 (top and bottom), 42, 43, 45, 46 (top), 47 (top), 50–51, 53, 54, 57, 58, 59, 60, 61, 71, 72 (right), 73 (left, right), 75, 76 (top, bottom), 77, 78 (top, bottom), 79, 80 (top, middle, bottom), 81, 86–87, 89, 90 (right), 91 (left, right), 92 (left), 93, 94 (top), 96 (top, bottom), 98–99, 101, 102 (left, right), 103 (left, right), 105, 108 (top, bottom), 109, 110–111, 112 (top, bottom), 113 (top, bottom), 114 (top, bottom), 115, 121, 122 (left, right), 125, 126, 130–131, 133, 134, 135, 136 (top, bottom), 137, 138, 139 (top, bottom), 140 (all five), 141 (all three), 156–157, 160, 162, 163, 164, 165, 166, 167 (top, bottom), 168, 169 (top, bottom), 170–171, 172 (top, bottom), 173, 174, 175, 176 (top, bottom), 177, 178, 179, 180–181, 182, 183, 185, 188, 189, 198–199, 206, 210.*

*Biville (Christian) 68–69, 118–119, 184.*

*Boutroux (Patrick) 24 (right), 63 (top), 116, 127 (top), 192.*

*Clément (Denys) 24 (left), 55 (right), 83 (top), 92 (right), 117, 123, 127 (bottom), 129, 150 (bottom), 151, 152 (middle), 191, 193.*

*De Martignac (Alain) 55 (left), 142 (bottom), 186 (bottom).*

*Deschamps (Michel) 6–7, 67, 97 (top), 186 (top).*

*Fablet (Bruno) 48–49, 64 (bottom), 64–65, 82 (top), 83 (bottom), 128, 194.*

*Fel (Jean-Louis) 84 (bottom).*

*Fèvre (Didier) 37, 66, 147, 149 (right), 154.*

*Lablatinière (Pierre) 74, 82 (bottom), 144–145, 148 (left, right), 149 (left), 152 (top, bottom), 152–153, 155.*

*Laudrain (Alain) 187.*

*Martin (Richard) 84–85.*

*Papon (Bernard) 25, 47 (bottom), 49 (top), 56, 62, 63 (middle), 82 (middle), 84 (top), 142–143, 195, 196, 197 (bottom), 207 (top), 208 (bottom).*

*Prévost (Jérôme) pages de gardes, 97 (bottom).*

*Rondeau (Pascal) 197 (top).*

**Presse Sports**

*Grippe (Patrick) 38–39.*

*Mons (Fred) 36.*

*Mons (Fred)/Ittel (Jean-Frédéric) 150 (top), 208 (top).*

**Roger-Viollet**

*13.*

**Sergent (Pascal)**

*15, 159, 161.*